# Adam

*Graphic Memoirs by Ariel Schrag*

AWKWARD

DEFINITION

POTENTIAL

LIKEWISE

# Adam

ARIEL SCHRAG

*A Mariner Original*
Mariner Books
Houghton Mifflin Harcourt
*Boston    New York*

For information about permission to reproduce selections from this book,
write to Permissions, Houghton Mifflin Harcourt Publishing Company,
215 Park Avenue South, New York, New York 10003.

www.hmhco.com

*Library of Congress Cataloging-in-Publication Data*
Schrag, Ariel.
Adam / Ariel Schrag.
pages cm
ISBN 978-0-544-14293-0 (pbk.)
1. Life change events — Fiction. 2. Lesbians — New York (State) —
New York — Fiction. 3. Nightclubs — New York (State) —
New York — Fiction. 4. Lesbian communities — New York (State) —
New York — Fiction. I. Title.
PS3619.C4616A67 2014
813'.6 — dc23
2013045641

Book design by Chrissy Kurpeski
Typeset in Garamond Premier Pro

Printed in the United States of America
DOC 10 9 8 7 6 5 4 3 2

Abridgment of "Cocky" by Julia Serano © 2003. Used with permission.

*For my mom, dad, and sister*

The mind commands the body and it obeys.
The mind orders itself and meets resistance.

— ST. AUGUSTINE (A.D. 398)

# 2006

# Chapter 1

ADAM STARED UP at the tree leading to Kelsey Winslow's bedroom window. He was holding a flower he'd picked on the way over — a golden poppy, the official California state flower, a conversation piece:

"*Did you know it's actually illegal to pick these?*"

"*Wow, really?!*"

"*Yeah, weird, right?*"

But now, about to climb the tree, he didn't know what to do with it. If he just held it in his hand while he climbed up, it would definitely get smashed; same thing with putting it in his back pocket. He racked his brain and finally decided he was just going to have to hold it in his teeth while he climbed: 100 percent Gay. But, whatever, he'd just make sure to get it back in his hand before Kelsey saw his head poking out over the window.

The whole climbing-into-the-girl's-window-through-a-tree-in-her-backyard thing was itself pretty ridiculous, but Adam didn't have much choice. He hoisted himself up. Kelsey's parents were cool — almost too cool — and they wouldn't have given a shit if some boy dropped by and asked if Kelsey was home. Kelsey was always saying things like: "My parents don't care about *anything*. They totally know I steal their alcohol. When Mom went on her 'I'm not drinking anymore' thing, and all the beer in the house disappeared, I was like, 'Just 'cause Mom doesn't wanna drink doesn't mean the *rest* of us shouldn't be able to!'" Their lack of caring was *why* Kelsey insisted everyone climb up the tree and through her window. It made things seem more exciting.

Adam transferred the flower from mouth to fist and rapped on the glass. He could see Kelsey sitting on her bed with her laptop. She came over and opened the window. She looked cross.

"I told you to come over at around six. You're early."

Adam scrambled into the room and peeked at his watch. It was 5:44. He had taken the bus from his house to Kelsey's and overestimated the time; he had actually arrived an entire hour early but walked around the block thirteen times until it was 5:40, and for some reason he had calculated that it would take him twenty minutes to climb the tree.

Adam shrugged. Kelsey mock-shrugged back. She went over to her bed and picked up where she had left off with her laptop. Adam sat down next to her. She was in socks with her feet curled up underneath her. Adam's sneakers looked huge and bulbous and were caked in mud, tree sap, and probably dog shit. He slouched against the wall so his shoes dangled off the edge of the bed, not touching any of the blankets. He considered for a moment kicking them off, all casual, like, *Whatever, I'm just gonna kick these shoes off.* But even the thought made him cringe. She'd think he was just trying to make out with her, which of course he was. Adam looked down and realized he was still holding the now-mashed poppy in his fist. He discreetly smushed it into his back pocket.

Kelsey was IM'ing with what appeared to be five different people on her computer screen and texting with someone on her phone. She was carrying on six conversations, none of which were with Adam. He gazed around the room, trying to pretend he didn't care or notice that she was ignoring him. His eyes shifted: desk cluttered with school stuff and *Buffy* DVDs; corkboard with photos of friends at school, everyone hanging off of one another; drawings that looked like they were done by a five-year-old (kid she babysat for?). *What the fuck was he doing here?* It was almost the end of his junior year of high school, and he'd still only made out with one girl in one piece-of-shit game of spin the bottle back in *eighth grade.* He probably shouldn't even count spin the bottle, but what was he going to do, say he'd never made out with *anyone?* He'd already exaggerated the kiss in his mind to include tongue and a little groping, when the reality was it had been one quick peck on the lips that gave him an instant hard-on. Kelsey was part of a group he hung around with at school, and everyone had been telling him she liked him. He thought she seemed 100 percent Indifferent to him like every other girl he knew, but Brad had insisted, "She wants you, man; she's totally *damp* for you," so he'd asked her if he should stop by after school, and she'd said: "Sure."

"Adam? Why are you being so weird and quiet?"

Adam looked at Kelsey, who was staring at him.

"I'm not."

"You are. You're, like, just sitting there staring."

Adam blinked.

Kelsey shoved her laptop off her stomach and walked over to her stereo. She fiddled with the iPod, and music started playing. *She's setting the mood.* Adam's body tensed. Kelsey started doing a flow-y dance to the music. She rolled her neck back and moved her arms in undulating curves. Her eyes were closed, and she mouthed the words along with the music as she swayed. She stopped and opened her eyes at him.

"Wanna get high?"

"Sure," said Adam.

There was nothing Adam wanted to do less, but if it meant making out with Kelsey, he was willing to risk it. He'd smoked pot a couple weeks ago with Brad and Colin, and spent the whole night praying for the feeling to go away. They'd smoked out of an empty Bud can that Brad had turned into a pipe by bending it in half and jabbing a little circle of holes in the middle with a ball-point pen. After only three hits, Adam couldn't tell the difference between what he was saying or merely thinking, and he was convinced Brad and Colin had masterminded the entire night just to fuck with him. "Adam's tweaking!" they kept saying, and laughing (secret looks between them), "Adam's totally tweaking!"

Now Kelsey wanted to get high, and before she'd even taken out the weed, Adam felt like he was completely stoned.

"I got this new bong on Telegraph," said Kelsey, rummaging through a drawer. She extracted a bra and flung it over her back across the room, just missing Adam, coloring his face red as it passed.

"Here it is," said Kelsey. "Shit goes straight to your brain with this." The bong was translucent purple with a giant weed leaf painted along the cylinder. Adam had seen ones like it propped up next to the FOR TOBACCO USE ONLY sign in the display case at Annapurna, the smoke shop on Telegraph Avenue. Kelsey dumped some leftover Diet Coke inside the bong and packed the bowl.

"Guests first," she said, standing in front of Adam and extending the bong to him. "Or is it ladies first?" She grinned and snapped her arm back, bringing the bong to her chest. The cylinder was stuck between her tits, making them spread out. Her nipples looked hard, and despite his paranoia, Adam could feel himself getting that way too.

"Ladies first," he said.

Kelsey flopped down on the bed, splashing Diet Coke from the bong on her pink ringer T-shirt. She lit up and inhaled long and deep. Adam scooted in closer to her. Their thighs were touching and his hand was resting just behind her back, right where her jeans went down and her shirt went up, exposing a slice of bare skin and underwear. Kelsey handed the bong to Adam and he lit it. He sucked in but closed his throat.

"What kind of pussy inhaling is that?" said Kelsey. "Open your mouth! Do you not like bongs 'cause it makes you feel like you're sucking a dick? Matt doesn't do bongs 'cause he says it makes him feel like he's sucking a dick." Matt was Kelsey's recently ex boyfriend. "I think he was just gay. *Dick.*" Kelsey shoved the top of the bong up into Adam's mouth, put her thumb over the carb, and relit the bowl for him. "Now *suck*," she ordered.

Adam inhaled with all his might, the bong bubbled, and Kelsey released the carb. Adam exploded in coughing.

"*Now* you'll be high," said Kelsey, satisfied. She took another hit and then performed the procedure with Adam again, resulting in another explosive cough.

"But I'm, like, what? Matt doesn't know shit," Kelsey rambled, apparently continuing a conversation she had started in her head. "He thinks all girls love to suck dick — I mean, some girls do; some of us like it to be a little more *equal.* Alice says she'll only suck dick after a guy's gone down on her. Frances says the only fair thing to do is sixty-nine first, and then it doesn't matter if the girl sucks dick or if the guy goes down first. I think it's OK to suck dick first, but only if you can tell it's the kind of guy who'll go down on you, and if you can't tell . . ."

Kelsey's stream was interrupted as she leaned over to suck on the purple bong shaft again, and Adam was now visibly hard under his jeans. He shifted positions so it wasn't so obvious and tried to press himself up a little closer to Kelsey. He could feel her move in a little closer to him. *Yes.* She passed him the bong, and he sucked in again. *They were going to make out. They were actually going to make out.* His eyes fixated on that slice of skin between shirt and jeans, and he imagined lifting the shirt up, exposing her smooth, soft stomach, putting his hands all over it, then pushing up onto her tits, inside her bra, then crawling on top of her, her legs spreading around him, his dick pressed up against her. Adam quickly looked up. Had he been staring for too long? What was Kelsey talking about?

"And so I told Harris, look, Amanda wants you, but it's not like *she's* gonna ask *you* . . ." Kelsey stopped and looked at Adam looking at her. Why did she stop? Did she think he was being weird again? Adam quickly tried to do something not weird.

"Yeah, heh, heh." *Why did he smoke pot? Why did he smoke pot?*

"What's funny?"

"Huh?" said Adam.

"Why did you just laugh? What's funny?"

"Nothing." Stuff was getting weird. He had to get back to that feeling, the feeling where they were moving toward each other.

Adam's hand inched over and sort of crawled onto Kelsey's thigh. He felt like his hand was a spider, each finger another spindly, sticky, unwanted black leg. Kelsey stared at the hand. The hand froze. Adam stared at it. It had to do something. Move the hand. It crept a little to the right, closer to Kelsey's knee, safer than creeping closer to the crotch, right? Kelsey abruptly stood up. The hand fell to the bed, dead.

"This . . . isn't working," she said.

"Uh, it's not?" Adam stood up too. Kelsey sat back down on the bed and pulled her computer onto her lap. She started typing something as she spoke. Adam stayed standing.

"I just, I need guys to be, like, more aggressive. Like, you know that whole girls-love-asshole-guys thing? Well, I'm *sorry,* but it's kind of true. Like, I think you're cute and stuff, but this, like, isn't working. Stuff feels weird."

"It doesn't have to be weird . . ." said Adam. *Shitfuckshitfuckshitfuckshitfuck.*

Adam tried to take a step toward the bed.

"No, it's weird," said Kelsey, looking up from her computer. Then she looked back down and began typing rapidly. Adam saw the IM in his head: Adam is here. Save me!

He stood there, silent. One second. Two seconds. Adam's brain was folding and contracting itself into horrible, convoluted shapes. Kelsey remained hunched over the laptop. Probably he should just go. He looked at the window. He looked at the bedroom door. He seriously thought that if he tried to climb back down the tree, he would fall and kill himself. The tree it was. He started toward the window.

"You can just leave through the door," said Kelsey, not taking her eyes off the computer. "My dad says I'm killing the tree."

Adam pivoted and headed to the door. He felt like he was being kicked off a reality TV show, making his grand exit of failure with the whole world watching, the audience at home marginally amused, but more likely, like Kelsey, bored.

He walked down the stairs from Kelsey's bedroom, through her living room, ignored the mom partially visible in the kitchen, and went out the front door. It was dark now, and this came as a relief. Like the change in setting could change his mood. He breathed in the cold air and could feel the high fading. Something he'd learned in biology ran through his mind: *Breathing through your nose cools your brain temperature and makes you happier.* He inhaled deeply again through his nose. It sort of worked. He made his way back to the bus stop.

...

By the time Adam got home, he was pretty much back to normal. He made a quick stop in the bathroom though to scrub his hands and swish some Listerine, just in case. His parents were not "cool." He had told them he'd be staying late at Brad's, studying for a government test, and now he had to come up with an excuse for why he was back so early.

"Brad barfed!" Adam shouted from the bathroom in the direction of the kitchen. His mom came out, soup spoon in hand, looking horrified.

"Is he all right? Do they think it's viral? Do you feel sick?"

She came at him with her free hand, lunging for his forehead. Adam ducked out of the way.

"I feel fine," he said. "I think it was something he ate."

"Well, dinner's almost ready," continued his mom, trailing after him down the hall, "and Daddy and I have something we want to discuss with you."

Adam could not figure out why his mom still insisted on referring to his dad as "Daddy," when he'd stopped calling him that, oh, nine years ago.

Adam took a seat with his dad and mom. His sister had been away at college for almost a year, but her empty chair stayed, reminding him how much better dinners were when she had been there. When she was around, there was always something to talk about. That something was usually her, but it was better than him alone, facing off against his mom's constant table-manner orders and gossip about people he didn't give a shit about.

"Adam! Elbows!"

Adam dragged his elbows off the table. His parents having something they wanted to "discuss" could not be good, especially since he was still a little out of it. He considered claiming he did feel sick, but he was hungry. He dumped A.1. sauce over his steak and started sawing off forkfuls.

"You seem down these days, honey. All mopey. Not like yourself."

Adam wondered who on earth his mom thought his "self" was.

"I'm fine," he said, chewing.

"No. It's been going on for a few months now. I notice these things. Daddy's noticed too. Richard?"

Adam's dad was concentrating on removing a strand of steak from his teeth with his pinkie fingernail and tongue. Adam felt his stomach turn. His mom continued.

"We think it's been hard for you this year with Casey being

gone. You miss her, don'tcha?" Adam's mom smiled at him like he was five.

"Sure, yeah, but I'm fine. Can I be excused?"

"No!" his mom said, switching quickly into angry-bitch mode. "We are trying to talk to you!"

"Well, I'm fine!"

"You are *not* fine! You shuffle around the house like some kind of . . . blind mole rat —"

"*What?*"

"— your grades are shit; your skin, frankly, is a mess. I know you *think* you need to shave, but, I'm sorry, honey, you don't yet, and —"

*Would she just shut the fuck up.*

"— by trying to shave before you need to, you're giving yourself acne that could result in scarring, right, Richard?"

"Leigh . . ."

Adam stood up and started walking away from the table.

"Of course whenever I mention calling Aunt Susan about her dermatologist, you just —"

Adam plugged his ears with his fingers and turned down the hall.

His mom stood up, shouting after him. "If you would stay put for five seconds, I could tell you how Daddy and I have been planning a special trip for you this summer to visit your sister in New York! But you probably don't want that either, so I guess we should just forget the whole thing —"

"Yes! Forget it!" shouted Adam, stomping up the stairs to his room. "I'm going to Lake Tahoe with Brad and Colin anyway!"

Adam slammed the door to his room. His most satisfying action of the day. He looked at his government book on his desk. A bald eagle frowning at an American flag. He did have a test tomorrow. That part wasn't a lie. He sat down at his desk, stared at the unopened book, and casually pushed it off the desk onto the floor with a thud. He turned on his laptop, and a barrage of Internet porn ads attacked the screen. There was really no way to avoid them. Once you looked at one porn site, it caused some freaking worm or virus in your computer that notified all porn sites in existence, and then they showed up every time you opened a browser. It didn't matter, really, since that was what he generally wanted to use the computer for anyway.

Adam scanned the selections of "real teen girls" and "barely legals." Sometimes it made him nervous, since he knew people got arrested for looking at child porn online, but *he* was only seventeen! He shouldn't get in trouble for looking at girls his own age. Adam found an appealing ad with a blond girl rubbing a lollipop in between her legs. He clicked on the "free trial" link to watch the five-second promo. That was what he usually did, watched the promo over and over again until he was done. Credit cards were too risky. Not that he had one anyway. The blond girl stuck the lollipop inside her vagina. Then another teenage girl, this one with brown hair, appeared on the screen, took the lollipop out of the girl's vagina, and put it in her mouth. The girls giggled and the screen froze. Adam wrinkled his nose. This was not the sort of video he liked. He didn't know if this meant he was secretly gay or something, but he just really preferred if there was a dick involved. He didn't want to see the guy's face or body or anything nasty like that, just his dick. Preferably being sucked on or plunged into some girl's hole. Adam scanned more ads. The lesbian thing was just really boring to him, especially since it was so obviously fake. He should know — his sister was a lesbian. And, yes, he'd seen her have sex.

It hadn't been his idea. It was Brad's, of course. Brad was obsessed with Casey — all guys were — and was always bugging him, "When are you gonna let me watch your hot sister fuck another girl?" as if Adam were the bouncer to his sister's bedroom door. "What's her girlfriend look like? She hot too?"

Adam had really liked his sister's (now ex-)girlfriend. Her name was Sam, short for Samantha, and she basically looked like a boy. She always wore baggy jeans and a baseball cap and was super-polite to his parents, even though his mom referred to her as "Casey's confused friend" behind her back. Their parents didn't know Casey and Sam were girlfriends, and Adam had been sworn to secrecy. "It's just easier this way," Casey would say. "The last thing I wanna do is answer a bunch of freaked-out Mom questions about lesbianism." Adam knew it was more than that. Casey didn't want their mom to know because Casey was the perfect child. Their roles in the family were immutable: Casey was perfect and Adam was troubled. Adam knew Casey loved him, but he also knew she loved being better than him. It wasn't that their parents were *homophobic* — it was just that *other* people were gay, and people in their family happened not to be. "Also, I wouldn't want Mom to tell Dad. The idea of him thinking about me having 'lesbian sex' makes me want to vomit." Casey saying this had, of course, put the image of Casey having "lesbian sex" in Adam's mind, though he also wasn't entirely sure what that was. And as wrong as it felt, he was curious.

It was last summer the night it happened. Adam's parents were out at "dinner and a movie" for one of their biannual pathetic attempts at romance. Casey and Sam were watching TV in the living room, and Adam had invited Brad over. When he went downstairs to let Brad in, Casey was sitting in Sam's lap, and Sam's hands were around Casey's waist, under her shirt.

"Get out of here!" said Casey.

"I'm just getting Brad," said Adam.

"Well, hurry up!"

When Sam was over, Casey acted as if she ruled the house.

"'Sup," said Brad, walking in and leering at Casey and Sam. Casey ignored him. She didn't like Brad. "Guys like Brad make me thank god I'm gay," she would say.

Adam and Brad went to his room, where they hung around doing nothing, being bored. It was around the time that stuff had first started feeling weird with Brad. They had always been best friends — since fourth grade — but for some reason it had begun to feel like whenever they hung out alone, Brad didn't really want to be there. Like hanging out with Adam was an obligation or something.

"You think they're fucking down there?" Brad asked.

"I don't know."

"Her girlfriend's kinda mannish, but whatever."

They heard Casey and Sam come up the stairs and go into Casey's bedroom next door. Brad smirked and raised his eyebrows. Then a song started blasting from Casey's room.

"Shit. How the fuck are we supposed to hear anything now?" said Brad.

"Gross," said Adam.

Brad picked up a Sharpie off the floor and scribbled on his shoe. Adam tried to think of something else to say, to suggest something for them to do, but everything he thought of seemed dumb. The song from Casey's room played on, highlighting Adam and Brad's silence. It never used to be this way with them. It was uncomfortable, awkward.

*"I actually know how we could maybe watch,"* Adam imagined telling Brad. *No. He would never.*

"I actually know how we could maybe watch," said Adam.

"No shit, Freedman."

Adam said nothing.

"Well?" said Brad.

"Never mind."

"Come on, you just said you know how we could watch."

*Fuck it. He was in it now.*

"Take off your shoes," said Adam. He looked around, even though there was no one else in the room.

"Yeah, OK," said Brad. He quickly started to unlace.

Adam took off his own shoes and stood up. "Now, whatever you do, do not make *any* fucking noise." As much as he hated himself, Adam was enjoying being the one to boss Brad. It was always the other way around.

The two of them crept out of Adam's room and softly padded down the hall past Casey's bedroom. Brad lingered by her door for a moment, but Adam waved him on, pointing down the stairs. Brad gave a quizzical look but followed. They walked through the living room and into the kitchen to the door that led to the backyard.

Outside it was dark and cold, and Adam realized how fast his heart was racing. Their house was built on a hill, so the backyard was a slope that led up to Casey's bedroom window. As they walked up the hill, Adam could feel his socks getting drenched from the wet grass. *This was a completely fucked-up thing to do.*

Adam leaned into Brad's ear. "Her shade is open just a crack — it's perfect," he whispered.

Brad swatted Adam away and wiped his cheek with the back of his hand. "Stop spitting on me," Brad said, not in a whisper.

They crouched behind the bushes in front of Casey's window. The crack in the shade glowed yellow against the darkened house. Adam groped for possible reasons why they were there if caught. *"Brad lost his baseball in the bushes,"* singsonged in his head like a Learn-to-Read book. They leaned in closer against the bush, and a sliver of the room came into focus. Casey and Sam stumbled into view — about mid-thigh to shoulders visible. They were sort of fake-dancing to the music, pushing and pretend-hitting each other. Sam grabbed Casey around the middle and began to pull her shirt up.

Adam glanced at Brad, whose mouth was opening and closing like a blowfish. He felt an urge to just *push* Brad, just sort of knock him over and watch him roll down the hill.

"Holy fuck," said Brad.

Adam looked back through the window crack. Casey was on the bed, and Sam was crawling in between her legs, undoing Casey's jeans. *Look away, just look away.* Casey reached up and tugged at Sam's shirt. Sam pushed Casey's hands off, but then hesitated and took her shirt off herself. She was wearing a black sports bra. Casey put her hands on Sam's tits, and they started kissing again. Sam was grinding herself into Casey. Adam imagined digging his fingers into his eye sockets, scooping out his eyeballs, and throwing them into the night. They would be light and slimy and hard to throw very far. Sam reached down and opened one of the drawers underneath Casey's bed. She took out a sort of black strappy contraption and turned her back to Casey. *What the fuck was she doing?* Sam pulled off her jeans, keeping her underwear on. She spread the contraption open, turned it around a few times and put her legs through some of the straps, tripping forward a little. She pulled it up around her waist and that was when Adam realized what it was. Coming out of the straps was a huge black rubber dick.

Brad went nuts. "No fuckin' way! No fuckin' way!"

Sam reached over and shut off the light.

"Fuck!" said Brad.

Adam felt a gush of relief, or maybe disappointment — he couldn't tell.

"Dude, you're a straight-up freak," said Brad. He grinned at Adam through the dark. "Watching your *sister?* What's wrong with you?"

And Adam pushed him, and they both rolled down the hill.

. . .

Needless to say, Adam felt he could speak with authority when he said that two girls sharing a pussy-soaked lollipop were *not* real lesbians. He found a video he liked, did his thing, and cleaned up with some dirty boxers off the floor.

. . .

It was 1:00 A.M. and Adam was still awake, lying in bed. His government book lay on the floor in the same spot, now illuminated by a patch of streetlight from the window. Like God was trying to remind him. He also had a five-page essay on *The Sun Also Rises* due yesterday. He had finished the book the day it was assigned, but writing essays depressed him and he'd put it off for weeks. He always felt forced to find a "point," one he often didn't even completely believe in but corralled the book into proving anyway. When he was done, he'd end up hating the book he had loved.

Adam stared around the dark, shadowy room. The lights from cars ran across his wall, soft sounds in the distance. The objects in his room were distorted, anonymous fuzzy gray blobs that looked alien and out of place. He liked finding the weirdest blob, usually two things melded together, and concentrating on it hard, feeling his brain working as it figured out what it actually was (a desk lamp and an old soccer trophy, a broken PlayStation 2 console and a pile of clothes). Sometimes he'd fall asleep doing this.

When he was little, he had these elaborate games he would play when he couldn't sleep. His favorite was "orphan." He would get out of bed in the middle of the night and lie on the cold hardwood floor in his pajamas and pretend he'd been abandoned in the middle of the woods. A small child left to die. He would grow colder and colder, huddling into himself, imagining the dark, towering trees above him, the open black sky, and the crack of mysterious noises. He would lie like this for as long as he could, eyes clenched in the forest, until his brain started to believe that it was true. Then he would hear the footsteps, the people coming to his rescue. *"We've found a child! There's a near-dead boy!"* And his brain would fast-forward — the ride in the back of the car, the nice big house in the neighboring town — the story would run through his mind as he almost sleepwalked back to bed. Then he would snuggle into the soft, clean pillow, imagining that his hands pulling the thick covers over his shivering body belonged to a warm, loving woman. He'd sometimes repeat this action, the pulling of the covers, the nestling into the pillow, three or four times. Warm and safe at last.

A few months ago, when he was having a particularly rough night, he tried the game again, even though it had been years. He got out of bed, lay on the floor, closed his eyes, and opened them about five seconds later, feeling like a complete retard. His body felt huge and lanky and, like, if he were in a fucking forest, he should get up and try to walk the hell out of it. He got back in bed and counted sheep.

Adam halfheartedly tried sheep-counting now, but he was too frustrated to stay focused. He fucking hated his mom. It was always, "Casey never acts this way; your sister always manages to stay pleasant around family."

"*Casey is fucking lying to you about her entire life!*" Adam imagined himself screaming back. "*You don't know the first fucking thing about her!*"

"Casey's at Columbia," his mom's voice rang on. "*Yes, we're all very proud . . . Adam's been struggling lately.*"

"*At least I'm not being fucked by a giant rubber dick five feet from your bedroom!*"

"*Adam?! What are you talking about?*"

"*Nothing, Mom, it's just my Tourette's.*"

"*Adam's been struggling with Tourette's syndrome lately.*"

The way Brad talked to his own parents blew Adam's mind. It was as if they were *his* children. "The folks are staying in, catchin' the late show," Brad would say, cocking his head toward his mom and dad, seated on the couch with a blanket spread over their knees, as Brad and Adam passed through the living room. "Ya gotta love 'em." And his parents would smile sheepishly, anxious for his approval. Brad was the perfect son. Good grades, played baseball. But when you got him alone, he was fucking foul. "Her pussy tasted like cat food." Adam didn't get how Brad could switch back and forth so seamlessly. He was also an entirely different person for the girls. Smooth Brad. Cocky Brad. "I know what you want and I can give it to you" Brad. "My dick is the most precious object on this planet Earth and you would be blessed to touch it" Brad. Like Kelsey said, girls go for aggressive guys. *You want aggressive?* Adam imagined himself back in Kelsey's room, standing in front of her, his dick still hard. *Suck on this, then, bitch.* He unzipped his pants and pulled his dick out, massive and throbbing. Kelsey dropped to her knees, falling on it with her mouth.

*No teeth, bitch!* Adam gave a quick swat to the side of her face.

*I'm thorry,* Kelsey said, mouth half full, looking up at him.

*Just be sure to swallow,* said Adam.

Adam reached under the covers to jerk off, but he wasn't even hard. He rolled over, squeezed his eyes shut, put the pillow over his head, pulled the covers over the pillow, and finally, finally fell asleep.

# Chapter 2

THE SCHOOL LUNCH BELL rang, and kids rushed out of their classrooms, bursting through the front doors to the concrete courtyard, where everyone ate lunch.

Adam went to East Bay Prep, a small private school in the Oakland hills. He'd begged his parents to let him go to Berkeley High, the public school that a bunch of his friends from middle school went on to, but his mom had refused: "I've walked by that school, and kids were smoking right outside the gate along with the teachers! The teachers were loaning them lighters!" "EBP has a ninety-seven percent top-college placement record," and of course the inevitable, "Your sister loves EBP!" Adam knew that Casey had *not* loved EBP. That she would in fact drive down to Berkeley High the minute school was over to hang out with Sam and her friends in the park.

It wasn't that Adam hated his school. He actually liked some of his teachers and was frankly (though he would never admit it) kind of scared by some of the stories Sam had told about Berkeley High. "This kid totally got jumped today; he's, like, in the hospital . . . No, no reason. Just looked like a nerd." What he hated was how small his school was. Only 152 students in all four grades. At a school like Berkeley High, with more than four thousand students, it seemed as if there were an endless supply of groups to

hang out with. You get in a fight with some friends, just go hang
around another group.

Adam's cousin Mark went to Berkeley High, and every time
Adam saw him at some family holiday gathering, Mark had a
new identity complete with a new pack of friends. It had started
two years ago at their cousin Sammy's bar mitzvah, when Mark
showed up with his hair (and hands and ears and back of his neck)
dyed green, wearing dress pants twenty sizes too big and carrying
a skateboard. "I'll probably go pro before I graduate high school,"
Adam overheard Mark telling Aunt Susan. Then, last year at
Thanksgiving, to Adam's mom's horror, Mark had been wearing
skintight black jeans, white makeup, and a T-shirt that read: HY-
MEN HOLOCAUST.

"I think I'm making people uncomfortable. Do I make you
uncomfortable?" Mark had said, hovering so close to Adam's face
that Adam could see the outline of Mark's lavender-colored con-
tacts. According to Casey, Mark was now a self-proclaimed "thug"
who wore designer sweatpants, dealt weed, and only hung out
with black people. "I just know Islam is around the corner," Casey
had said, snorting.

Adam didn't want to follow in Mark's path, but the range of
possibility seemed liberating. At Adam's school there were only
two groups: Popular and Nerd. And he felt like he spent most of
his time struggling to hold on to his place in Popular.

Casey had complained about the same thing. "The only thing
worse than spending all my time with EBP brats is knowing I'm
one of them." But then she had met Sam at a joint school field
trip organized by all the gay-straight alliance groups from different high schools in the East Bay. Casey's membership in such a
club had been, of course, a total secret, but the teacher sponsor
who "totally 'gets it'" had drafted an elusive permission slip for
an "exploration of San Francisco for students interested in local
culture." That culture being the rainbow flag–adorned, gay-men-

with-their-balls-hanging-out street called Castro. Adam had occasionally seen the strip through the windows of their family car, always wishing they would drive slower so he could take it all in. For the field trip, Casey and fifteen other gay teens from the Bay Area, along with some teachers, had spent the entire afternoon walking up and down the street. With no other purpose than to, as Casey had put it, "You know, be gay." "Retardedly gay," is what she called it when she came back. "They bought us little rainbow flags to wave around, and one kid, this fag from Kensington, even tried to convince everyone to get rainbow sherbet ice cream." Adam had been surprised to hear his sister use the word *fag* so casually. "I'm allowed to," she had said, "'cause I'm gay. You're not allowed to use it." Then Casey had launched into a description of Sam, the girl from Berkeley High who was "so fucking hot I want to fucking kill myself." The rest was history. Or "Herstory," as Casey had written on her history binder.

Since Adam wasn't gay, this sort of life-changing field trip wasn't exactly an option for him. He'd given up soccer after middle school, and the groups at his school (Chess Club, Environmental Action, Junior Classical League) were hardly appealing. Also, his mom was always bugging him to join one ("Extracurriculars, Adam, have you even thought about your extracurriculars?"), and that in itself was reason not to.

Adam often felt like he was teetering on the edge of Popular, a pit full of Nerds waiting to catch him below, shrieking and giggling with outstretched arms and drooling smiles. Being best friends with Brad had been his ticket into the right crowd. The problem was that Adam felt totally dependent on Brad, and if Brad decided he didn't want him around anymore, the rest of the group would eagerly kick him to the Nerds. They knew he was faking it. He could see them see through him.

It was the usual at lunch that day. The group: Brad, Colin, Colin's girlfriend Andrea, Stephen and Stephanie, who'd been dating since the fifth grade (barf), Fletcher, Fletcher's girlfriend Alice, and Kelsey Winslow. Fletcher was busting everyone up imitating teachers and various Nerds.

"So, Mr. Stewart is all, '*Fletcher,* you need to pull yer pants up! I can almost see yer *bare ass!*'"

"It's true! He totally said that!" Colin chimed in. Colin was always trying to insert himself into Fletcher's jokes. Fletcher ignored him and continued.

"And I was like, 'Um, excuse me, Mr. Stewart, you have a little chalk . . .' Because you know his entire dick area is caked in the shit. So he starts brushing away furiously at his crotch. Dude totally looks like he's beating off, and just at that moment, *Talitha* walks into the room and is all, *'Oh!'*" — Fletcher put his hand up to his O-shaped mouth in a perfect prude imitation. "Shit was hilarious."

Everyone in the group doubled over laughing, Alice louder than everyone, though her laugh struck Adam as painfully fake. He couldn't believe someone with a name like Fletcher was so popular. Weren't people named Fletcher supposed to be Nerds? Like how fat people were supposed to be named Bertha or stupid people, Dewey? In Fletcher's case, his dork name just made him cooler.

Colin, attempting to ride out the rest of Fletcher's wave, started his own joke.

"That totally reminds me of that time in Eleanor Meyerhoff's hot tub? You guys know what I'm talking about?"

Brad burst out laughing, but everyone else looked kind of vacant. Adam felt a prickle up the back of his neck.

"So it's me, Brad, Andrea, Eleanor, and Adam." Colin swallowed some Coke and then cough-snorted it out, laughing pre-emptively at his own joke.

"We were all stoned, just chillin' in the tub, and Adam starts telling some long-ass story . . ." Colin's eyes shifted quickly over to

Adam and then back. Not long enough to actually make contact but a kind of token gesture like, *I looked at you and you didn't stop me, so I'm allowed to go on.*

"So, Adam's talking and talking—I don't even know about what—and he's, like, leaning back in the water, kind of floating as he goes on. And we're all staring at him, kind of laughing, but trying to act like we're *really* interested in what he's saying, when what we're all staring at are his boxers, which are, like, billowing up from the water jets, and his fucking schlong and balls"—Colin leaned over to try to catch his breath—"like, hanging out, all wafting back and forth in the water!"

The entire lunch group exploded. Adam could tell that this time Alice's laugh wasn't fake.

"Finally, we just had to tell him," finished Colin.

Adam tried to cover his red face with his hands and laugh a little too, like he didn't give a shit, like, you know, it was funny to him too or whatever. The worst part hadn't even been his exposed dick. It was what he'd been saying when it happened. Some stupid joke about his mom that had gone on way too long because he thought everyone was super into it, the way they were all staring at him so intently. The moment they all cracked up, right before they told him about his boxers, he thought they were laughing at the climax of his joke. He remembered how cocky and pleased with himself he'd felt for those few seconds.

"Is there gonna be a hot tub at the cabin in Tahoe?" Andrea interjected into everyone's laughter.

"Yeah, what are you gonna hook us up with, Stephen?" asked Fletcher. The group was staying at Stephen's parents' cabin for the first two weeks of summer.

"Fuck yeah, there's a hot tub," said Stephen. He draped his arm around Stephanie so his hand rested limply on her breast. "But my folks only want two in at a time. After that crap when my brother's friend went unconscious. So it's couples taking turns. It's better

that way, anyway." Stephen grinned and his hand grazed back and
forth across Stephanie's tit. Adam swore he could see her nipple
getting hard. She giggled and squirmed in closer to Stephen.

"So, my car's got room for three more," said Colin. "The rest of
y'all fools have to ride up with Stephen's parents." Colin was the
only one with his own car.

"No problem," said Fletcher, "the Explorer's sweet. Alice and I
call back. Got those TV screens on the car seats and everything."
Fletcher and Stephen knuckle-bumped. "Better than your piece of
shit." Fletcher laughed at Colin.

"At least I can call her my own, bitch," said Colin. "So who's
with me? Brad, you taking Sandy or Jennifer?"

"Sandy," said Brad with an expression like, *Duh*. And he and
Colin shared a grin that meant: *The girl that puts out is the girl who
comes to Tahoe*. Sandy went to Bishop O'Dowd High, and Jennifer
went to Berkeley High. Brad had managed to pick both of them
up just by walking down the street and saying "hi."

Adam was getting nervous. Everyone was coupled up. When
the trip was first planned, it had been assumed he and Kelsey
would be a couple. But after yesterday, he wasn't sure. Well, whatever, they were a couple by default anyway, right?

"OK," said Colin, "so you and Sandy ride with me and Andrea."
Brad shrugged. The chillest person on the earth.

"I guess we gotta ride separate." Adam smiled at Kelsey. There
were two seats left, one in Stephen's parents' car and one in Colin's.

"Actually, Stephen, I wanted to ask if it would be OK if I
brought Matt up with us?"

Matt. Kelsey's ex-boyfriend. *What the fuck? She was supposed
to hate him*. Suddenly, as if on some kind of magical cue, Matt
appeared on his skateboard next to the group. In one swift movement, he flipped the board up with a kick, it landed on the ground,

and he sat on it with a space left for Kelsey. She eagerly took her place.

"Heard you guys are hittin' Tahoe," said Matt.

"Colin," continued Kelsey, "Matt can ride with you guys, right? If I go with Stephen?"

Adam felt his face grow hot. He shifted on the concrete, trying not to make eye contact with anyone.

"Sure, I guess," said Colin. Adam saw Colin looking at him out of the corner of his eye. Like he was waiting for Adam to speak up, defend his spot or something. Colin didn't care whether Adam went or not, Adam knew that.

"Dude," said Brad to Colin, "you could squeeze four in your back seat, right? I'll put Sandy on my lap."

"Naw, my parents are all up in my shit about that shit," said Colin. *Was he lying?*

"Adam could drive up by himself," said Alice, giggling a little. *What the fuck was that retard bitch talking about?* Everyone knew Adam didn't have his license yet.

"Stephen, what about the Explorer?" said Brad. Adam felt stupid letting Brad talk for him, but his entire body had shut down. Like, even if he wanted to talk, he couldn't.

"I could ask my dad if we could squeeze . . ." said Stephen.

"I thought this was a trip for couples," said Matt, swinging his arm over Kelsey's shoulder. "You bringing anyone, Adam?"

Adam stared at the giant zit perched on the tip of Matt's nose — a huge red mountain with a quivering chunk of white ready to burst out. Adam shook his head.

"Yeah, who's Adam gonna go in the hot tub with?" said Alice, more giggling.

"We gotta be in couples for the Jet Skiing too . . ." said Stephen to no one in particular.

*If Brad was the odd man out, they'd never try to kick him out of the trip. They'd all wanna take fucking turns being his Jet Ski/hot tub/whatever-the-fuck partner. He had to just act like he was Brad, just be Brad for five fucking seconds and —*

"So whatever the fuck, you guys can take turns being my couple, I mean, or whatever," Adam found himself saying.

Everyone in the group stared at him.

"Yeah, like, I'll go in the hot tub with you" — Adam nodded at Kelsey — "and you" — he nodded at Andrea — "and you" — he nodded at Alice — "and you" — he nodded at Stephanie. "And . . . *you!*" Adam jerked his head toward Matt, the word coming out like *Boo!*

Matt slowly lifted his hands up, as if Adam were pointing a gun at him.

Everyone was silent. Adam looked at Brad, thinking he would laugh, turn it all into a great joke. But Brad just looked embarrassed for him.

"Whatever, I, like, wasn't even sure I could go anyway . . ." Adam trailed off. And someone changed the subject.

. . .

Adam crumpled his lunch bag, the majority of his lunch still in it, and threw it in the trash. He walked up the steps of the Language Arts Building, passing a group of Nerd boys huddled together playing Magic: The Gathering.

"OK, I'm bringing out my five/four dragon. Fear me the wrath of my wingèd foe!" said a kid named Marvin, absent-mindedly scratching his balls through his thin sweatpants.

Adam hustled up the steps faster. He got to his Spanish classroom, kids laughing and racing around before class started. Barely aware of what he was doing, Adam turned down the hall, ducked into the boys' bathroom, and locked himself in a stall.

He listened to make sure no one else was in there and then

kicked the stall door. He felt like he wanted to cry. There was something wrong with him. He didn't know what it was, just that it was inside him and it was wrong. "*Fuck* me! *Fuck* me!" he said through clenched teeth. He slammed his fist into the metal divider and then jerked over in pain, massaging his knuckles with his other hand. *Fuck you, Adam Freedman, you stupid fucking pussy.*

. . .

Adam walked through the front door to his house and headed straight up the stairs to his room. He caught a glimpse of his mom in the kitchen, bent down on her hands and knees, scrubbing hard at the bottom of the stove. They had a housecleaner who came once a week, so Mom in crazed-cleaning mode only meant she was upset about something.

"Adam?" she called out. Her voice was weak, anxiously apologetic.

"What," he yelled back. A statement, not a question.

"Could you come here for a minute?"

Adam rolled his eyes and turned back down the stairs. He was so fucking bored of this routine. Mom nice. Mom freaks. Mom nice.

His mom was still hunkered down by the stove. She was wearing her nice blouse and skirt — like she'd gotten home from work, walked into the kitchen, was suddenly struck with an undeniable urge to clean, and had immediately fallen to her knees, grabbing a scrub brush on the way down.

"I just wanted to tell you that I'm sorry for last night. I know I shouldn't —"

"It's OK," said Adam.

"Friends?" she said.

"Uh-huh," said Adam. "I gotta go do homework." He started to

walk away when it occurred to him that since Mom was in mak-
ing-up mode he should take advantage while he could.

"Hey, Mom?" Adam said, turning around.

His mom poked her head up from underneath the stove. "Yes,
honey?"

"I think I might actually want to go visit Casey after all . . ."

"I thought you were going to Tahoe with Brad?"

"I just miss Casey. It'd be cool to see New York."

His mom stood up, wiping her hands on the rag hanging from
the stove handle.

"Yes, I think we can still arrange it — the last week and a half of
June?"

Adam had a flash of the entire summer ahead of him. The gang
going to the movies — couples only! The gang going swimming
at Lake Anza — couples only! The gang getting high and going
to the Laserium in San Francisco — couples only! Adam sitting
alone in his room, jerking off for the fiftieth time that day.

"What if I went to New York for, like, the whole summer?"

His mom's face did a little twitch back.

"You're paying for Casey to stay in an apartment. I could live
there too . . ."

"First of all, we're *helping* Casey to stay in an apartment; she'll
have a job. And she already has roommates —"

"I'll get a job! I'll find something! If Casey says it's OK, can I
just do it? Please?"

All of a sudden, spending the summer in New York City was
the perfect and only solution to every single problem in Adam's
life. He knew, he just knew, that if he could do this, everything
would be OK. He had to do this. There was no going back. This
was the answer. "Please, Mom? Please?"

His mom stared at him. She appeared genuinely impressed by
his desperation.

"OK, well, we'll have to discuss it with Casey and see if she even has room . . . Though I do think that as your sister she should make room. And I'll also expect you to make some money — this will not be some paid vacation for you."

"Of course! I know! I'll call Casey right now, OK? And you think it will be OK with Dad?"

Adam's mom sighed. "Oh, we both know it doesn't really matter what he thinks. I'll convince him." And she smiled.

Adam grinned back.

# Chapter 3

IT WAS SETTLED. Casey was spending the summer living with friends in an apartment in Brooklyn, and Adam was going to live with them. The apartment was in the Williamsburg neighborhood of Brooklyn. "Actually, it's Bushwick," Casey had told Adam on the phone. "But Mom read about Williamsburg in some fashion magazine, so she thinks it's safe and cool." They would be living with two other people: a friend of Casey's from Columbia and someone who Casey referred to as "Craigslist" (who their Mom was told was also a friend from Columbia). The apartment had an extra sort of glorified closet-room that they were originally going to use for storage, but that Adam could cram a single mattress (and nothing else) into. He (well, his parents) would pay $900 for the room for the summer, which cut everyone else's rent down, so they were into it.

At first Adam had worried Casey wouldn't want him there — that she'd think he'd be a tagalong, or that she'd have to be responsible for him the whole time — but when he'd called to bring it up, she had been really nice. Casey knew how it had been at EBP for him that year, and she loved playing the role of cool older sister who could solve any problem.

"Fuck Brad and Colin and all those pathetic people," she said the next time they talked. "We're gonna find you some hot older hipster girl, and you'll come back with the entire school wanting to suck your dick."

Adam saw an image of everyone in the school, teachers and maintenance staff included, all standing in a line that snaked down through the hallways and out into the courtyard, everyone patiently waiting their turn to blow him.

"Everything is different here," Casey continued. "It's like my life at EBP never even happened or was just some shitty dream. This is my real life, where I was meant to be all along."

Adam remembered how during the month before she left for school a year ago Casey's response to anything anyone said to her was "I'm supposed to be in New York."

*"Casey, do you have plans this weekend?"*

*"I'm supposed to be in New York."*

*"Casey, it's your turn for the dishes."*

*"I'm supposed to be in New York."*

Now this became Adam's mantra too, albeit a silent one. Sitting at lunch, watching the couples paw and giggle at one another — *I'm supposed to be in New York.* Taking his finals, knowing he'd get a C average at best — *I'm supposed to be in New York.* And sitting at the dinner table, Mom telling him to stop chewing so loudly and to sit up straight and to put Neosporin on the zit on his chin before it gets infected — *I'm supposed to be in fucking New York.*

He couldn't wait.

. . .

The night before Adam left for New York, Brad spent the night. Adam's mom had booked his ticket to leave at 6:15 A.M. (His mom always booked these butt-crack-of-dawn flights, which was *so* annoying, though not as annoying as booking the ticket himself.) Since they had to leave for the airport at 4:00 A.M., he and Brad decided to stay up all night.

They played Xbox, ordered a pizza, drank beer from the fridge that they snuck down to get at 1:00 A.M., and IM'ed with Brad's girlfriend Sandy, who didn't know Adam was there and gave Brad a verbose, poorly spelled online blowjob. It was fun. It had been so long since he and Brad had had one of these nights where the two of them synced up perfectly, felt like doing the exact same thing at the exact same moment. Adam missed them.

They were sprawled on the floor, buzzed from the beer and playing two-player *Killzone: Liberation* on their PSPs, when Adam started to get nervous. Why was he going to New York again? To hang out with Casey and her lesbian friends for an *entire summer?* Maybe if he stayed here, it wouldn't be so bad. He'd just hang out with Brad, and maybe Sandy would have a friend from Bishop O'Dowd that he could go out with. They'd say fuck it to the rest of the group and just the four of them would hang out all summer.

"You're such an asshole for leaving," said Brad, as if he were reading Adam's mind. "I can't believe I have to hang out with Colin and Fletcher all summer. I'm gonna get brain damage. You'll come back and I'll be retarded."

Adam locked on to his missile launcher and threw a grenade. "So you're saying you'll be exactly the same."

Brad laughed. "Dick."

Adam imagined walking out into the hallway and creaking open his parents' bedroom door. Dad would be snoring. He'd tiptoe through the dark over to Mom's side of the bed. *"Um, Mom, I think I changed my mind ... can we, like, cancel the whole New York thing?"* He looked over at the clock: 3:09 A.M. In less than an hour, his mom would be knocking on his door, freshly dressed and ready to drive him to the airport. She'd surprise him with that care package he saw on the dining-room table when he and Brad had snuck downstairs for the beers. A neatly folded little brown bag with Keebler cheese and crackers, a chocolate bar, and dried apricots for him to eat on the plane. The thought of it killed him. He had to go to New York, if only because of that stupid care package.

. . .

"Adam? Adam!"

Adam opened his eyes. He and Brad had crashed out on his floor, their PSPs still in their hands. His mom was in the doorway, fresh and dressed just like he'd imagined she'd be. She was holding a camera.

"Adam! Now get all your bags together, and I'm going to take a picture of you."

Adam kicked Brad awake.

"What the fuck?" said Brad. He looked around, disoriented. "Ugh, I can't believe you're getting on a plane." He got up and crawled into Adam's bed.

"Hurry up!" said Adam's mom. "We have to leave in ten minutes, and I want this photo."

Adam grabbed his red duffel, strapped it onto his back, and hoisted up his two other bags, one in each arm.

"Ready?" said his mom. Her eyes were bloodshot. Adam could tell she was trying not to cry.

"Ready." He plastered on a big toothy grin.

*Flash*

. . .

Adam had only flown by himself once before. He had been eight, going to visit his grandparents, and a stewardess had clung to his side the entire time. She snuck him extra bags of M&M's and ruffled his hair with her long fingernails that dug into his scalp with the most pleasurable sensation imaginable. He remembered trying to hold on to that tingling feeling for as long as he could after she'd do it. It was the first time he felt in love. Now he was seventeen, and he felt old and cool, a young man getting on a plane to go seek his fortune. Even if his fortune was his parents paying for him to live with his sister for the summer.

In the boarding area, he looked for girls his age who might be traveling by themselves too. He'd go up, introduce himself, and they'd end up sitting next to each other on the plane, maybe even have sex in the bathroom. (*"Ever heard of the mile-high club?" "I've been waiting my whole life to join."*) They'd decide to be boyfriend/girlfriend, go into New York City to meet his sister together (who'd be really impressed), and then it would turn out that the girl had an apartment Adam could live in with her, and at the end of the summer they'd move back home, and she'd transfer to EBP, and he would show up at school with her on his arm, and everyone would be like, *"Who is she?"* and he would be like, *"Guys, this is . . . this is . . ."* What would her name be? Adam's eyes floated across the boarding area: A fat couple. An old couple. Another fat couple. A Hasidic man. Woman with three screaming children. Adam slumped on the floor to wait.

On the plane, seated next to the Hasidic man who was reading the Torah or whatever, Adam dozed, the muffled airplane sounds incorporating into his half-conscious dreams. The early morning sun cut through the window, blinding him in a pleasant, hypnotic way. His eyelids hung down, and he saw murky orange-redness — *capillaries,* he thought, millions of them. A thickly woven blanket of blood. And then the orange-red became a drowsy brown, and then through the brown, a blurred-out face. Wavy red hair, light eyes, pink lips. *This is the girl I'm going to New York to meet.*

# Chapter 4

CASEY HAD TOLD Adam to take the M60 bus for $2.75 all the way from LaGuardia Airport to 116th Street, which was right in front of Columbia.

The bus arrived and Adam claimed the corner seat in the back, as he always did, as every teenager he knew always did. It was weird to him that the whole civil rights movement had pretty much started over a fight to not have to sit in the back, and now the back was the only cool place to sit. Especially for black kids. A lot of times Adam had gotten on a bus, hoping for a back seat, but had to take something up front because a crowd of black kids had already staked the area. And, no, he could not just "join them."

Adam looked out the window. The inside of the bus was a pretty mixed group of people, but out on the streets every single person he saw was black. The storefronts read: JAY'S BARBER SHOP BEAUTY SUPPLY, DRUGS AND SURGICALS, SOLANGE HAIR DESIGN, HAIR AND BODY CONTROL, FOOT CARE CENTER (foot care center?), a fake Kentucky Fried Chicken called KENNEDY FRIED CHICKEN, and SHAE SHAE'S SALON. He wondered what part of New York this was.

There were nine black kids who went to EBP. Yes, nine. Out of 152. Adam wasn't friends with any of them. Even though they were spread out among the grades, they were all friends and ate lunch together (all except Nyiema, who didn't eat lunch with anyone except the six stuffed animals safety-pinned to her backpack). There was this one girl, Kandis, who Adam was kind of scared of. She had transferred to EBP mid-semester and was the only black kid in Adam's American history class, and whenever they were talking about civil rights or racism, Kandis would get all huffy and groan really loudly any time a white kid had an opinion. Their teacher, Mr. Grossman, totally played into it, always making sure Kandis got the last word on whatever they were discussing — like she was the necessary period to any sentence. Other teachers tried really hard *not* to single out Kandis or the other black kids when race topics came up, acting overly nonchalant about their opinions, like: *"Hmm. Maybe, maybe not. Just because you're black doesn't make what you say any more valid."*

Or maybe Adam was just crazy. He hated the way he'd think obsessively about race whenever he talked to one of the black kids. One time Adam had come to school in a new hooded sweatshirt, and this black kid named Jonari had told him he liked it when they passed in the hallway. The sweatshirt had immediately become the coolest item Adam owned. Colin had a black friend who lived in San Francisco that he'd been friends with "since before they were born," because their moms were in some baby group together. Colin was always going on and on about how tight he and Devon were, even though Adam had only met Devon a couple times over the years at Colin's birthday parties and Devon had always looked as if he were just waiting until he could leave. One of Colin's favorite things to say was that he "totally forgets Devon is black." What did that even mean? Adam was pretty sure if Devon went to EBP, he'd be hanging with the nine other black kids — not Colin.

Berkeley High was racially mixed, though, according to Sam, still really segregated. As far as Adam could tell, most of the gay kids Casey and Sam hung out with there were white. Casey had never really talked about race much, and Adam had been pretty sure she felt just as awkward about it as he did, but ever since Casey went away to college, all that had changed. Now Casey was constantly throwing around phrases like "white privilege" and "white guilt" or, most often, just plain referring to things as "white." As in: "I just don't want my summer job to be really white, you know?" Apparently Columbia had given her a "change of consciousness about race" — but as far as Adam could tell, that just meant talking about being white all the time.

The bus pulled up to the 116th stop, and Adam gathered his bags and got off. He was here. New York City. Columbia University. Where Jack Kerouac used to hang out and play football and stuff. *On the Road* was Adam's all-time favorite book. Of course Casey hated it. "*On the Road* is responsible for probably ninety percent of America's white male jerks and their fucked-up idea of what it means to be 'cool.'" Adam thought she was just jealous.

He crossed the street to Columbia's tall wrought-iron gates. Two Greek-looking sculptures stood guard on either side — to the left, a man holding a sphere that read, SCIENCE, and on the right a robed woman holding an open book. Adam lugged his two heavy bags and duffel on his back across the bricked quad in search of Casey's dorm. He would never get into a place like Columbia. More like Diablo Valley community college. Living at home and taking the bus there every morning. Or, possibly worse, when the time came to apply, his mom would send out some desperate mass e-mail to everyone she knew who worked at a "real" college to try to get him in. *"I'm writing on behalf of my son, Adam, who, despite everything, really is a good boy and tries very hard."*

Adam rounded a corner with his bags. Columbia certainly was a classic-looking place. The towering stone buildings with names like HOMER, HERODOTUS, PLATO, ARISTOTLE chiseled on them. People who went here turned into people like that. In the center of the campus sat a giant sculpture of a woman, her arms outstretched — a serene welcome to those who had been accepted, and inert bronze disinterest to those who hadn't. Adam passed a guy and a girl reading together on the crisp green lawn. The guy held his book with his arms wrapped around the girl, who leaned in between his legs, her book on her knees. They were both reading Thucydides' *The History of the Peloponnesian War,* the two identical books bobbing up and down on top of each other, making Adam feel as if he had double vision.

JOHN JAY. *Finally.* Adam walked in and released his bags with a *thud* onto the floor of the foyer. He gave the guy at the desk his name to call up to Casey. As Adam waited, two men in security uniforms unlocked the large doors to his right. The doors parted and Adam could not believe what was revealed inside — the most magnificent, elaborate, mind-boggling buffet banquet he had ever seen. He stepped over to get a better look and was hit with a puff of warm, buttery air. There were rows of grilled chicken breasts, crispy roast beef, pork chops with mushrooms, heaps of greasy French fries, mashed potatoes, butter-drenched corn on the cob. In the center of the room was a sprawling salad bar; to the left, a sandwich-making station; to the right, a glass tower sectioned off with Lucky Charms, Cocoa Puffs, Froot Loops — every kind of sugared cereal he was never allowed to have. Next to it there was a fucking ice-cream-sundae-making station. He was *starving.*

"ID," said the banquet security guard, bored.

"Uh, no, just looking," said Adam. He awkwardly pivoted around, pretending to be immersed in the various flyers taped to the walls: "Ultimate Frisbee on the Quad — Saturdays," "Stand-Up Comedy Night at the Village Pourhouse," "Horror Movie Club, This Tuesday: Wes Craven vs. John Carpenter," "CU Bellydance Presents!" Jesus. College was like some perfectly crafted, honest-to-god *utopia. Fuck.*

Casey appeared before him. "Took you long enough, loser!"

"Shut up, retard." They greeted each other with their customary kicks to the shins.

When they got off the elevator onto Casey's floor, the unbeliev-able Pleasure Island that was college continued. A bunch of doors were open, and Adam could see beanbag chairs and widescreen TVs. Rap music mingled with rock, drifting out from different di-rections. Nailed to the hallway wall was a little plastic basket filled with colorful condoms, a sign reading: FREE!

"This is my shithole," said Casey, opening the door to her room. "And this is June."

June was clearly gay. Like, no doubt about it, this was a lesbian. Casey, who had long hair and often wore skirts, wasn't obviously gay—which is probably why she got away with Mom and Dad not knowing. June, meanwhile, had a shaved head and a giant bull nose ring, and she was wearing a baggy T-shirt that read: I WON'T GO DOWN IN HISTORY, BUT I'LL GO DOWN ON YOUR SISTER. Just in case the shaved head and bull nose ring hadn't tipped you off.

"Hi," said Adam, offering his hand.

"He's so polite!" June said to Casey, laughing and ignoring Adam and his hand.

Adam decided that he hated her. *"And you're _so gay!"_* he said back to June in his head.

"June is living with us in Brooklyn," said Casey, flopping onto her bed.

*Great.*

"You'll meet Craigslist when we get there. God, it's gonna be so weird not calling Craigslist 'Craigslist' anymore!"

"I *know*," said June, flopping down next to Casey, staring at her with drooling eyes. June was clearly in love with Casey. *Loser,* thought Adam. *No way are you good enough for her. Sam would beat you to a pulp.*

Casey rambled on. "We're totally gonna be like, 'Um, Craigs-list—*I mean Ethan.*'" Casey and June burst out laughing.

*Ethan?* Adam had just assumed they'd be living with another girl. Well, that was cool. He'd have a guy there to be on his side, maybe show him around a bit. He could already tell he'd want to be spending as much time as possible out of the apartment and away from June.

Casey and June chattered away about the apartment, debating whether they should make a cooking/cleaning chore wheel ... Adam tuned them out. He sat on the floor, leaned up against the bed, and stared into the dorm room across the hall from Casey's. A girl's shorts-clad legs lolled on her bed, a giant economics book obscuring her face, calculator resting on her stomach. Suddenly, she let the book drop, revealing a gorgeous face and loads of heavenly red hair. Was *this* the girl Adam had seen in his daydream on the airplane? Had she actually arrived so soon? Adam's heart was racing. What if this was her? What if God was giving him this chance? It was now or never. Use it or lose it. But what was he supposed to do? Just get up and go introduce himself? Casey would think he was off the fucking wall. Fuck Casey, he wasn't going to let her get in the way of him and his destiny girl. But if it was destiny, shouldn't it happen without him really needing to make any effort? Wasn't that the point of destiny? But maybe he did need to do something. Just give her a certain look. Then she would do the rest, bring them together. Adam sat up straighter against the bed, made eye contact with the girl, and formed a tentative smile. The girl stood up, walked over to the door, and slammed it shut. A piece of paper taped to the door with the name LINDSEY wafted briefly: a sad little wave goodbye. *So long, Lindsey. . . . It was nice while it lasted.* Adam turned back to Casey and June.

"God, I cannot wait to leave this fucking place," said Casey.

"Really?" said Adam. "It seems pretty cool to me."

June snorted. Adam grimaced. *People with bull nose rings should never snort.*

Casey continued, "Ugh, you have no idea. I have to listen to two sets of nasty sex happening twenty-four/seven on both sides of my walls —"

"Nasty *straight* sex," interjected June.

"Plus the food is making me fat. Plus I hate everyone."

"You don't hate *me!*" said June.

"I don't mean I hate everyone at *school*," said Casey. "Mainly just everyone on my floor. Did you know most buildings don't even have a thirteenth floor? 'Cause it's unlucky, you know? This floor shouldn't even exist."

"You should have signed up for a Carman suite like I did," said June. "But, whatever, at least we're rooming together next year."

Adam noticed Casey flinch almost imperceptibly.

"I'm just ready to start living in the real world already," said Casey. "Enough of this sheltered-bubble stuff. It's, like, we're nineteen — we shouldn't have to be signing people in, checking in with the fucking RA about everything. And I'm sick of not being able to drink in my room."

"I'm gonna spend the whole fucking summer *baked,*" said June.

Adam glanced at Casey. He knew she didn't like smoking pot either. They'd bonded over it at least a million times.

"Hell yeah!" said Casey, knuckle-bumping June.

*Traitor.*

"Let's get the fuck out of here!" said Casey, and she jumped off the bed.

. . .

It took two trips to load all of their stuff into the cab that was waiting for them at the corner of Amsterdam and 117th. June made a big show of rolling her sleeves over her shoulders and acting all chivalrous carrying Casey's heavy things — "Hey, lemme get that one." "Put that down! I got it" — and didn't even thank Adam when he in turn carried down all of June's heavy shit. The cabdriver didn't want anyone up front, so the three of them squished in the back with all their stuff that didn't fit in the trunk. Casey in the bitch seat.

Adam had only ridden in a cab a couple times in his life. The idea of it freaked him out. You're supposed to get in a car with a total stranger and just trust that they'll take you where you want to go? All your life it's *"Never get in a car with a stranger, never get in a car with a stranger,"* then, all of a sudden, you're in New York and it's *"Get in a car with a stranger!"*

Casey and June were blathering on, oblivious, but if their driver — who was currently conspiring into a headpiece in a language Adam couldn't understand — decided he wanted to kidnap them and rape the girls (or at least Casey), it would be up to Adam to stop him. What kind of surveillance did they have on these cabs anyway? Were they connected to a GPS in some headquarters? Adam imagined a clean office with a friendly white man monitoring the cabs on a computer system. He realized if their cabdriver looked like the white man he imagined in the office, he probably wouldn't feel nervous right now. That thought made him uncomfortable though, so he decided to think about something else. He looked out the window at all the old brick buildings going by — there were barely any brick buildings in California. It was because of earthquakes.

After a long drive through different neighborhoods and over a bridge, the cab pulled up in front of the apartment in Bushwick. Adam, Casey, and June piled out, unloaded their stuff from the trunk, and dumped it onto the sidewalk. Casey paid the driver and the cab sped off.

This was their building: 206 Scholes Street. A bunch of tough-looking guys were sprawled out on the front steps, drinking and smoking, listening to music. Adam saw them looking at him and felt dumb standing there in a huddle with Casey and June and June's five-foot-tall pink flamingo lamp.

"I'm supposed to call the landlord," said Casey, taking out her cell. "He said he'd meet us with the keys."

Adam looked over at the guys on the steps again.

"I like your lamp," one said to him.

Adam looked away.

Finally, Casey spotted a Hasidic man hustling up the street toward them — his long black coat and curly hair things flowing behind him.

"That's him," whispered Casey. June and Adam nodded. For some reason it seemed like you should be quiet around a Hasid. Adam remembered the man he'd sat next to on the plane this morning. Maybe Hasids were going to have some special significance in his summer in New York. It gave the whole thing a biblical gravity. God was working with him.

"Hello," the Hasid said to Casey, and then to Adam, "I am Jacob." Adam shook his hand.

June offered her hand. "I'm June."

"I do not touch women; it is my religion," answered Jacob.

June glared at him.

Adam was impressed Jacob could tell June was a woman.

"You have three keys," continued Jacob, taking out a key ring. "The front door to the building and a top and bottom key for your door. Very safe. I will give you these, but any additional copies you must make yourself."

"Do you know a place around here that makes copies?" asked Casey.

"I only know a place where I live. The Hasidic neighborhood."

"We could go there," said Casey. "I wanted to buy a menorah anyway . . ."

Jacob's face lit up.

"You are Jewish?!" It was as if he'd just heard the most marvelous news of his life.

"Well, half," said Casey. "Our dad is Jewish. But we celebrate Hanu—"

"Not Jewish." Jacob cut her off. His face retracted to cold and businesslike. He handed the keys to Adam and abruptly walked off, disappearing around the corner.

"*Of course* he gives *him* the keys," said June. "What is he, sixteen?"

Adam wondered if he should start referring to June in the third person all the time too.

"I'm seventeen."

"Yeah, *huge* difference."

Adam ignored her. He hoped they did go to the Hasidic neighborhood to get the keys. He'd always been curious about Hasidic Jews. He'd never really understood the difference between them and Orthodox Jews until his class read this book *The Chosen* in ninth grade. It was by Chaim Potok—a name he and Brad had become obsessed with and repeated nonstop to each other for about two weeks—*Chaim Potok, Chaim Potok*—the *Chaim* coming out like they were hawking loogies. The book was about this Orthodox kid befriending this Hasidic kid and realizing how weird and sheltered the Hasidic kid's life was. The Orthodox kid's dad was a Zionist, which the Hasids were really against because they didn't believe in Israel—they thought only God should be able to create the homeland. This was the part that struck Adam the most—he'd always assumed the more Jewish you were, the more into Israel you were, but it was actually the opposite with Hasids. He wondered if maybe the girl he was supposed to meet in New York was a redheaded Hasidic girl. Their love would be tragic and revolutionary like *Romeo and Juliet* or *West Side Story*. It would end with Adam being gunned down outside the menorah shop where they first met, the redhead throwing herself on his twitching, soon-to-be-lifeless body. All they ever wanted was love.

Casey and June were gathering up their stuff and Adam followed. They said some awkward *heys* to the guys on the steps, dragged everything into the foyer and then up the stairs.

"You know why Hasidic people all look so weird and sickly like that?" said June. "It's because they're inbred. They can only have sex with each other."

Adam gave her a look.

"I can say that because I'm Jewish," said June.

"You're only half, too!" said Casey.

"Yeah, but I'm the *right* half!" said June.

"The inbred half," said Adam.

Casey laughed.

June scowled.

"I heard they can only have sex through a hole in a sheet," said Casey.

This idea complicated Adam's redheaded Hasidic girl fantasy. Or perhaps improved it . . . He would be the first guy to have sex with her without the sheet. Her mind would be blown.

Casey undid the two locks on their door. Number 9F.

"Ta-da!" she said.

The apartment was disgusting. Adam had always thought of Hasidic people as especially clean and fastidious, but apparently that didn't transfer to the apartments they rented. The floor was covered in trash — nasty trash, like leftover food. Mouse shit was scattered everywhere, and the molding looked chewed on. Spastic flies buzzed in the windowpanes.

"So it's a little messy," said Casey. "But it's *ours,* guys. It's all ours."

Adam grinned at her. The place was their mom's worst nightmare, and that made him love it. "I think I just heard Mom scream from three thousand miles away," he said.

"I think that was someone being shot outside," said June.

"Fuck, we should really clean it up before Ethan gets here, though," said Casey.

"You mean Craigslist?" said June.

Casey ignored her and June blushed. The Craigslist joke was apparently over.

"He might be really neat or something," said Casey. "What if he decides he doesn't want it!"

"No!" said June.

"We should start cleaning immediately. We can't lose Ethan — he's *perfect!*"

"I *know.*"

For a couple of lesbians, Casey and June sure were obsessed with this Ethan.

"I'm kinda starving," said Adam. "Is it OK if I go get something to eat real quick before I start cleaning?"

"Typical," muttered June.

Adam indulged a quick fantasy of punching her in the face.

"Sure," said Casey. "Just go to any corner store. They're called bodegas, and they all make sandwiches. And the best part, the sandwiches all come with American cheese — the kind we love that McDonald's uses."

. . .

Adam made his way past the guys lounging on the front steps again. He gave them the slightest hint of a nod that could be interpreted as friendly, if that was the right thing, or non-existent, if that was the right thing.

He stood on the sidewalk and looked around. So this was *New York.* It was a sentiment he'd conjured up about five times already since getting off the plane, but it still felt fresh and exciting, and he wanted to keep the feeling going for as long as he could. He started off in a random direction in search of a deli. *Bushwick Av-*

*enue,* he noted, looking up at the street sign. He imagined himself two months from now, this street as familiar as anything, comforting instead of strange.

"Boy! I'ma beat the shit out of you!"

Adam whipped around. A fat, balding woman with her hands on her hips was staring him down.

"E-excuse me?" said Adam.

"You get the fuck back in here, or I'ma beat the shit out of you. You think I'm playin'?"

Adam started to shake his head no when he realized the woman was looking past him at a kid on a Razor scooter. The kid grumbled and rode toward his mom. She grabbed the kid's arm and yanked him off the scooter.

"Ow!" he screamed.

Adam glanced around to make sure no one had seen him think the woman was talking to him. He went to cross the street — the light was green — when *HONK!* a car screeched in front of him. He jumped back to the safety of the curb. The traffic light switched to the red-hand sign, and several people barged past him into the crosswalk, barely looking. *What the hell?* Adam hustled after them.

Across the street was a shabby-looking store called E-Z Stop. Adam peeked his head in, and, behind the shelves of canned food and cleaning supplies, sure enough, there was a little sandwich counter. He went in and stared up at the menu. *Ham. Turkey. Salami. Liverwurst.* Liverwurst? The only time Adam had ever heard of liverwurst was in the book *A Wrinkle in Time,* which he'd never bothered to finish. In the book, some kids had made a liverwurst sandwich in the kitchen late at night, and then some fantastical stuff had started to happen that bored him. Adam wasn't even sure what liverwurst was, but, for some reason, right then it seemed like the most delicious thing ever.

"Ah, a liverwurst sandwich, please?" he said to the guy counting money behind the register.

"Liverwurst?"

Maybe you weren't supposed to order liverwurst.

"Uh-huh," said Adam.

"Everything on it?"

Adam had no idea. What went on a liverwurst sandwich? He didn't want to do it wrong. "Uh, just the liverwurst."

Another man appeared behind the meat counter and slapped together the sandwich while Adam paid the first guy. He took the sandwich outside and had just unwrapped the paper when two girls wearing giant sunglasses, threadbare tank tops with visible bra straps, and short shorts strolled up to him. The blond one had a cigarette in her hand.

"Hey, do you have a light?"

Adam did not have a light. But he brushed his hand across his front pocket, acting as if he were checking anyway.

"Sorry."

"No problem, cutie." And the girls flounced off.

Adam's face flushed. Was something like this going to happen every time he stepped out of the apartment? A thrilling prospect, if it wasn't so horrifying. He quickly turned back to his sandwich. "Liverwurst" was a thick wedge of grayish stuff squeezed between the bread. Adam was going in. He took a giant bite, and it was salty and creamy and smoky all at once. Amazing. Liverwurst was officially his new favorite food. His cell phone dinged in his pocket. Continuing to cram the sandwich into his mouth with one hand, he pulled out his cell with the other and read the text from Casey.

Ethan's here!

. . .

When Adam got back to the apartment, Casey, June, and Ethan were sitting around on some milk crates sharing a six-pack that Ethan had brought. There wasn't a fourth milk crate, so Adam tried to look casual leaning against the wall.

"'Sup, dude," said Ethan, popping open a beer and handing it to Adam. "I'm Ethan."

"I'm Adam," said Adam. He took a swig and his beer immediately foamed all over his shirt. Ethan chuckled, but it wasn't mean. It actually made Adam feel kind of warm.

Ethan was really good-looking — the kind of expertly-tousled-hair-movie-star guy that girls in Adam's class went nutjob for. He was wearing a clean white T-shirt and crisp dark jeans with brand-new bright white Adidas. Adam looked down at his own shit-caked dork Reeboks, a flash of them dangling off Kelsey Winslow's bed. He needed to go shopping immediately. What was he even thinking dressing the way he did? Obviously, cool clothes were the way to get girls. He wondered if Ethan would notice if he showed up the next day in his own brand-new Adidas.

"Yeah, it's shit pay, but I can see all the movies I want for free. I can hook you guys up, too."

Casey and June were hanging on Ethan's every word. Casey looked positively entranced, and June looked as if she were being batted back and forth between her own entrancement and jealousy of Casey's entrancement.

"I'm working at this YMCA summer camp," said Casey. "It's, like, nine dollars an hour, but I really love kids, so it should be fun."

"I'm still looking," said June.

No one asked Adam what his job was going to be, and he didn't volunteer. He had forgotten until this moment he was supposed to get one.

They talked about when the mattresses were being delivered

and who was going to take which bedroom. Ethan said he really didn't care, and June *insisted* that Casey take the large one. Like Casey was June's pregnant wife or something.

Ethan busted out his iPod dock and put on some weird electronic music while everyone moved their stuff into their respective rooms. All of Ethan's things looked new and expensive. An iMac, with a 36-inch monitor. Some kind of recording gear. A plastic tub lined with spotless sneakers: Pumas, Nikes, more Adidas. Maybe he and Ethan were the same size? Adam also noticed that all of June's stuff looked like shit. She walked into her room carrying a CD-player boom box that still had cassette decks.

Adam dumped his bags into his room and examined the closet-size space. It looked like solitary confinement — no windows, low ceiling. He wondered if it would make him go crazy. The idea was sort of exciting. He saw a small object in the corner he couldn't identify and went over to examine it. It was a black plastic square, about an inch and a half long on each side, with a round plastic circle on top. The whole thing was caked in dust. Adam poked it with his toe. Nothing happened. He considered picking it up, but then decided to leave it. He'd put his mattress on top of it and pretend it wasn't there.

...

That evening Casey and June were going to some girl's apartment for an *L Word* party. The girl's name was Schuyler, and she was a friend of their friend Roxanne from college. Schuyler was older and lived in Williamsburg. Casey and June seemed really excited to have been invited.

"We're in the neighborhood now," said Casey. She was leaning against the wall drinking from their third six-pack of the day. "We're not some dorks all the way up on Morningside Heights."

They'd plugged a couple of the desk lamps in and set them on the floor, giving the near-empty living room a cozy glow. Casey, June, and Adam were all drinking, but Ethan was in his room. Adam wished he would come out.

"I was totally down to go with Roxanne when she used to go," said June. "You were the one who was always like, 'It's too far! It's a school night!'" June followed this with a nervous laugh, waiting to see if her poking fun at Casey would fly.

"It's not like I actually gave a shit about schoolwork," said Casey. (Adam was pretty sure she did — Casey was obsessed with doing well at school.) "It would have been embarrassing to trek all the way across the city just to watch a TV show with people we barely know. It would totally look like we were trying too hard."

June nodded as if she'd already thought that herself.

"This is way more casual," continued Casey. "It's like, we're in the neighborhood; sure, we'll stop by." Casey took a nonchalant swig of beer, and Adam instinctively did too. He was feeling nice and buzzed.

"God, if Casey isn't there, I'm gonna kill myself," said Casey.

June gave a weak smile. "Isn't Casey, like, Schuyler's best friend? I wouldn't worry about it."

Casey sighed. "This is a good outfit, right? I look hot, right?"

"You look hot."

June still annoyed Adam, but he couldn't help feeling a little sorry for her. It was just too tragic.

"Wait, you have a crush on someone named Casey?" he asked Casey.

Casey laughed and rolled her eyes. As if she'd heard it a million times but wouldn't mind hearing it a million more. "*Yes.* I have a crush on someone named Casey. I *know.*"

"I guess that's just something you have to deal with when you're gay," said Adam.

Casey and June exchanged a look.

*What? That was offensive?*

"OK, we should leave in, like, fifteen minutes," said Casey, moving on, "and I need to be at least thirty percent drunker." She guzzled her beer.

"What are you up to tonight?" June asked Adam. Adam shrugged. *What was he up to? How the hell was he supposed to know?*

Casey stood up, wobbled a little, and walked toward the faint music coming from Ethan's closed door. She paused and gave June a teeth-clenched nervous grin. June mirrored the grin back. Casey knocked lightly on the door.

"What's up?" said Ethan, poking his head out.

"Uh, we're going to an, um, *L Word* party over on Lorimer Street . . . if you wanna come?"

*Ethan does not want to go to a fucking* L Word *party,* thought Adam. He imagined Ethan stepping out, declining the invitation, then mentioning a hot club in the city he was going to tonight and saying, *"They don't card. Adam, you wanna come with?"*

Ethan gave his customary little chuckle. "No thanks. I'm gonna stay in tonight." And he shut the door.

*Fuck.* Was Adam just supposed to stay here in the apartment while Ethan was in his room with the door locked? That just seemed so awkward . . . so pathetic. Whatever Ethan was doing in his room was definitely cool, but the only thing Adam could think to do alone in his room was surf Internet porn. And, the truth was, he was too scared to go out into the city alone. He wouldn't even know where to go. Adam saw Casey looking at him. He could never hide how he felt from her.

"You wanna come?" she asked. "I know you like *The L Word* — even if it's for the wrong reasons."

Adam liked *The L Word* because it showed hot girls making out. Isn't that why Casey and all her friends liked it too? He glanced back at Ethan's closed door.

"Uh, sure, whatever," he said. And he started to chug his beer, too.

...

Outside, the warm New York night spread out exciting and exposed. Police cars with their sirens blared by, and groups of older guys slouched and murmured in the corners. Adam wondered if they were drug dealers. He imagined a phone call to Brad back home. *"Yeah, picked up an ounce from the guys on the corner. . . . Naw, they give me a good deal. Neighborhood price. It's gonna blow when I get back to the Bay and have to pay regular again."* Brad had mentioned coming to visit him for a week, but Adam wasn't so sure. Everything would have to be perfect. He'd need to have a girlfriend, all new clothes, and a gang of cool dudes he hung with that were not Casey's lesbian friends. He imagined Brad being jealous of Ethan.

*"What, so now this guy's your best friend?"*

*"We live together; you just get super tight that way."*

*"Isn't he, like, twenty-one? Why's he hanging out with a seventeen-year-old?"*

*"He, like, didn't even know how old I was for a couple months . . . He was totally shocked when I told him."*

A man pushing a ratty ice-cream cart jostled up next to them. Casey and June bought Chocolate Eclairs, and Adam got a Cherry Bomb pop. He took a sweet, icy bite, and as he swallowed was hit, blindsided really, by a sudden, momentary elation. For those two seconds, he knew — he just *knew* — everything in New York was going to turn out exactly as he dreamed.

...

"*Hola,*" said a lesbian, opening the door. Schuyler wasn't far from how Adam had imagined her. Short cropped hair with bleached tips, lip ring, boy's clothes.

"This is my brother, Adam," said Casey.

Schuyler looked Adam over. "Nice lipstick."

Casey looked at him. "The popsicle."

Adam quickly rubbed at his mouth with his fist.

Inside, a bunch of other typical-looking lesbians lounged around on a couch and pillows on the floor. No one seemed to notice them walk in.

"You guys want some beers . . . whiskey . . . water?" asked Schuyler. "Roxanne's not here yet."

Adam saw Casey blush, embarrassed that apparently their only excuse for being there was Roxanne.

"I'll have some whiskey," said Casey.

"Me too," said June.

"Me too," said Adam.

Casey gave them an annoyed look.

"Hey, Casey," Schuyler shouted to a super-butch lesbian talking with people in the kitchen. "Hook these guys up with some Jack."

Adam watched his sister stare at the other Casey, panic, then check her cell phone for no reason. June looked down at her own body as if she wished she'd left it at home.

"Have a seat wherever you can find one," continued Schuyler, then abruptly turned around. "Bitch, I know you did not take my spot! No one fucks with my *L Word.*"

Casey and June sat on the floor, leaning up against the couch, and Adam huddled by the ficus tree in the corner. He tried to catch a glimpse of himself in the window reflection to see if his lipstick was still there. Not that there was any girl here for him to impress. Every single one looked gay — like manly lesbian gay. It might be fun to talk with a girly lesbian, just for the night, even if it went nowhere, but none of these girls were even remotely hot. Why would you want to make yourself look so unattractive? And why was Casey — who *was* hot — so batshit for these girls?

Adam looked over at Casey and June, who were talking to Butch Casey. Casey was doing all her flirty stuff she used to do when Sam first started coming around. Constantly brushing her hair behind her ear. Talking really fast and using lots of hand gestures. She was also downing her drink as if it were on the verge of evaporation. June was doing likewise. Casey turned toward Adam and started waving for him to come over. *Great.* She'd probably run out of things to say and was now going to "introduce her brother" as a new conversation topic. *Awkward.* Adam made his way over, almost tripping over a lesbian in a baseball cap sitting on a skateboard. He hunkered down next to the group.

"Adam's in high school hell right now, so I'm letting him live with us for the summer," said Casey.

Adam didn't like the word *letting.* Even if it was true.

"Yeah, high school's a cunt," said Butch Casey. Adam stared at her. He'd seen lesbians with faint mustaches before, but this was out of control — this girl had a straight-up *beard.* What the fuck was Casey thinking? This girl was disgusting!

"Casey works at MoMA. He gets to go to any museum in New York for free."

*He? Oh. This person was a guy.*

"I thought you were *gay?*" Adam blurted out to his sister. Boy Casey laughed. June made a quiet, strange little noise.

"Uh, OK, weirdo," said Casey. "Anyway, I'm *queer,* or whatever." She was trying to play it off like it was nothing but still let Adam know she was mad at him for saying it. How could she not expect him to be surprised? His entire life all she'd ever done was go on and on about how much she loves girls and has zero interest in guys.

Adam looked back at Boy Casey — it was insane. Right before his eyes, a butt-ugly girl transformed into an actually not-bad-looking guy. It was like that optical illusion when you look at the black vase that then turns into two white profiles facing each other. Ugly girl. Attractive guy. Same face. He could tell he was staring, so he quickly took a gulp of whiskey. He was getting drunk.

"It's starting! It's starting," someone shouted. "Shhh! Shhh!" The TV was on and the lights went out.

The show began with a woman running out of another woman's house, both of them crying. The woman got into a car with a different woman waiting outside.

Adam had only seen the show a couple of times and didn't know who anybody was.

"Oh, Alice! I can't *believe* Dana dumped her for Lara!" someone said.

"You're telling me you'd rather have sex with Alice than Lara?"

"Well, maybe not, but . . ."

Everyone laughed.

"This is why Dana got cancer," said someone else. "Karma."

This time no one laughed. There was an awkward silence and then the opening credits blasted on the screen, and everyone started singing along to the theme song.

Adam was the only one not singing. He shifted uncomfortably.

A title card read, SEVEN MONTHS LATER, as two women, one with a giant headscarf, strolled down the street.

"Um, can we talk about Dana's outfit?" someone said.

"Just because you're bald and wear a headscarf doesn't mean your entire wardrobe has to become Africanized," said someone else.

This one got a couple chuckles.

The screen cut to a girl pinning up a flyer that read: '80S TRANS PROM — TOP SURGERY BENEFIT PARTY.

The entire room exploded.

"What the fuck?! What the fuck?!" said one girl. She stood up from her seat on the floor. "*My* benefit was a prom theme! They totally stole that!" The girl whipped out her cell phone. "Get me Ilene Chaiken's phone number."

Everyone laughed more and the girl sat down. Adam looked back at the TV, totally confused. Now a guy and a girl were pinning up flyers together. Apparently this was not a show you could just jump into midway.

"OK, I'm sorry," said someone on the couch. "But we need to talk about Max's facial hair."

"You mean the Brillo Pad glued to his chin?"

More laughter.

"I mean, *what the fuck,* I've been on T for six months, and I've got, like, seven hairs! Max has been on it for, eh, a week and a half — full-grown beard."

"That shit wouldn't look normal on a bio guy."

"Cis guy."

Adam peered through the dark at all the lesbians, their faces flickering in and out of the TV light. Now that he was really looking, he saw that a bunch of them had facial hair. What was going on? Was everyone here some kind of *hermaphrodite*? Wasn't that supposed to be really rare?

"I still think Shane is hot," someone said. "I don't care if it's not cool."

"*Carmen* is hot. Look at her."

The girl on the screen *was* hot. She had huge tits and was wearing a really low V-neck, and you could see her bra strap. When were they going to get to the sex already? The screen cut back to a hospital.

Adam heard his sister's voice calling out next to him. "So Max *wants* to get his breasts removed, but Dana *has* to get her breasts removed. Symmmmmbolism."

Everyone laughed and through the dark Adam saw Casey

beam. She was leaning against Boy Casey, who had draped his arm over the couch behind her. June was separated from them by one person.

Adam turned back to the TV. A woman and man floating in a swimming pool, each holding babies, were talking.

"Fucking Tina, I always knew she'd turn straight," said someone.

"At least that means she'll be off the show next season."

"Seriously, no one wants to watch Tina trolling for dick."

Adam wrapped his arms around his knees, hunching into himself.

The screen cut to a party, and there was another full-room attack of laughter. A woman wearing a white tank top with TRANNY PROM on it was dancing on a table.

"Lord have mercy," said Schuyler.

The cancer woman was talking to a guy about how much she used to love her breasts.

The girl sitting next to June sighed loudly. "I told my aunt I was getting top surgery, and she was like, '*Why?* I *love* my breasts!' I was like, 'Well, I don't. I'm a *guy*.'"

On the screen, the guy with the Brillo Pad facial hair butted into a girl and a guy dancing and yanked the girl away, shouting at her.

"Oh, that's fucked up," Boy Casey's voice called out. "I bet they're trying to say that taking T is making Max all aggro. That is seriously fucked."

"Yeah, like you become a guy, so of course you're suddenly an asshole."

Everyone kept talking, and all of a sudden it hit Adam. He got it. The lesbians here weren't hermaphrodites—they were girls who wanted to be guys. And somehow this was possible. He looked back over at Boy Casey, whose arm was now wrapped around Casey's shoulder. Boy Casey wasn't a boy; he was a girl who became a boy. But how much of a boy? Did he have a penis? And why the fuck didn't Casey just tell him all this from the beginning? It was so like her: she just loved having something cool and different that she could think Adam wouldn't understand. Fuck that. He was going to pretend as if he knew all along. He'd bring it up all casual, like, *"So, since Boy Casey used to be a girl . . ."* No big deal. Fuck her. He would *not* give her the satisfaction of thinking she was revealing something special and shocking to him.

The show chugged on as Adam tuned in and out, returning to the fantasy of Brad's potential visit. Brad would knock on the apartment door, and Adam would be in the middle of having sex with his hot redheaded girlfriend. *"Oh, shit! Brad's here!"* he'd say, and Redhead would exclaim, *"Where are my clothes?!"* They'd open the door all flustered and half-dressed, and Brad would totally know what was up. He'd give Adam a *"you asshole"* grin, and Adam would give a cocky grin back.

Everyone in the room was getting riled up again. On the screen, the woman and man from the pool scene were now alone in a bedroom, making out. The man took off his shirt.

"Ewwwwww!!!" everyone shouted.

The woman caressed the man's chest. Everyone was making gagging noises. Adam could feel himself getting hard.

The woman and man fell onto the bed, and the man pulled the woman's underwear off. It looked like he was about to go down on her.

*"N-n-n-n-n-n-no,"* the woman said. "That's not what I want."

A girl next to Adam snorted.

The woman and the man stood up and stared into each other's eyes. She reached down into his underwear.

The room was surprisingly quiet. Adam was definitely hard now.

The man lifted the woman up and started fucking her against

the wall. She was moaning and gasping as the guy thrust himself inside her.

*This was amazing.* Adam had thought he'd see lesbians having sex, but this was a million times better.

Someone made a faint repulsed sound.

"'Do-me, red-faced man!'" said June.

And everyone laughed.

. . .

On the walk home, all Casey could talk about was Boy Casey and the date they'd planned to go see *Donnie Darko,* which played every Saturday at midnight at some theater. June was overly enthusiastic, telling Casey, "Don't worry, he's *obviously* into you."

"He is, isn't he? Oh my god."

When they got back to their building, Adam realized he was starving again.

"Hey, do you think that sandwich place is still open?" he asked. Another liverwurst sandwich sounded perfect.

"Everything's still open in New York," said Casey.

"I'm gonna go hit it again," said Adam.

"What are you getting?"

"Turkey sandwich."

For some reason, he didn't think he should tell them he was eating liverwurst.

"Pick up some toilet paper and paper towels while you're there," said Casey.

Adam did not want to pick up toilet paper. What if he ran into those girls again?

*"Hey, you got a light?"*

*"No, but I've got some toilet paper."*

"Fine," he said.

Casey and June went into the building, and Adam was alone

on the street. It was after 11:00 P.M. but the air was still sweet and
warm. It made his limbs feel antsy, keyed up. Adam had a sudden, crazy idea. He would text Casey that he was "going out for a
while" and just fucking go anywhere he wanted. He really *could* go
anywhere he wanted! It was a rapidly intensifying, reckless feeling
he'd never had before. No one knew him here. He could go anywhere, talk to anyone, do anything. It was as if instead of life being
this confusing, awkward thing he had to bumble his way through,
it was a brand-new video game, fresh from the shrink-wrap, where
he was the hero and every single thing was possible. The most fan-
tastic game ever invented. On a sudden impulse, Adam bolted —
sprinted down to the end of the block as fast as he could run. He
stood on the corner, gulping in breath, the pavement stinging his
feet, looking around. He really could do *anything* he wanted.

A gang of thug-looking guys rounded the corner and came toward Adam. His body tensed. But he knew if they attacked him,
he'd fight with everything he had. If he died, he died, but he'd give
it every fucking thing he had. The gang passed by him without
notice. He could do whatever he wanted, but right now he mainly
just wanted to eat. He crossed the street to get his sandwich.

. . .

Back in the apartment, Casey and June were in Casey's room, lying side by side on the mattress, watching *But I'm a Cheerleader*
on Casey's laptop. Casey apparently never felt the need to watch
any other movie. Ethan's door was closed, but light snuck out of
the crack, along with the faint secret-code sounds of synth music.
Adam went into his room to eat his sandwich. He splayed out on
the bare mattress and turned on his laptop.

*Knock*

"What?"

"Mom on the phone," said Casey through the door.

*Not in the mood.*

"Tell her I have diarrhea."

"Gross!"

Adam heard Casey, muffled, to their mom, "Uh, he's gonna call you back later." Then to Adam, louder, "Just text her or something, OK?"

"Fine."

Adam wondered if Casey was going to turn bossy this summer, acting like she was Mom. She might . . . but he wasn't too worried. She could act like the boss all she wanted, but he'd never actually have to do what she said. There were too many secrets between them. More that he kept for her. Like if she got all huffy about him staying out late, he could say, *"Oh yeah? Well, I'm gonna call Mom and tell her your new boyfriend she's so thrilled about used to be a girl, so, as long as that's cool . . ."* Not that he would ever really do that. But the fact that he could was still there. He sometimes thought about how Casey and his relationship would be different if she weren't gay or if their parents knew and were OK with it. If he didn't have that power. Or what if he was the one who were gay, and she kept the secret for him. The troubled younger brother who, on top of everything else, was gay. Thank god it wasn't that.

Adam tried to check his e-mail, but there was no signal. He went out into the living room.

"Casey? What's up with the Internet? It's not working."

"It's not set up yet, dork," she said, not taking her eyes off the movie.

"You can try to steal someone else's signal," said June. "Ethan said it was working this afternoon."

June was wearing plaid pajama pants and a baggy tank top that her large breasts spilled out of. *Ugh, don't look. Don't look.*

Adam went back to his room and scrolled through the wireless networks: 59AC. kozyshack. Jordan. DressedforSuccess. They were all locked. Fuck it. He was really tired anyway.

He spread his sleeping bag out on the mattress, pulled off his jeans and T-shirt, turned off the office lamp he'd borrowed from Casey, and climbed into bed. Because there were no windows, the room was solid black. Like if he didn't have a memory of what the room had just looked like, he would have *no* idea where he was. He could wake up in the middle of the night and think he'd been buried alive. Adam shivered at the thought. A siren and honking cars blared outside. The sounds that had been thrilling and fun when they walked to the *L Word* party now seemed scary. But Ethan was here. Adam wasn't the only boy. If someone busted in and tried to rob them, he and Ethan could totally take the guy.

Adam stared into the dimensionless black as a thought morphed into focus in his brain: *What if Ethan was like those guys at the party? A girl.* It seemed impossible, but how could he even tell? Ethan was taller than Boy Casey, taller than Adam. And, besides, Ethan just *seemed* like a guy. For some reason, the thought that Ethan was a girl . . . scared him. Adam tried to blink his eyes and have them adjust to the room, but nothing. It was as if there were bandages wrapped around his eyes. He remembered a book his class had read at the beginning of the school year, *Johnny Got His Gun.* It was about a guy who'd lost his sight, hearing, and all of his limbs in World War I. The book was just the guy's thoughts racing through his head as he lay in the hospital, imagining rats chewing on his fingers — his fingers that didn't exist. Adam shivered again and burrowed deeper in his sleeping bag. He thought about his mom taking his picture in his bedroom before they left for the airport. He couldn't believe that had been this morning. It was a million years away. He remembered how when she took the photo, she was smiling really big, but her eyes were red and she was crying a little, trying to hide it. Adam banished the thought from his brain. It hurt too much. He couldn't even think about it. He leaned over the side of his bed and fumbled in the dark for his jeans on the floor. He found them and pulled his cell phone out of the pocket. The tiny little light flipped open, and with just that small green glow he felt better. He scrolled down to Mom and texted: NY is great! love it here. talk tmrw. He put the phone down by the mattress and slid back into the sleeping bag. He imagined that his redhead was with him. He'd have his arm around her, and she'd be curled up into his chest. Her hair would be in his face, and it would tickle but feel kind of nice. He'd fall asleep breathing her in.

# Chapter 5

THREE WEEKS LATER and everything had changed. First of all, it was fucking *hot*. As in, Adam's laptop broke because the sweat dripping off his hands had messed up the keyboard. Ethan had gotten an air conditioner installed in the window of his room right away, but Casey and June insisted they didn't need one for the living room. Casey liked to sprawl out on the futon in her underwear and "pretend it's a shaman's sweat lodge and I'm getting cleansed." June liked to watch her sprawl out. Every day Adam witnessed June veer between the sheer joy of being around the object of her obsession and the horror of getting to do that without getting to have her. The whole thing was sort of fascinating, if not totally depressing.

Everyone had also started jobs. Casey was working at a YMCA summer camp and came home each day babbling about how much fun she'd had, demonstrating how a kid named Kelvin had taught all the counselors the Crip Walk, or completely exhausted, tipping like a felled tree, face first onto the futon. "All I want to do is pass out, but I can't stop hearing their screaming voices in my head."

June had had some trouble finding a job, what with her bull nose ring and shaved head and all. "Fucking homophobes," she would say, coming back from a failed in-face interview.

"Why don't you just take the nose ring out?" Adam had suggested.

"This is my identity," June answered, tugging hard on the ring, making Adam wince. "I'm not *removing* my identity for some piece-of-shit job — I'm a fucking lesbian, and they're gonna have to fucking deal." Adam hadn't bothered to point out that plenty of lesbians got by being lesbians just fine without bull nose rings.

Eventually, June got a job at a crummy comic book shop where all the employees had labret, philtrum, and other previously unknown facial-part piercings and aggressive tattoos, and the owner paid them five dollars an hour "under the table."

"Everything about the place is illegal," June would say, "we make $1.75 under minimum wage — I checked; we never get any breaks — also illegal — and we have to eat while we're working, but if a customer comes in while we're eating we have to, like, hide our sandwich in the coat check." Still, all of this was apparently better than removing the nose ring that made her look like a hog.

Ethan still had his job at Film Forum — an art house movie theater in Manhattan. One night they were showing *Touch of Evil* — this movie Ethan was obsessed with — and he'd invited Casey, June, and Adam and let them all in for free. They'd gotten all the popcorn they wanted, and Ethan had made them foamy chocolate egg creams from the soda fountain. The movie was pretty great too — one of those that made you feel cool just for watching it. Adam sat next to Ethan in the theater, and every fifteen minutes or so Ethan would go *"uhn"* and punch Adam in the shoulder, like it was just so good he couldn't take it.

It also turned out that Ethan was totally rich. Adam and Casey's family was rich too, but Ethan was *rich* rich. His parents had a trust fund for him that was supposed to be for college, but when Ethan had decided he didn't want to go to college, they'd just let him use the money to move to New York. He wanted to make movies.

Because Adam wasn't eighteen, he needed something that didn't require a work permit. So far, he'd had one job that Casey found for him on a Columbia listserv. The job was stuffing envelopes for a rich artist woman named Mags Mumford, who needed to "remind people that I fucking exist, god damn it." The job was at Mags Mumford's house on the Upper East Side, and the first time Adam went he had gotten completely lost. Casey had told him to take the green number 4 train to Ninety-Sixth Street, but when they got to Ninety-Sixth, the train just zoomed on past the station and then past the next station, and the next, and before Adam knew it, they were stopped at 125th Street. He'd thought maybe he could just walk back to Ninety-Sixth, but when he got out of the station, he was by some river and there were no white people on the street and he was pretty sure this wasn't anywhere near where Mags Mumford lived. He'd gone back into the station, got on the wrong train again, this time ending up at something called West Farms Square–East Tremont Avenue, finally figured out the right train, and showed up at Mags Mumford's apartment an hour and a half late. She didn't even notice. She was on the phone and pointed Adam toward the dining-room table, which was heaped with empty envelopes and shiny cards announcing the words *Mags Mumford*. He was supposed to sit there for six hours and at first felt assaulted by boredom, but as the first half hour turned to an hour, and then the next, the monotonous stuffing and licking ended up lulling him into a pleasant trance. He went back every day for a week, but then Mags Mumford ran out of people to remind and the job was over. He'd made only $275, but it was something, and he still had his savings (from birthdays, Christmas/Hanukkah) to cull from as needed.

Mainly, Adam's favorite thing to do was hang around Ethan, who it turned out did *not* used to be a girl. That Adam had even considered it just made him laugh now. The first week they were all living there, it had obsessed Adam. He kept trying to figure out *how he could tell.* Ethan shaved like a guy, had a flat chest like a guy, sounded like a guy . . . but it was apparently possible to be all those things and still be born a girl. Boy Casey had started coming over to the apartment and liked to go on and on about being "trans" — which is what you called it when you were a guy who used to be a girl (and vice versa). Pretty much all Casey and Boy Casey ever talked about was how Boy Casey was trans and how complicated life was because of this. The two of them would lie, intertwined, on the living-room futon, having some variation of this conversation:

> BOY CASEY: *"Nobody fucking understands me."*
> CASEY: *"I understand you . . ."*
> BOY CASEY: *"Yeah . . ."*
> CASEY: *"Nobody fucking understands us."*

And then they'd make out, right there on the futon. It was kind of fucked up. Casey had the biggest room of everyone, but apparently she and Boy Casey just preferred making out where everyone else had to watch.

June, of course, had to pretend as if she *really* liked Boy Casey and was *super* supportive of the relationship. Casey and June talked about Boy Casey nonstop, barely noticing if Adam was in the room too. Which was weird since they could get pretty personal.

> CASEY: *"He let me touch him, you know . . . 'down' last night."*
> JUNE: *"Really? Has he . . . had bottom surgery, or . . . ?"*
> CASEY: *"No! Most trans guys don't . . . It's too expensive and not even really that good. But you know what the T does to his clit . . ."*

JUNE: *"Wait, so that's true?"*
CASEY: *"Mmm-hmm."*

Adam wasn't sure what they were talking about half the time, but he was totally fascinated and able to piece together different facts. He'd usually pretend to be engrossed in whatever TV show was on so they would forget about him and really get into the details, but sometimes, if it seemed right, he'd ask a casual question or two. "So, like, how did Boy Casey get to grow a beard and stuff?" Whenever he asked a question like this, Casey would leap at the opportunity to launch into some long, show-offy explanation.

CASEY: *"OK, so the hormone that makes you grow hair on your face — or one day grow hair on your face, ha-ha!"*
ADAM: *"Eat shit."*
CASEY: *"That hormone is tes-tos-ter-one."*
ADAM: *"Duh."*
CASEY: *"Listen! So you get it naturally in your body, but Boy Casey's body doesn't make it, so he injects it into himself with a syringe."*
ADAM: *"Gross."*
CASEY: *"It's not gross. He's doing what he needs to do to be himself. So, anyway, the testosterone — T — makes him grow hair on his face and lowers his voice and makes him lose fat, like, around the butt and hips."*
ADAM: *"Sounds like you need to inject some T."*

Adam didn't ask too many questions, though — he didn't want Casey knowing he actually gave a shit. But how could he not? I mean, *what the hell* — you could actually transform yourself from a girl into a guy. Adam didn't know what the fuck he'd spent the last few years studying in school when *this* was going on in the world.

One night, when Ethan was out, Adam had decided to just up and ask Casey and June about him. I mean, why not? Casey and June were having a typical gabfest about Boy Casey and whether or not Boy Casey had ever dated another trans guy, when Adam, flipping TV channels, asked in his best verging-on-bored voice: "So, is Ethan, like, trans?" and Casey had answered: "Ethan? No." And that was that. Adam had felt a flood of warmth for Ethan fill his body. They were brothers, in it together.

Adam tried to hang around the house whenever Ethan was home and would bring up random things — "Do you think this bread is stale?" — but really he barely knew him. Ethan spent most of his time locked in his room, and there was an understanding that unless it was urgent, you did *not* knock on his door.

Then, one night, it happened.

Casey, Boy Casey, June, and some ugly girl June had found on the Internet were all out on a double date, and Adam and Ethan were alone in the apartment. Adam was watching TV when Ethan poked his head out of his room.

"Hey, can I get your opinion on something?"

"Uh, sure," said Adam.

Stepping into Ethan's room for the first time was like opening the wardrobe into Narnia. Immediately upon entry the air shifted to clean and cold, the colors relaxed into blues, blacks, and grays. Everything was meticulously organized, rows of DVDs in an as-of-now-unknown-but-certain order, the sheets tucked tightly under the bed. It was hard to believe this room even existed in their apartment. Ethan was fussing with a video program on his giant iMac.

"OK," said Ethan. "Check out these two sequences and tell me which one you like better."

Ethan hit PLAY. A pretty, dark-haired girl with arched eyebrows was standing in a room, her arms wrapped around herself, staring at the ground. After remaining in that position for about a full minute, the girl brushed a strand of hair out of her eye, looked up at the camera, and said, "I don't want to." Cut to black.

"Or . . . this," said Ethan. He clicked PLAY on a new file. The exact same video played. Girl staring at the ground. Girl brushing away hair. "I don't want to." Cut to black.

"Uh, I don't get it," said Adam. "What's the difference?"

Ethan smiled. "I'm not gonna tell you," he said. "That's the point. It's not about what's *actually* different — it's about what you feel. The actual difference is a subtle technical change only film nerds will notice. But for regular people, like you, it's about the *feeling* you get. Which one gave you a better feeling?"

Adam was disappointed Ethan thought of him as a "regular person." But more than that, he was flattered that he wanted his opinion.

"Uh, the first one," said Adam. His choice was completely random. They both made him feel exactly the same.

"Awesome," said Ethan, nodding his head.

"So who's the girl?" asked Adam.

And then Ethan started talking and didn't stop for half an hour straight. The girl was Rachel, and she was the love of his life. They had started dating in high school in Greenwich, Connecticut. He knew, was certain, he would never be able to be with anyone else.

"I know that sounds like dumb kid stuff . . . no offense," said Ethan, looking at Adam — Adam shook his head, none taken. "But it's true," Ethan continued. "I just know. It's like she was there while my brain was still developing, and she's part of the way it's structured now. I loved the way she saw. You know how each person sees the world differently?"

Adam nodded, even though he wasn't entirely sure what Ethan was talking about. He just wanted Ethan to keep on talking. Adam was getting this tingly feeling sitting there listening to him, and he didn't want it to go away. It was almost as if Ethan were talking to himself, the way his eyes sort of glazed over as he spoke. But then he'd turn and look straight at Adam — like he knew Adam was following him — and that Adam *got it*.

Ethan went on. "I know it sounds really obvious, like, 'Oh, people have different personalities, they experience the world in different ways' — but it's more than that. Imagine how the world actually *looks* to each person. Visually. Physically. It's like this: You know how if you're happy, the street you're walking down can look full of life? The trees glorious and vibrant? The people good and kind? But if you're depressed, the exact same street looks ugly, suddenly all you can see is the trash, the sky is menacing, and the people, grotesque. Our visual worlds are a constantly shifting metaphor for our internal moods. But what about person to person? What about all the time? How do I see the world all the time versus how you see it? The things Rachel would point out ... I don't wanna repeat them, it doesn't work ... but her world was beautiful. Mine just felt so bland in comparison. All I wanted to do was live in hers."

Adam nodded again. He wanted to know how Ethan saw the world. He was positive it was better than the way he saw it.

"That's what I love about movies," Ethan went on. "Trying to capture all those different viewpoints. Make a movie that literally re-creates someone else's visual world. There's not one world we all live in. There are a billion different worlds overlapping each other. Falling in love is finding the world you want to fuse with your own."

"Why did you guys break up?"

Ethan stared at the blank wall behind his computer and shook his head. "Shit happens, right?"

Adam nodded, as if he'd been through it, too. He was getting a little self-conscious about all the nodding.

"So what about you?" asked Ethan. "You got a girlfriend . . . boyfriend?"

"I was kinda dating this girl at school," said Adam. (He had been at Kelsey Winslow's house . . . that counted as dating.) "But, you know, shit didn't work out."

Ethan nodded. "You're gonna meet a girl here in New York. Bet you anything."

Adam looked down and smiled. He considered for a second telling Ethan about the redheaded girl he'd seen in his mind on the plane but decided it sounded too weird. There had been a couple more false alarms. A girl on the subway. A girl at the 99 Cent Store. But he still hadn't met her.

"Yeah, I just gotta figure out where to meet them . . ."

"That was pretty sad watching June leave with that Internet girl and the Caseys," said Ethan.

Adam laughed.

Ethan continued, "I know people who have met online and it's cool and they're happy and all, but when someone goes on an Internet date and the person sucks, it's just so much more depressing."

"June is depressing," said Adam.

Ethan laughed really loud and Adam beamed. "Oh, man," said Ethan, "she and your sister have got some weird S & M thing going on. It's like June *likes* torturing herself."

"I know!" said Adam. He paused for a moment and looked down at his jeans, picked casually at a stray thread. "So, like . . . what do you think of Boy Casey?"

Ethan snorted.

Adam gave a tentative smile. "He's, like, kind of annoying . . ."

"He's just young . . ." said Ethan. Which was weird, since Ethan was twenty-one and Boy Casey was twenty-three.

"He's always looking at himself in the mirror," said Adam, "and making me take all these pictures of him and Casey. All he and Casey ever talk about is *him*."

"He'll grow out of it," said Ethan. "Now get out of here — I gotta get back to work." He smiled at Adam and punched him in the shoulder, just like he had done during *Touch of Evil*. Adam grinned and punched him back.

. . .

It was around 2:00 A.M. that night, and Adam was cocooned in his bed, having just fallen asleep, when he heard Casey and Boy Casey come home. They were drunk and talking loudly. He didn't hear June's voice. She must have gone home with Ugly.

> BOY CASEY: *"I'm hungry!"*
> CASEY: *"Les get some cereal!"*

There was some crashing in the kitchen.

> BOY CASEY: *"First I wanna fuck you, you look so fucking hot."*
> CASEY: *"Aaah! Not on the futon! Adam an' Ethan!"*
> BOY CASEY: *"They're sleeping! Shhh! Come on . . . I'm pgkjgdkjkf . . ."*

*What did he say?*

> CASEY: *"I love it when you pack."*
> BOY CASEY: *"Uhhn, that feels good."*
> CASEY: *"Lemme suck on it."*
> BOY CASEY: *"Yeah . . . suck it. All of it."*
> CASEY: *"C'mon, les go in my room."*
> BOY CASEY: *"You gonna let me fuck your ass?"*

*\*SHUT\**

Silence. Adam looked from side to side in the dark, needing a witness — *someone* to acknowledge what had just happened. His mind was swimming. What had Casey been sucking on? The rubber dick? Like Sam had? Boy Casey must have one too. He did *not* want to imagine what was going on in Casey's room right now. Fuck. He was never going to fall back asleep. *Think about something else. Anything.* He shifted onto his right side. Then onto his back. His room felt unbearably hot. He needed to splash some water on his face.

Adam creaked his door open and stepped softly into the front room. He really was going to go to the bathroom, but then heard muffled voices coming from Casey's closed door. He took a cautious step closer to her room. It was Boy Casey.

BOY CASEY: *"I told you. No."*
CASEY: *"Why not?"*
BOY CASEY: *"I'm just not jkrjkll."*
CASEY: *"But I want to lkjlkjslk."*

Then there was nothing. Adam stayed poised, hovered between Casey's door and the bathroom. They could burst out at any moment. *"What are you doing here??"* He would pivot. *"I'm going to the bathroom, Jesus."* Then:

BOY CASEY: *"I hate my bkjhjhjk."*

Another silence.

CASEY: *"But I like it . . . I lhjhkh it . . ."*

"I hate it." Boy Casey's voice was icy dark. Adam had never heard him sound like that before. He squeezed his eyes shut and willed his ears to open wider.

Casey's door swung open. Boy Casey stared at Adam.

"Oh, sorry, just . . . bathroom," said Adam.

"That's cool, you can go first," said Boy Casey. He was wearing boxer shorts and no shirt. Adam had never seen him without his shirt before. He instinctively looked down at Boy Casey's chest, not sure what to expect. It looked mostly like a guy's chest, but was sort of loose and droopy, and through the dark Adam could make out two curved scars, one under each nipple. Boy Casey's hips bulged out of his boxers. They looked womanly. Like Adam's mom's body. Adam whipped around and went back to his room, forgetting all about the bathroom. He closed the door, and in the safe, still dark of his room, he tenderly ran his hand over his own smooth flat chest.

# Chapter 6

FRIDAY NIGHT AND everyone was going out to a club called The Hole. The Hole was in "The City," which was what you called Manhattan if you lived in Brooklyn. Casey and June were really excited about The Hole, and for some reason Ethan had decided not to stay in his room looking at Rachel on the computer screen and instead go with them.

"It's not like I'm gonna *date* anyone, but, whatever, I could hook up with a girl . . ." said Ethan.

"So this is, like, a straight club?" Adam asked. He couldn't believe it, they were finally all going out to a straight club. It was actually happening.

"Why the fuck would we go to a straight club?" said June.

*Right. Of course.* Well, if Ethan was going, that was good enough for Adam. He didn't even care where they were going. It was him and Ethan, out in the city, looking for action.

Everyone wanted to take a shower before they went out, which was a problem, since the bathtub had stopped draining a few days after they moved in. It would eventually drain; it just took about five hours. If you wanted to take a shower right after someone, you had to stand in their scummy water. The tub was some varying degree of cesspool throughout the day.

"Ugh! Those fucking hebes!" said June. They were arguing over who got to take the first shower.

"I know," said Casey. "I've been calling them, like, every day since it stopped. They keep telling me someone's on their way to fix it, and then no one shows up."

"They don't care about anyone who isn't Hasidic," said June. "There's probably lead in the walls, too." June glanced around the apartment, as if she realized a bomb could be lurking in any corner.

"I say oldest gets to shower first," said Ethan.

"Second oldest second!" said Casey.

"Fine," said June. "I'm next." *Thrilled* to get to shower in Casey's filth.

"Wait, that's not fair," said Adam.

Everyone ignored him.

While Ethan was in the shower, Casey's cell rang. Their mom always called Casey first. Casey chattered away on her bed until Ethan came out of the bathroom with a towel around his waist, and Casey handed the phone to Adam.

"Casey just told me all about her new boyfriend!" his mom said, as though in the throes of religious rapture.

"Uh, yeah, I've met him," said Adam.

"Is he just marvelous? Is he wonderful?" she said.

"Not really," said Adam.

"Oh, how wonderful," said his mom. She then moved on to how the roots of their neighbors' bamboo plant were growing on their property from under the fence, and their dad had had words with the neighbors, but they hadn't cut the bamboo down, and legal action might need to be taken . . . and then they hung up.

By the time it was Adam's turn for a shower, the brown, oily water was sloshing out the sides of the tub. *Whatever,* he thought, naked and stepping in. He was going out to a club in the city with

Ethan to look for girls, and a little flare of excitement sparked inside him. He closed his eyes, opened his mouth, and let the fresh spray hit his face.

. . .

Adam, Casey, June, and Ethan walked down Bushwick Avenue to Boy Casey's apartment, where everyone was meeting to "pregame" before The Hole. A few of Boy Casey's best friends were going to be there, and Casey was nervous.

"He's always telling me how important his bros are," said Casey. "What if they don't like me?"

"Why wouldn't they like you?" said June.

"I don't know. Why would they?"

"Because you're funny and smart and beautiful and —"

"I know. But they're all so *cool*."

"We're cool!" said June.

But everyone knew she didn't believe it.

"I don't know, he seems pretty into you, to me," said Adam.

Casey smiled at him. The good thing about spending 75 percent of your time insulting someone is that if you do actually say something nice, it counts.

They got to the apartment, and Casey rang the buzzer. She applied lip gloss and tugged the collar of her V-neck T-shirt down lower.

"Come up," said Boy Casey over the intercom.

Boy Casey's apartment was full of *Star Wars* paraphernalia: *Star Wars* posters on the wall, pillows on the couch, and a giant R2-D2 model in the corner.

"I guess you hate *Star Wars*," said Ethan.

"*Star Wars* is my jam," said Boy Casey. "You guys want some beer?" He gestured to the couch. "You know Schuyler, and that's Jimmy."

Schuyler and Jimmy were watching skateboarding on TV. Schuyler didn't bother to look over at them, but Jimmy cocked his head.

"Whassup." Jimmy was wearing a crisp Orioles hat tilted to the side, his tiny body engulfed in a baggy T-shirt and baggy jeans stuffed into puffy, colorful Nikes. Adam recognized a PSP sticking out of his jeans pocket. *How old was this guy?*

"Uhhhn, *brutal,*" said Jimmy, as a skater wiped out. The skater had bit it on a rail slide. "You know that's gotta hurt." Jimmy grabbed his crotch.

Boy Casey handed out beers. He sat down on a sofa chair and patted his lap for Casey. Casey perched on his knee. Adam could tell she was uncomfortable but didn't know what to do. Ethan took the other free chair, and Adam and June sat down on the floor.

"Yo, Jimmy, kill the TV," said Boy Casey. "Put on some tunes."

"*Man,*" said Jimmy in a whiny voice. He did some things with the remotes, and emo music started playing.

"Man, I had a shit day," said Boy Casey, taking a swig. "What have you guys been up to?"

"Just work," said Casey. It was awkward because she turned her head to answer his question, but her face was already right next to his.

"I'm at Cooper Square Comics," said June.

"I need some new comics," said Boy Casey.

"Can you hook us up?" asked Jimmy.

"Well, not really . . ." said June. "We don't get, like, a discount . . . but you guys could come say 'hi,' if you wanted. I work Tuesdays, Thursdays, and —"

"Work's a cunt," said Boy Casey. "I hate my job."

"I thought you liked the MoMA?" said Casey, turning her head at that awkward angle again.

"I like *art,*" said Boy Casey. "I don't like people."

"Where do you work?" Schuyler asked Casey.

"At the YMCA day camp in Bed-Stuy," said Casey. "Oh my god, today this little girl — it was the sweetest thing. I was working with the kindergarten group, and everyone was doing free play — just drawing or playing with whatever game they wanted. And this one kind of pudgy girl, Elizabeth, had this handful of shells, and she kept walking around to every group of kids saying, 'Who wants to play with shells? Who wants to play with shells?' But nobody wanted to play with shells. I almost died."

"I hated camp when I was a kid," said Boy Casey. "Capture the Flag! Red Rover, Red Rover! That shit was not for me."

Adam and Ethan exchanged a glance. Adam looked down and smiled to himself. He wished he and Ethan could talk telepathically: *Ten dollars says Boy Casey can't go two minutes without bringing the conversation back to himself.*

"What do you do?" June asked Jimmy.

"I sell weed. Four years of college, stamped on that ass, and I'm sellin' weed." Jimmy grinned and slapped himself on the ass.

"Let's get that shit going," said Schuyler.

"Y'all a bunch of fiends," said Jimmy. He rummaged in his pockets.

Fuck. Why did everyone always want to smoke weed? Adam seriously could not tell what anybody saw in it. *Hey, wanna get totally paranoid and make everything you say sound stupid and fake? Awesome!* He looked over at Casey and could tell she was nervous too.

Jimmy packed a pipe and lit it. He passed the bowl to Schuyler, who took a hit and passed it to June on the floor. June inhaled greedily.

"This isn't bad," she said, exhaling. "I'll have to get your number. All the weed I've smoked in New York sucks." She passed the pipe to Adam. There goes the evening.

"Where're you from?" said Jimmy.

"Indiana," said June.

Jimmy laughed as if June had told a joke.

"You're from California, right?" Schuyler asked Casey. "*That's weed.*"

"Yup," said Casey.

Adam exhaled and passed the pipe up to Ethan.

"You guys from L.A., the Bay, or what?" said Schuyler.

"We're from San Francisco."

*San Francisco?*

"We live in Piedmont," said Adam.

Casey glared at him. "Nobody knows Piedmont. We're from the Bay Area — people know San Francisco."

Ethan finished his hit and walked the pipe over to Boy Casey. Boy Casey took a hit and handed it to Casey.

"No thanks," said Casey, waving her hand, and Boy Casey casually passed the pipe back to Jimmy. *What the hell?* Adam didn't know you were allowed to pass. And he couldn't just pass the next time it came around because that would show he'd changed his mind, was weak. He had to commit to getting high now.

"*Lodi Dodi, I likes me a shawty, titties D to the double, gettin' crackas in trouble . . .*" Jimmy bobbed his head up and down as he rapped.

June passed the pipe back to Adam. Maybe he could get so high, he'd forget he was high. He took a big inhale.

"Isn't Piedmont kind of rich?" said Schuyler.

"It's near Oakland," said Casey.

Why didn't Casey want people to know they were rich? At EBP, the richer you were, the cooler you were . . . Isn't that how it works? Adam glanced over at June. For the first time, he tried to imagine what she would look like normal — with long girl-hair and without the bull nose ring. She might not actually be that ugly. He looked around the circle of people and imagined that everyone, including himself, had a shaved head and a bull nose ring. Like they were all in a creepy cult. The weed was a special potion. Soon they would all enter a collective consciousness like the future human-robots in the movie *A.I.* June's thoughts would be Jimmy's thoughts; Casey's thoughts would be Ethan's thoughts. Adam's nose would itch, and Boy Casey would scratch his own nose.

Adam scratched his nose. Was everyone staring at him? No. A conversation was going on. A conversation about . . .

"I like her," said Schuyler. "I mean, she's hot. But I don't know if I wanna date a femme right now. I feel like she'll push me to be trans, and I just wanna stay genderqueer for a while. I don't know, maybe I'll fuck her."

"What about Sailor?" said Boy Casey. "I think ze has a crush on you. I bet ze'll be there tonight."

"Ze's all right. I just feel like I could kind of do better than hir."

"I met hir. Ze's kinda annoying . . ." said Casey. "Roxanne was dating hir and said all ze ever did was talk about hirself."

"Ze and I just go way back . . ." said Boy Casey.

"Who's Zee?" said Adam.

Boy Casey, Schuyler, and Jimmy all laughed.

"There's no 'Zee,'" said Casey. "Hir name is Sailor, and ze uses the pronouns *ze* and *hir.*"

Adam started to open his mouth, but Schuyler cut him off.

"I go by *ze* too."

Adam looked up at Ethan to see if he was getting all this. Ethan looked totally out of it. He was just staring into his lap, not paying attention at all.

Boy Casey continued, "Ze'll be there tonight. If you want, I can ask hir what's up. I'll be casual about it —"

"Can we change the song?" said Ethan. He was still staring into his lap.

"You don't like Neutral Milk Hotel?" said Schuyler.

"I love them," said Ethan.

"Hey, pack that bowl again, Jimmy," said Boy Casey. "I don't feel high at all."

Adam had never felt more high in his life.

Ethan was speaking really soft. "It just . . . reminds me of my ex. Can you please switch it?"

Schuyler cocked her head at Jimmy. Jimmy picked up the remote and the song changed.

"Dude, I feel you on that," said Schuyler.

"Word," said Boy Casey.

"No. It's different," said Ethan, looking up. His eyes were bloodshot. "It's not that I can't listen to it because it reminds me of her. I can't listen to it because I save it." His eyes fell back to his lap. "I don't want to ruin it. I only listen to that song when I'm alone, when I want to think about her. If I listen to it too much, it won't give me that feeling anymore." His voice was slow and monotone. "The world means more if you compartmentalize. Songs belong to different people. A food can taste like a person. Put on the shirt you wore when you met, and she's touching you. You only wear it when you want to wear her. But if you overwear it, you lose that. Everything fades. Before you know it, your world's just a washed-out wasteland."

There was an uncomfortable silence.

"I know what you mean, man," said Boy Casey. "I used to have this shirt I *loved* — I just looked *good* in it. Losing that shirt was like losing a person —"

"I gotta go," said Ethan, standing up. "I'm sorry. I'm a dumbass. I shouldn't smoke pot."

"Are you sure?" said Casey. "Do you want another beer?"

"You're sure?" echoed June.

"No, I really just gotta go. Thanks, though." He turned to Schuyler and Jimmy. "It was cool meeting you."

"Yeah, man," said Schuyler.

Ethan looked at June and Adam. "I'll see you guys later."

Adam started to panic. Ethan was the reason he had wanted to go to this club. Ethan was his ally. He couldn't go there alone.

"Wait, I think I'm gonna go too . . ." Adam said. He stood up.

"No, man, go out, have fun," said Ethan. "Don't be lame just 'cause I am."

"No, I'm . . . tired anyway," said Adam.

"Bye," said Casey. She shifted awkwardly on her lap perch.

Adam nodded and looked at June. She gave him a nervous smile, like she wanted to ask him to stay. Adam felt kind of bad but waved goodbye. He followed Ethan outside.

Adam and Ethan walked down the steps of Boy Casey's building into the night. A motion sensor went on, and the stoop light lit up. Ethan paused.

"You really don't have to go home just 'cause I am," said Ethan.

"I know . . ." said Adam.

Ethan turned the corner and leaned up against the wall of the building. He slid down till he was sitting. Adam did the same.

"Jesus, I really wigged out up there. I'm such a retard. I wish I still smoked. I need a cigarette."

"We could go to the store . . ." said Adam.

"Nah," said Ethan. He paused, staring at a crack in the ground. "I texted her at, like, four in the morning last night. Fucking stupid."

"Rachel?" said Adam.

Ethan nodded. "I just feel so guilty. I fucking hate myself."

"I thought she broke up with you?" said Adam.

"She did."

"Did you . . . cheat?"

"Hell no. You do *not* cheat on Rachel."

Adam wanted to know what had happened, but for some reason, he felt like he shouldn't ask.

"Fucked-up thing is . . ." said Ethan. "What I really wanna do when I feel like this, like if I could do *anything,* is cry. You know? But I just can't."

Adam did know. At some point in middle school, he'd decided that crying was not a thing he was going to do anymore. He knew it felt good though. He was eleven when they'd put their dog Lucy to sleep. She had tumors all over her face, distorting her expression, and smelled so bad their dad wouldn't be in the same room as her. Adam had forced himself not to cry in front of the vet and his mom and Casey, but had done it alone in his room when they got home. It had made him feel better.

"It's cool to cry," said Adam.

"I know, man," said Ethan. He smiled at Adam.

They sat in silence for a moment.

"How about that Jimmy?" said Ethan.

"*'Titties D to the double, gettin' crackas in trouble,'*" recited Adam.

Ethan laughed. "You really should still go out," he said. "Seriously, you're never gonna meet a girl staying home, watching TV on that scabies futon all night."

Adam laughed. "I know . . ." He paused for a moment, and then, "I have this idea of this redheaded girl I'm supposed to meet in New York. It sounds stupid but . . ."

"Redhead is at The Hole right now, as we speak!" said Ethan.

"She is?"

"She totally is."

Adam was getting that recklessly impulsive feeling again — the one he'd had on the street after the *L Word* party the first night they'd moved in. A feeling like anything was possible — all he had to do was act.

"You really think I should go?"

"I'm gonna kick your ass if you don't go," said Ethan. "Now get back up there."

. . .

Adam, June, Casey, Boy Casey, Schuyler, and Jimmy walked to the end of the line outside The Hole. When Adam imagined a "club in Manhattan," he thought of red-velvet carpets and roped brass barriers and big bald bouncers in suits. This was not the case with The Hole. The Hole didn't even have a sign that said: THE HOLE. How everyone found it was beyond him. It was a concrete wall covered in competing graffiti and old peeling posters with a fat butch lesbian checking IDs at the front. At least the burly bouncer part was right.

"Wait, there's a cover?" said June.

"It's only ten dollars," said Schuyler. "Anyway, Riley always lets me in for free."

"I thought you said I would be able to get in?" Adam whispered to Casey. "They're checking IDs."

"They usually don't do that," said Boy Casey. "This place is getting too popular."

"June and I have fakes," said Casey, "but we need something for Adam."

"Just come back out and give him yours after you're stamped," said Boy Casey. "You guys look enough alike. It's just like you got a haircut."

"She's a girl!" said Adam.

"Half the guys in here have girl IDs," said Schuyler.

"You could use mine," said Boy Casey, "but I'm taller than you." Boy Casey was about a half-inch shorter than Adam.

"He and Jimmy kinda look alike," said June.

"Watchoo say?" said Jimmy.

Boy Casey grabbed Jimmy's Orioles hat and put it on Adam. "Ahhh! Fuckin' doppelgängers!" Jimmy barely cleared Adam's shoulders.

"Gimme that!" Jimmy jumped up and swiped the hat back.

Boy Casey continued, "OK, so Jimmy'll go in, get stamped, then bring his ID back out to Adam. Adam, you go hide behind that building."

Casey gave him an encouraging nod.

"Uh, OK," said Adam. He walked in the direction Boy Casey had pointed.

Waiting in the alley between two buildings, Adam watched girls get on line for The Hole. Unlike the *L Word* party, a lot of them were hot. Like *really* hot. One girl noticed him staring, and Adam whipped his head around. He fixed his eyes intensely on the dumpster in front of him, as if he were waiting for someone to jump out. Maybe some of these girls *were* straight . . .

Jimmy slapped his ID into Adam's palm. "Wait ten minutes or I'ma *kill* you!" Then he turned around and ran back into The Hole.

Adam looked down at the ID. It was Jimmy's photo, but the name was "Francesca diSessa," and she was a girl and she was twenty-six years old.

. . .

Inside, The Hole was dark, pounding pop music, and clogged with cigarette smoke. It was also completely packed with girls. Most of them were butch lesbians, but there were a good number of straight-looking girls as well. The interior walls were the same as the outside ones, concrete with spray-painted tags everywhere. It was like someone had gutted a building, stuck a bar in the middle, and called it a club. And for whatever reason, *this* was the place to be.

Adam scanned the club trying to get a glimpse of the Caseys, Schuyler, or Jimmy. He couldn't find them anywhere. It was better this way, right? He was on his own. A man in a giant pulsing throng of women. *Something* had to happen. A butch dyke with giant breasts rammed into him.

"Sorry, dude," she said.

A drink. First things first, he needed a drink. Whether he was going to meet a girl was yet to be determined, but at least he could get fucking wasted. Adam pushed his way through the hordes. The closer he got to the bar, the tighter everyone was packed in. He stood on his tiptoes to get a glimpse of the bartender. She looked like she was making five drinks at once, and everyone was leaned in toward her with money in their hands. Adam swiveled his shoulders, trying to squeeze in closer. He was almost to the edge of the bar when a lesbian wearing a beanie and a backpack shoved him out of the way.

"Hey! Su Jin! Two whiskey sours for me and Ramona! You're awesome!"

Adam glared at the back of the girl's head. *Fuck this.* He couldn't even get a drink. He couldn't even get a fucking drink. *Fuck everything.* His eyes fell down to a button pinned to the beanie girl's backpack that read: THAT'S WHAT 'ZE' SAID.

"Hey! What do you want?!"

Adam looked to his left. A cute blond girl was smiling at him.

"Uh ... whiskey sour!" said Adam. He had to shout over the music.

The girl laughed.

*Shit.* He should have just said a beer. But what kind of beer? Heineken.

The girl leaned over the lip of the bar, her low-cut shirt slinking down.

"Suji! When you get a chance — one whiskey sour and a grey-hound!"

The girl turned back to Adam. "Bitches are bruxjkkxjkxjxk!"

Adam smiled big. He had no idea what she'd just said. It was too loud. The girl got the drinks and handed Adam his. He took a swig, and then realized he hadn't given the girl any money. *Fuck.* He was doing absolutely, every single minuscule thing wrong. He reached into his back pocket, took out his wallet, and tried to extract some bills with one hand while still holding his drink with the other. The whiskey splashed all over his T-shirt. The girl looked at him like he was crazy.

"Just get the next one!" she shouted. "It's not like I paid for these anyway!"

"Thanks! Thanks a lot!" said Adam. *Retarded, retarded, re-tarded.*

"I'm Calxnxknxkmsk!" she said.

"What?!" said Adam.

The girl leaned over and shouted into his ear, her lips brushing against his cheek. "I'm Calypso!"

The whole right side of Adam's face and neck tingled from where she had touched it. *Calypso.* He couldn't explain it, but all of a sudden, he felt 100 Percent in Love. The girl he'd imagined on the plane had probably really had blond hair and he'd just misin-terpreted it.

"I'm Adam!" he shouted back.

Adam and Calypso moved to the back of the room, where it was slightly less crowded and easier to talk. There were ratty couches strewn about the place and couples making out all over them. Calypso swayed as she drank. Adam had the impression she'd had several already.

"So do you, uh, you come here often?" said Adam. *Jesus fucking Christ.*

Calypso burst out laughing. "You're hilarious. Wow. Are you a Sagittarius or something?"

Adam was a Virgo, but he didn't want to disappoint her so he just nodded yes.

Calypso grinned and rolled her eyes. "Thought so. Always the comedians . . . but you guys are *awesome* in bed."

Adam blushed and downed the rest of his drink, ice and all.

Calypso continued, "My ex-boyfriend was a Sag. Cubs is gonna *kill* me when she finds out I spent all night talking to a Sag. Ha-ha! No pressure."

*Ex-boyfriend? Was Calypso straight? Was this actually happening?*

"Uh, so . . . what sign are you?" said Adam.

"Leo," said Calypso, smug. "Triple Leo!" She shook her long beaded necklace in Adam's face.

Adam wanted another drink but was scared that if he went to get one, Calypso wouldn't be there when he got back.

"Should we . . . go get some more drinks?" he asked.

"Thanks! Another greyhound!" She smiled.

*Look,* he told himself. *If this is destiny, she will be there when you get back. She will be there, she just will.*

"Cool, be right back," he said. Adam turned around and barged his way through the crowd. He was on a mission now. He needed to get these drinks and get them fast. No bullshit.

Adam got to the bar and elbowed his way to the front, pushing two girls out of the way. They barely seemed to notice.

"Two greyhounds!" he shouted. The bartender didn't hear him. "Two greyhounds!" he screamed. He didn't give a shit if he looked lame — he was *getting these drinks.* The bartender slammed two frothy yellow drinks in front of him.

"Fourteen bucks."

Adam slammed down a twenty, grabbed the drinks, and

whipped around to plow back to Calypso. Adrenaline was rushing through him. He felt cool, with purpose. He had a girl waiting, and he was bringing her a drink.

"Took you long enough," said Calypso, accepting her drink. "I almost got roped into a threesome." She jerked her head toward one of the couches where two people were going at it. Adam looked a little closer and saw that one of the people was Boy Casey. The other was *not* his sister. He took a huge swallow of his drink. He didn't know how it was possible that alcohol made everything seem like not a big deal, but it just did.

"You're so over this place," Calypso said, shaking her head at Adam. "You're totally over it."

Adam tried to look nonchalant.

"I came here with my friend Cubs, but she ditched me for some girl. Whatever, we'll totally laugh about it tomorrow. We always do . . ."

Adam nodded, sipping his drink.

"It's my birthday," said Calypso.

"Happy birthday," said Adam.

"Big Three-O," said Calypso. "This is the year I really get my poetry going."

"Cool," said Adam.

"So, like, what's your deal? What do you do?"

Adam nodded, pretending not to have understood her.

Calypso took a big gulp of her drink. "Can I tell you a secret?"

Adam took a big gulp of his drink, too. "Uh-huh."

Calypso put her hands on Adam's shoulders and leaned in. Her voice was loud in his ear. *"I want to be a star."*

Adam nodded again, not sure how to respond.

"You're so cute," she said, backing up, looking him over. "Your little boxers sticking out . . ."

Adam looked down to where his shirt had ridden up on his pants a little.

Then he realized Calypso was kissing him. Really kissing him. Her tongue was in his mouth, and her hand was tugging at the side of his T-shirt, pulling him closer. He had a full-on erection and swiveled a little, embarrassed she would feel it. He tried to think about how he was kissing her back. He had never done this — what were you supposed to do? Were you supposed to move your tongue in any particular way? A thing Brad had once said to him popped into his head. *"And then I fucked her mouth with my tongue, you know?"* He tried moving his tongue in and out. Calypso stopped the kissing and looked at him.

"You are fucking hot," she said.

Calypso grabbed Adam's hand and pulled him into the crowd. "We need to take this shit to the bathroom."

The two of them swerved and pushed through the dancing, sweaty mass, making their way to the other end of the club where the bathroom was. Adam saw Jimmy dancing with an extremely tall girl, his head bobbing in front of her breasts. Jimmy noticed Adam, saw that he was with Calypso, and gave him an *"Aww yeah!"* grin. He pointed his finger out at Adam while continuing to bounce up and down to the music.

"Shit!" said Calypso, dropping Adam's hand. "It's my ex-girlfriend."

"Oh, uh . . ." said Adam.

"You know what? Fuck that. She canjnjkjkjkjkj." Calypso linked arms tightly with Adam and continued pulling him along.

They got to the front of the club where the bathroom was.

"Yes! No line," said Calypso. She smiled at Adam. "It was meant to be."

They went into the bathroom, and Calypso locked the door. Bright fluorescent light and a muffled quiet. The walls were covered in frenzied, colorful writing, and the toilet was plugged to the top with yellow toilet paper and bloody tampons. Calypso

backed into the corner and shot Adam a coy look. He was suddenly really nervous. It was just like in Kelsey Winslow's bedroom.
He was supposed to make a move, but he felt paralyzed. His body
felt alien, as if it weren't supposed to touch anything. Like if he
touched her, some blaring alarm would go off. Everyone in the
club would evacuate.

He heard Kelsey Winslow's voice in his head, *"I need guys to be
more aggressive."* Calypso was staring at him, thinking the same
thing.

"Awww, you're shy," said Calypso. "That's soooo cute." She
reached out and tugged the bottom of Adam's shirt, pulling him
close to her.

"Don't worry," she said, speaking softly in his ear, "I like guys
like you." Her lips moved across his face. "I like guys like you a lot."
She flattened her hand out onto his chest and slid across, stopping
on his nipple. Her middle finger made a slow little circle around
it. Adam's hard-on was back in full effect. They started kissing
again, and this time Adam wasn't nervous. All he was, was one
giant human-shaped concentration of pleasure. He fucking loved
being alive.

Calypso took his hands and put them under her shirt. "My
body is for you," she said. He moved his hands all over her smooth
round breasts and under her bra, where the nipples were hard. He
felt about five seconds from coming in his pants. Calypso grinded
into him. "You like that?" she said.

"Uh-huh," said Adam. His mind was mush. He didn't even
know where he was anymore.

"Oh god, you're packing," said Calypso. "That is so fucking
hot."

*Packing?* Adam didn't know what she was talking about and
didn't care. He pushed in closer, squeezing her tits as his tongue
shoved into her mouth.

"I want you to fuck me right here," she said. "Feel how wet I am?" She grabbed his hand and plunged it down her jeans. Adam didn't know what he was feeling — it was wet, it was soft. He suddenly felt kind of terrified.

"Uh, I . . ." he said.

"Come on," she said. "Fuck me with that dick of yours."

*OK, wait, he needed to think. Was this actually happening? Was he going to have sex? Shouldn't they use a condom? You're supposed to use a condom. Fuck the condom.*

"I think I have a condom," he said, reaching for his wallet. *Was he ready to have sex? Yes! No. Should he just do it?*

"A condom?" Calypso laughed. "What, it's dirty? You already fucked another girl tonight?"

"No!" said Adam.

"Then let's just do it — you didn't come here packing unless you wanted to use it. Don't be shy. I love tranny cock."

*Tranny cock. Packing.* What Boy Casey had said to Casey that night. *"I'm packing."* A fake dick. Calypso thought Adam was trans. He had to get out of there.

"I — I have to go," said Adam.

"What?" said Calypso.

"My sister, she's . . . waiting." Adam pulled his phone out of his pocket. He did have a text from Casey: Where r u?

"She texted me. She's drunk. I have to go."

Adam backed out of the bathroom into the throbbing dark club. He pushed his way through the dancing mob. *Where the fuck was everyone?* He felt like he was going to cry. June appeared in front of him. She shouted something, but he couldn't understand her.

"What?!" he shouted back. "Where's Casey?!"

June grabbed his arm and pulled him toward the exit. "We've been looking for you!" she said.

They walked out of the club, and Adam saw Casey sitting hunched on the curb, her head in her knees. She looked up at Adam and June, her cheeks soaked and flushed from crying.

"Let's go," she said. "Let's just take a fucking cab home." She stood up and stumbled a little, catching her balance on a parked car. She really was drunk.

June hailed a cab, and the three of them piled into the back seat. The cab was air-conditioned, and the black leather seats felt smooth and cool.

"Bushwick," said June. "Scholes between Humboldt and Bushwick Avenue."

The driver pulled into traffic. Casey was slumped against the window, Adam was in the middle, and June stared out the other window. Adam was surprised June wasn't consoling Casey as usual. Nobody talked. As they drove over the bridge, back to Brooklyn, the lights from the city spread out on all sides around them. Adam had never seen this view before, and for the first time, New York looked as he had always imagined it would.

Casey started giggling to herself. It started out quiet, but then got louder, mixed in with drunken hiccups.

"All I have to do is stay black and die," she said.

Adam and June exchanged a look.

"What?" said Adam.

Casey giggled more, trying to catch her breath.

"All I have to do is stay black and die. At camp today, this kid Christine didn't want to go to Drama Group, and I kept saying, 'Christine, you have to go to Drama Group,' and she was like, 'No, I don't. All I have to do is stay black and die.'" Casey started hiccupping again. She turned her head and stared back out the window. "I didn't really know what to say to that."

. . .

Back at the apartment, Adam was relieved to see that Ethan's door was closed and his light was out. Half of him wanted to burst in there and tell Ethan everything that had happened, but for some reason he couldn't. He wasn't sure why, but it just seemed like what happened with Calypso was something he shouldn't tell anyone. He would tell Brad the making-out part and maybe Ethan that part, too. But the other part, no one.

June went into her room and shut the door. Had she and Casey had a fight? What could they possibly fight about? June just did everything Casey wanted and complimented her all the time. June being mad at Casey was a little scary. Like nothing was dependable in this world. If June could be mad at Casey, god knows what else could happen.

Casey was splayed on her mattress with her laptop.

"Fucking asshole!" she said, to the screen.

Adam paused halfway to his room, unsure if Casey wanted a response.

Casey looked over at him. "What are you doing?" she said.

"Nothing."

"Come here."

Adam walked into her room and sat down on the floor.

"They're already friends on Facebook," said Casey. "They couldn't wait *five fucking seconds!* Oh no! Had to *immediately* go home and make sure the *whole world* knows they fucked at The Hole tonight. I mean, people need to know. This is serious business."

"Casey sucks," said Adam.

"No . . ." said Casey, her tone changing, recalibrating itself into *mature*. "It's complicated. I mean . . . it's not like we were exclusive."

"You guys were dating," said Adam. "He sucks."

"It's just, it's kind of a trans thing, though," she said. "He's new to his body, his sexuality. As an emerging trans person, he needs to be free to explore sexual experiences now that he's not constricted by his assigned gender."

Casey was doing that thing where she repeats something someone else told her and it sounds totally weird coming out of her mouth.

"I guess," said Adam. He'd learned that anything that had anything to do with "being trans" was not a thing you questioned.

"That girl's ugly, anyway," said Adam, peering at the profile open on Casey's screen. "I mean, if he needs to explore what it's like to be with an ugly person . . ."

Casey didn't laugh. Adam looked over at her. Two tears slid in uneven lines down her face.

"Hey, don't be upset about that lame-ass," he said.

Casey was really crying now. Wiping at her nose with her fist. Her nose always ran a ton when she cried.

"I'm not . . . crying . . . about Casey . . ." she said, in between cries. "I'm *crying* about *Sam*." She let loose, giving herself over to heaving sobs.

Adam didn't say anything. In a weird way, he missed Sam, too. He wished Sam was in the next room, instead of June. He wondered if Sam would get along with Ethan.

"What's she up to?" Adam asked. It wasn't the most sensitive question, but he wanted to know. He suddenly felt angry at Casey for dumping Sam. Sam had wanted them to stay together, even though they were going to different colleges. All Casey cared about was becoming an entirely different person in New York. But here she was, same person, just without Sam. Adam looked at Casey, snorting and blowing her drippy nose into her shirt. She looked pathetic.

"She's got some *girl*friend," said Casey, spitting at the word *girl* as if Sam had been the one to switch her sexual orientation, not

Casey. Casey clicked on the computer and brought up Sam's Facebook page. "The girl's ugly, right?"

Adam looked at the photo of Sam and a girl snuggled together on a couch. The girl was actually pretty cute. But Casey was cuter.

"You're better," he said. Casey clicked off Sam's page with a self-righteous jab. She went back to Boy Casey's profile. Stared at it blankly.

Adam perused it as well.

SEX: Male. Adam felt defensive. Boy Casey wasn't *really* male. He was trans male. He knew if he said this out loud, Casey would flip and go on one of her "trans guys *are* real guys" rants, so he didn't say anything.

ACTIVITIES: kicking it with my boys, crashing fancy museum parties, f#%*ing.
ABOUT ME: I'm an artist.
MEMBER OF: Facebook's finest T-Boys, FTM YouTube, Facebook should have other gender options: Official Petition, LAID Dance Party, Transbromance!, Pretending to Text in Awkward Situations

"So, how was your night?" asked Casey, her crying jag apparently over.

"It was fine," said Adam. His heart was beating fast. If he started talking about Calypso, Casey would know something weird had happened. There was no way he could hide it from her. With Brad and Ethan, he could lie, cover it up, pretend it was just any normal make-out. But Casey would look at him and know something else was up. She'd hound him until he confessed everything. So he had to say nothing.

"I'm kind of tired," he said. He stood up from the floor.

"OK, weirdo," said Casey. "Did something happen tonight? What did you *do?*"

"I didn't do anything," said Adam, walking out of her room. "I have to go to the bathroom."

Adam went into the bathroom and pissed. His dick was still semi-hard. Like it was grasping at the chance that Calypso might come back. *Calypso.* Just saying her name made his dick get harder. Shit. Now he couldn't pee. Adam leaned awkwardly over the toilet so he wouldn't spray piss all over his stomach. God, why *didn't* he go further with her? *"Fuck me with that dick of yours."* Fuck! Adam was fully hard now. He needed to go to bed and jerk off immediately.

In his sleeping bag in the dark, Adam recalled every second of what had happened in the bathroom with Calypso. The way her big tits had felt under her bra. When she'd grabbed his hand and shoved it down her pants. It was wet, it was soft. Adam imagined ramming his dick up inside her, oh god it felt so fucking good —

Adam came all over his hand.

He was a dumb-ass. He shouldn't have bailed! He didn't have to tell her he wasn't trans. Then he could have put his fingers back inside her. His tongue inside her. Fuck! Did he just totally blow his chance?!

Adam slammed his head into the pillow. *But at least he did it, man. At least he fucking finally made out with a girl!* He rolled over and grinned into the dark. *He did it!* And he went pretty far, too! Adam pumped his fist in the air like a nerd and laughed. He didn't care how stupid he looked. He was *happy.* Happy. He closed his eyes, and a lulling calm fell over him. He tugged the sleeping bag tight and rolled onto his side. *Calypso.* And as his brain filled up with thick, dark sleep, one last thought squeezed out: *I wonder what she's doing this very moment.*

# Chapter 7

A COUPLE WEEKS later and the thing everyone was excited about was the Gay Marriage Rally happening in the city that weekend. "All the kids are going," Casey had said. "The kids" referred to anyone in "the scene" that Boy Casey was a part of and that Casey and June were obsessed with.

Stuff between Casey and June was still weird. June was officially dating the ugly Internet girl and went around talking about how hot she was all the time when everyone knew she was lying. It wasn't just that the girl — Agnes — was ugly. It was that she and June didn't seem to have any kind of connection. Observing them around the apartment was painful. June would say something normal, and Agnes would respond with some baby-voiced non sequitur. As in:

JUNE: *"Hey, wanna go to McCarren Park?"*
AGNES: *"Hee-hee, my burp tastes funny."*

People like Agnes disturbed Adam. People that were both profoundly unattractive and stupid. Not that he was some handsome genius or anything, but he knew he was good-looking enough and smart enough. Agnes — with her weak chin and bug eyes and lack of ability to say anything on the fringe of interesting — had nothing. I mean, couldn't God have given her *something* to work with? Even her name sucked. Adam knew he shouldn't believe in God because people were being tortured and murdered and wiped out by tsunamis, but it was people like Agnes who really made him doubt there was a higher power.

Casey, meanwhile, had spent the last two weeks figuring out ways to make Boy Casey jealous. "It's not about *him*," she would say. "It's about *me*. How dare he think he can get more action than I can. I'm hot shit and he knows it." Adam loved it when Casey got cocky. She *was* hot shit. He was proud. She'd brought home another trans guy and a butch girl, but wasn't too interested in either of them. Her main focus was this girl Hazel who posted on the same queer message board as Casey. Casey had never met Hazel but would go on and on about the latest way Hazel had "burned" someone during a political argument on the board. "This other poster, OnionBagel, told me Hazel got a perfect score on her SATs," Casey had announced, apropos of nothing, during breakfast one morning. Hazel was also apparently "*ridiculously hot*" — according to some Facebook pics. Hazel was going to be at the Gay Marriage Rally, and Casey had taken to doing nightly sit-ups and facial cleanses in preparation.

Ethan was, of course, not going to the rally. "I fainted at Disney World when I was a kid. I try to avoid crowds." But also, he had a date. A girl who kept coming into Film Forum had asked him out, and he'd said yes. Adam was floored when he heard this. "She just asked you out? I thought guys always had to do the asking."

"That's just retarded high school shit," Ethan had said. "Girls ask guys out all the time. I don't know, I wasn't gonna do it, but she's really cute . . ."

Adam could tell Ethan was more nervous than he was letting on. It was his first real date since Rachel. Ethan said he wasn't allowing himself to work on the Rachel movie for two days before and after the date, because he couldn't let the date with the new girl taint his energy when working on the Rachel movie. "But what if you want to keep dating the girl?" Adam had asked.

"Maybe that means the Rachel movie is finished," Ethan had answered, somber. And then he'd gone into the bathroom to shave and mess with his hair for the fifth time that day.

The night before the rally, Adam hung out in his room, surfing porn on mute. It had been two weeks since the Calypso incident and then — nothing. Just the fucking usual: hanging around the apartment, reading, watching TV, eating liverwurst sandwiches in secret. He'd tried taking the subway into Manhattan and exploring a little by himself a few times, but he'd felt lonely walking around the Museum of Natural History with no one to talk to and self-conscious eating alone at a restaurant. One evening he got up the courage to stop by a bar on Bushwick Avenue, but the bartender had just looked at him and shook his head. It was all old men inside, anyway. He'd thought about suggesting to Casey they all go back to The Hole but couldn't do it. *"You want to go back to The Hole? Why?"*

He missed Brad. They had only IM'ed and texted a little. Brad was spending the summer hanging out in couples with Fletcher and Alice and Colin and Andrea and Stephen and Stephanie, just like Adam had feared. Brad also didn't seem too bummed about it. He had always complained to Adam how obnoxious Fletcher and Colin were and how ditzy Alice and Andrea were. But now, every time they got on IM, Brad was in some hurry to go off and meet the group. During one IM chat, Adam had written, You brain-damaged from hanging out with those fools yet? and Brad had just written back, What? It made Adam nervous. His New York trip was almost half over, and he was going to have to go back to school. The whole point was to come here and get action, become different, experienced, and return to EBP with everyone dying to be his friend. But what if when he got back, everyone had forgotten about him? What if instead of New York making him cool, it just erased him? Before Adam had left, Brad had said he wanted to visit. But a month and a half had gone by, and Brad had never mentioned it. Adam didn't even know if he wanted Brad to visit. He was supposed to have a hot girlfriend, a cool group of friends, a whole new life that would blow Brad's mind. After Calypso, he'd texted Brad that he'd scored with a hot older chick, and Brad had texted back, Word! But that was two weeks ago, and Brad had never even called to get details. Didn't even seem that interested. Adam felt like he'd lost his life in Piedmont but didn't have one here, either. He felt like a ghost.

Adam closed his laptop and walked out into the front room. Casey and June were slumped on the futon, watching TV. The noise was loud and jarring. He went into the bathroom and closed the door. What was he doing in here? He didn't even have to go to the bathroom. Adam stared into the mirror. His face looked weird. Like all the right parts were there, but they didn't add up. He couldn't recognize himself. He smiled and the face smiled back. It felt creepy. Wrong. Adam thought he had been standing over the sink but realized he was backed up against the wall. How did he get there? What just happened? His heart was racing. He felt sweat dripping down his forehead and his hands were buzzing. What was happening to him? There was a loud ringing in his ears, and he plugged his fingers in, trying to make it stop but he couldn't. He splashed water on his face. *Just make this feeling go away, just make this feeling go away.* He sat down on the toilet. Leaned his head over his knees. *It's OK. It's OK.* He started to feel a little better. He straightened up. Casey and June would wonder why he was in here for so long. They would ask him what happened. He had to get back in his room. He stood up and exited the bathroom. It felt like returning from outer space. He walked into his room. Casey and June didn't even look up. He closed the door and sat down on his mattress. He put his hand over his chest.

His heart was still beating fast, but it wasn't racing. He picked up his cell phone and stared at it. He should call Brad. He should just call Brad. Adam scrolled down to Brad's name and dialed. *Please let him be cool, please let him be cool . . .*

Brad picked up. "What's up?"

"What's up?"

"Nothing."

"Nothing."

"How's New York?"

"Boring."

"I thought you hooked up with that older girl?"

"Yeah, that was cool."

"You gonna see her again?"

"Probably."

"When?"

"Soon."

"When?"

Adam started to panic; did Brad know he was lying?

"Tomorrow, at this rally thing." *Fuck! Why did he say that?*

"No shit. What rally?"

"Gay Marriage."

"Sounds gay."

"Ha-ha."

"Why don't you go on a normal date?"

"I don't know . . . she's into this. She's, like, political. We'll probably go to a club in the city afterward. And then have sex. She, like . . . can't get enough of it." *What the hell was he talking about?*

"No shit. She got some friends?"

"No one that wants your ugly ass."

"I'm bored of Sandy. Her pussy's weird. She's Asian. Hook me up with some New York girl."

"Get the hell over here if you want a New York girl."

"Cool. My parents want me to go with them to Hawaii in a few weeks. Boring. I'll tell them I wanna visit you instead."

"Cool."

"You're not making this shit up, are you?"

"No!"

"Good."

They hung up. Adam felt nauseous. He needed to get a life *fast*.

. . .

NO SECOND-CLASS CITIZENS!

Casey, June, and Agnes were kneeled on the living-room floor painting large cardboard signs taped to wooden rulers. It was the morning of the rally, and it was blazing hot. Casey was wearing a wife-beater over a black bra and short red seventies shorts. June was wearing her usual dark baggy T-shirt and jeans. Agnes was in khaki shorts and a pink T-shirt with the word EQUALITY written in marker across the front.

"Want to come?" Casey asked Adam.

"Sure, whatever," said Adam. He wished she'd just assumed he was coming. He hated having to acknowledge he never had anything of his own to do. Calypso might be at the rally, and maybe she would recognize him. It was a total fucking long shot, but at least it was *something*. Brad would be here in less than three weeks, and Adam certainly wasn't going to amass a whole new life and identity hanging around the apartment. He had to go out if anything was ever going to happen. Plus he, like, supported gay marriage and stuff.

"What'd you do, raid Ethan's closet?" said Casey.

Adam blushed. He was wearing a white T-shirt, new Diesel jeans, and new Adidas sneakers. Pretty much Ethan's uniform.

"Whatever, this is just what guys wear," he said. "What'd you do? Get off from your job at Hooters?"

Casey rolled her eyes.

Adam saw June chuckle to herself.

The four of them took the subway into the city. You could spot all the people on the train going to the rally. People carrying signs that read: END HETEROSEXUAL PRIVILEGE and AGAINST GAY MARRIAGE? DON'T GET ONE! Some of the signs Adam didn't understand, like one that read: WHO DO YOU THINK DESIGNED YOUR WEDDING DRESS? Those were the ones Casey and June pointed to and laughed hardest at. All the people carrying signs or who looked "queer" were extra friendly to one another and talked as if they'd known each other for years, even if they were just introducing themselves. Adam knew if he was alone, he wouldn't look like he was one of them, so he stood close and chatted with Casey and June, asserting himself as part of the group. The queer people were cheesy and "in your face," but he liked the idea of being part of something. He supported gay marriage, supported his sister. He was an "ally," as Casey had described him — an essential part. He'd much rather be that than one of the boring, solitary people on the train, reading their books or staring into space.

When they got out of the subway at Bryant Park, the streets were swarmed. People jumped around, waving their signs, chants of *"What do we want? EQUALITY! When do we want it? NOW!"* in a kind of musical round with *"No to Hate! No to Hate! We Will Not Dis-crim-i-nate!"*

June was fired up. She started pumping her EQUALITY sign up and down in the air. "Equal Rights! Equal Rights!" she screamed.

"Equal Rights!" said Agnes. Then stopped to pick her nose and eat it.

Casey scanned the crowd, anxious. "I know Boy Casey's here with Schuyler and Jimmy, so if you see any of them, you have to tell me immediately. Also Hazel."

"I don't even know what Hazel looks like," said Adam.

"Cute curly hair, *really* pretty face, probably all black clothes. And she uses a cane."

"She uses *a cane?*" said Adam.

"Yes!" said Casey, annoyed. "So if we see her, don't go using the word *lame,* OK?"

"What?"

"The word *lame* is offensive to differently abled people."

"To what people?"

"*Differently abled.* People with disabilities."

"That's retarded," said Adam.

Casey groaned. "Adam! Just try not to embarrass me, OK?" She picked an abandoned EQUALITY sign off the ground and shoved it at him. "Come on, let's go."

The sign Adam was carrying said EQUALITY on one side and SMILE IF YOU ARE GAY on the other. He discreetly dropped it and picked up a normal EQUALITY-on-both-sides sign.

Adam, Casey, June, and Agnes weaved their way into the thronging march, which had started thumping down the street. Adam could feel himself shrinking as the mass of people expanded around him.

They reached a police-manned intersection, and Adam noticed a clump of old, ugly people leering on the street corner, passing out pamphlets with a picture of Jesus. One of them held a sign that read: AIDS ISN'T A DISEASE, IT'S A CURE.

"AIDS affects everyone!" June shouted.

"Go home, creeps!" Casey yelled.

The clump began chanting in response. *"One Man! One Woman! One Man! One Woman!"* Adam saw a little girl mouthing along with them. She was holding a sign that read: CHILDREN NEED A MOMMY AND A DADDY, which Adam found especially dumb. Plenty of kids didn't have a mom and a dad, and it had nothing to do with gayness.

Adam thought about his own mom and dad. It was weird how he didn't really miss them. Their mom sent e-mails and called every Sunday, pestering them with questions and giving the latest news from "the homestead" — news that Adam and Casey couldn't care less about. Sometimes she'd put their dad on the phone, and it would be really awkward because no one would have anything to say. Their dad had never been all that interested in Adam or Casey. He wasn't a "deadbeat dad," just more of a "bored dad." The only thing Adam knew his dad really loved was golf. There were trophies all over the house.

Adam saw a gang of teenagers sitting on newspaper vending boxes, eating pizza, laughing and pointing at the people marching. He felt nervous. They were his age. He couldn't tell if they were for or against them.

"Show your tits for Gay Marriage!" one of them shouted at Casey. Adam thought Casey might go off on the guy, but she just looked embarrassed and marched faster.

"Shut up!" Adam yelled, except it wasn't really a yell, more like a cracked-voice stutter that no one but Adam seemed to hear.

"June, tell me if you see Boy Casey or Hazel," said Casey.

June linked arms with Agnes. "Sure."

God, it was hot. Adam's face was swathed in sweat and his eyes stung. When he looked ahead, the thousands of bodies blurred into a colorful pixelated sea. The chances of running into Calypso were pretty slim. He wasn't even sure what he would do if he did see her. They were so drunk when they'd talked at The Hole, a sober conversation seemed impossible:

*"How's your tranny cock doing?"*

*"It's good, doing good . . ."*

"EQUALITY!" shouted Casey next to him. "Say it, Adam!"

"Equality!" he said.

And then he saw her. Not Calypso. The redhead. His redhead. No fucking joke, all those other times he thought he saw her, he was on crack — *this was her.* She did exist. She was marching with a group and was wearing jean cutoffs and a gray tank top and had this unbelievably cute round face framed by red hair with bangs and the hugest smile. And if anyone ever did anything to make her stop smiling, Adam would ram his fist in their face. His heart was pounding. He took a step closer — a pack of fat hairy men shouting "Bears for Marriage!" barreled past, obscuring everything for thirty seconds.

She was gone. He had lost her. *Fuck* — but she was *here.* Adam felt like he might throw up.

"Hey, look at them, right on!" said June. She pointed to a pack of marchers all wearing white T-shirts with a picture of a crossed-out diamond ring printed on them and the words I DON'T. A few in the middle held up a banner that read: BOYCOTT STRAIGHT MARRIAGE — WE WON'T MARRY UNTIL EVERYONE CAN!

"Yeah!" said Casey, pumping her fist at the group. Several members of the group pumped their fists back.

"I love that!" said June. "It's, like, seeing that means more than everything else."

"I know," said Casey. "You should go join them, Adam!"

"Uh, what?" said Adam.

"You would get married when your sister can't?" June cut in. She glared at him.

"I don't know," said Adam.

"Wait, what?" said Casey. She stopped marching and looked at him.

"I don't know!" said Adam. He felt hot and sick.

"If that's how you feel, I don't think you should be here," said Casey. She looked genuinely hurt. Unlike June, who seemed thrilled.

"So you just get to stroll on down the aisle with your *bashful bride,*" said June, "your family *so happy,* everyone full of *love,* thinking how *wonderful* this is, such a *beautiful rite of passage,* while your sister sits and watches with her 'girlfriend' everyone likes to pretend doesn't exist."

Adam wondered if in June's fantasy Casey's "girlfriend" was June.

"You're getting married?" said Agnes.

"OK, I wouldn't do it," said Adam. "You're right, it's not fair . . ."

"You're just saying that," said Casey.

"I'm not," said Adam. "Really, I wouldn't . . ."

"I wanna get married, too, you know," said Casey. She looked away and continued marching.

*Would he get married?* Adam imagined himself, age twenty-nine. He was handsome, a . . . lawyer. He'd been with the red-headed girl for years, knew it was time to get married.

REDHEAD: *"Adam darling, why haven't you popped the question?"*

ADAM: *"Well, you see, my sister . . ."*

REDHEAD: *"I know, she's gay. And I support gay marriage. We met at the Gay Marriage Rally, remember? In fact . . . I'm gay."*

ADAM: *"I know . . . that's why I'm so confused right now . . ."*

Adam's fantasy faded, unsure of where it was going. Would he get married if Casey couldn't? He supported gay marriage — he was here marching with this dumb-ass sign — but did he have to sacrifice getting married himself, too? Why should he give it up, just because she couldn't? It wasn't his fault it was illegal. But he didn't want to hurt Casey. Hopefully gay marriage would just be legal by the time he wanted to get married, so he wouldn't have to think about it.

"Hey, there's Boy Casey," said June. There was a weird tone to her voice. "What's he doing?"

"Where?" said Casey. Her head spun, frantic.

June pointed to a small table set off to the side of the march. There was a banner over the table that read: QUEERS AGAINST GAY MARRIAGE. Boy Casey, Schuyler, Jimmy, and some others stood behind the table. Casey, June, Agnes, and Adam walked over.

"Uh, hey," said Casey.

"You're marching?" said Boy Casey.

"Uh, yeah," said Casey. "I thought you were, too . . ."

"I said I was going to the march," said Boy Casey. "I thought you knew what was up." Boy Casey pulled his baseball cap down over his eyes, "Man, it's fucking hot out. I hate it when it's too hot."

A girl with spiky hair, holding a pamphlet, came up to Adam. "Hey, you want a copy of our statement? We're Queers Against Gay Marriage."

"Uh, sure," said Adam. He took the piece of paper and tried to scan it. It was too hot out; he couldn't read.

"I don't get it," said June. "Why are you against gay marriage?"

Adam saw Casey glance nervously at June. He could tell Casey was quickly realizing there was something *not cool* about being for gay marriage. She didn't know what it was yet but did not want to be aligned with June. Casey stepped behind the table, next to Boy Casey.

"At least you guys have this banner for some shade," said Casey. "And a cooler? Damn. Can I get a Coke?"

"We are against the prioritization of gay marriage in the queer political movement," said the spiky-haired girl to June.

Adam looked down at his pamphlet again. It began: "We are against the prioritization of gay marriage in the queer political movement."

The girl continued, "The gay marriage agenda is about assimilation. It's about granting rights to an exclusive, privileged group of people, while the more serious problems our other marginalized allies face are de-prioritized. We should be focused on keeping trans people safe, immigration reform, changing the prison system — not whether or not rich white gays get to have the wedding they always dreamed of."

Adam looked at Casey. Her face was bright red.

"OK, I get that," said June. "But gay marriage isn't just about weddings . . . I mean, whether we like it or not, marriage holds a lot of symbolic and economic weight."

Adam was surprised by how calm June was. Unlike Casey, she didn't care what this group thought of her.

"I *like* being different because I'm queer," said Spiky Hair.

"I like being different now," said June. "I didn't like it when I was fifteen, got beat up, and had to have my jaw wired shut for three months."

Jimmy came out from behind the table and sidled up next to Adam.

"Lotta pussy at this rally, huh?"

"Uh, yeah," said Adam. All he could think was, *Your name is Francesca diSessa, and you're twenty-six years old.*

"I'm 'bouts to get lucky tonight!" said Jimmy. He cocked his head over at spiky-haired girl.

"So are you, like, against gay marriage?" said Adam.

"I'm against getting blue-balled again like last time," said Jimmy.

"Check it out," said Spiky Hair. "*Embarrassing.*" She pointed to a tall, skinny, blond-haired boy wearing short pink shorts and nothing else. He was cheering and waving a sign that said: WEL-COME TO SELMA.

"It's, like, the fucking greatest day of his life," said Spiky Hair.

"Gay rights are civil rights," said June. "He's making an analogy."

"It's a *fucked-up* analogy," said Spiky Hair. "We should not be equating the gay rights movement with the African American civil rights movement. It's insulting, divisive, and alienating to queers of color."

Adam noticed that all the people behind the Queers Against Gay Marriage table were white. The majority of the people at the whole *rally* were white. *Why?*

"I hear that," said June.

"Gay is NOT the new black," yelled Boy Casey at a woman carrying a sign proclaiming the inverse. Casey stood behind Boy Casey, sipping a Coke, looking troubled.

"You guys coming to the party at Carlisle's tonight?" asked Schuyler.

"Yeah, we might stop by," said Casey. "Where is it again?"

"Upper East Side. His parents are out of town. Perfect timing. Get ready for some Cristal and shit . . . Carlisle's such a little faggot."

"Awesome," said Casey.

"Yo, what the fuck be happenin'," said Jimmy, pointing.

Everyone looked over at a police car stopped in the middle of the rally. People were crowded around the car, chanting, and some were climbing on the hood.

"Dude! Let's go check it out!" said Schuyler.

A woman by the police car shouted into a bullhorn, "Lawyers! Lawyers! We need some lawyers!" One of the hood jumpers was getting arrested.

"Schuyler, it's your turn to stay behind the table," said Boy Casey.

"What?! No."

"I'm in law school," said Spiky Hair. "They might need me." She and another girl behind the table took off.

"Come on!" said June to Adam, Casey, and Agnes. They all started jogging toward the scene. Boy Casey and Schuyler were beside them.

"Hey, Jimmy, watch my bag!" Boy Casey yelled back at the table.

"What! I gotta stay here?! Suck ass . . ."

Over at the police car, two gay-looking boys were getting arrested. People had formed a circle around them and were shouting, "Let — Them — Go! Let — Them — Go!"

"Man, I cannot fucking risk getting arrested," said Boy Casey. "They'd fucking throw me in the bitch cell. You know they would."

Adam didn't get it. Wouldn't Boy Casey rather be with the women? If he was with the men, he could get raped. Adam took a few steps back.

"Fuck that," said Casey. She looked at Boy Casey, serious. "I'll stay right with you. I won't let them."

"But in case they do," said Boy Casey, "take these." He put a pack of cigarettes in Casey's hand. "I want you to put one in my mouth and light it while they're cuffing me. Then take a photo of me just fucking standing there smoking while they lock me up."

The commotion died down. The two hood-jumpers were in the back of the police car, and it slowly moved forward.

"Failure to disperse," said a butch lesbian standing in front of them. "It's all bullshit so the police can flex their dicks. They'll let them go where no one can see them and just give them a citation."

"Hey, you're . . . Hazel," said Casey. "I'm Casey!"

"I know," said Hazel. She grinned and winked.

*This was the disabled girl?* Hazel had short, curly hair and was wearing a black tank top, black cargo pants, combat boots, and had a utility belt around her waist holding a police baton, two knives, and what looked like a can of Mace. She also had a long black tube slung over her back. She whipped the tube around and extracted a thin black cane, which she twirled between her fingers.

"Play party at Dungeon tonight. You coming? I promise to beat the shit out of you."

Apparently Casey had been confused about the use of Hazel's

"cane." Adam glanced at Casey, but she was ogling Hazel. He knew that look. Casey was in love.

"We've got the party at Carlisle's," said Boy Casey, stepping in. He slung his arm over Casey's shoulder.

"You should come," said Casey to Hazel. She stepped out from under Boy Casey's arm and took out her phone. "What's your number? I'll text you the address."

Casey and Hazel traded phones and exchanged numbers. Casey had a huge glowing grin and was doing that twisting-her-hair thing. Adam thought Boy Casey might say, *"Fuck it,"* and walk away. That was the sort of thing Brad or Colin did if a girl rejected them. They'd act as if they couldn't fucking care less. But Boy Casey looked nervous. He hovered.

"Hey, we're Queers Against Gay Marriage." Spiky Hair again. "Here's our statement." She tried to hand Hazel the pamphlet, but Hazel didn't take it. Spiky Hair awkwardly retracted her hand, saying, "We don't believe gay marriage is the solution."

"What do you mean 'gay marriage is not the solution'?" said Hazel. "It's the solution to gay people not being able to get married."

"Hey, honey." A black girl came up and kissed Hazel on the mouth. "I lost you." The girl was carrying a sign that read: SLAVERY WAS TRADITION TOO. Adam wondered if Spiky Hair would inform the black girl that *"gay is not the new black."* She did not.

Hazel took the black girl's hand. "Maybe I'll stop by that party," Hazel said to Casey. "If you come to Dungeon afterward." She stared straight at Casey with this really intense look.

"Um, maybe," said Casey, flustered.

"You're coming back to my place afterward, right?" said Boy Casey.

"I'm not sure what I'm doing," said Casey.

"Come on," said June. "We're stuck in the dregs of the march; let's get back up to the front."

"I gotta get back to the table," said Boy Casey. "I'll see you at the party." He turned his head to Adam. "You coming to Carlisle's, dude?"

"Sure, yeah," said Adam.

*Of course now Boy Casey acts like he exists.*

. . .

The sky turned dark and the rally dissolved. No Calypso. No re-appearance of Redhead. Adam had a sinking feeling but tried to fight it.

"It's almost eight-thirty," said June. "Shouldn't we just head up to the party?"

"Eight-thirty? Are you retarded?" said Casey. Then caught herself and put her hand to her mouth.

"Ha-ha," said Adam.

Casey flipped him off. She was in a bad mood. All she'd done the past couple hours was complain, switching off between "It's too hot" and "I'm hungry." Adam knew what she really meant was: *"I wanted Boy Casey, but now I want Hazel, but she's with someone else, at least I think she is, and now Boy Casey wants me back and I don't even care."* He wondered if Casey was reading his mind, too, right now. I mean, how difficult could that even be? *"I wish I was having sex, I wish I was having sex."*

"So . . . should we get some pizza or something?" said June.

"Right. 'Cause what I really need right now is to get fat," said Casey.

"You're so skinny," said Agnes.

"Let's just go to Starbucks," said Casey.

There was one on the opposite corner, and the group pivoted en masse and headed in that direction.

Adam remembered how the night of The Hole he'd had that crazy, elated feeling that *something was going to happen*. And something *had* happened. How crazy was that? Did it mean he was psychic? Could he actually predict what was going to happen in the future by how he felt in the present? He tried to focus really hard to see if he was getting that same feeling now. If something would happen tonight. But the harder he focused, all he could feel was himself focusing.

They got Starbucks, then June, Agnes, and Adam got pizza, then they browsed Barnes & Noble, got Starbucks again, and walked aimlessly until finally it was 10:19 and Casey decided it was OK for them to make their way uptown to the party.

The subways were air-conditioned, and now that it was night, they were surprisingly cold. Casey and Agnes, who were wearing shorts, shivered and tried to cover the goose bumps on their legs. June reached into her backpack and pulled out a sweatshirt to drape over Agnes's knees. Agnes smiled and leaned in closer to June. Adam thought about their dog Lucy and how she'd always liked to sleep on the heater grate. Casey read the subway ads.

. . .

The party was in a super-fancy building with a giant marble lobby and a doorman.

"We're here for, uh . . . Carlisle," said Casey. The doorman gave her a look like: *Really? Because I couldn't tell.*

"Floor seventeen," he said.

They waited for the elevator, and another group of "Carlisle" people came up behind them. The elevator dinged, and they all crammed in.

"We got room for everyone!" someone shouted. "This elevator is *inclusive*."

Adam got pushed against the wall. More people were squeezing in, and as Adam shifted to try to make room, he realized right in front of him was the redheaded girl. The elevator jerked, and Redhead's back slammed up against him.

"Aaah! Sorry," she said, turning her head around briefly.

Her body was fully pressed against his as the elevator chugged slowly up. He could smell her hair. It smelled delirious. Adam moved his hand to cover his crotch. *Oh god, his dick was totally sticking out.* He fixed his eyes on her tiny little soccer ball ear stud.

*\*Ding\**

Everyone flooded out. Redhead followed her crowd. Adam stayed in the elevator, his hands around his crotch.

"What are you doing, Adam?" said Casey. "We're here."

"I think I dropped something in the lobby," he said. "I'm just gonna ride back down and come back."

"Uh, OK," said Casey, like Adam was crazy, but she wasn't interested enough to care. "It's apartment seventeen-E." Casey, June, and Agnes rounded the hallway as the elevator doors closed.

Adam pressed the STOP button. He'd never done that before. Part of him was scared it would transmit a signal to some room where a man was watching all the elevators on TVs. But he just needed a minute alone. He needed to chill the fuck out. She was here. This was his chance. This was motherfucking destiny and he knew it. Forget Agnes — there *was* a fucking God, and for whatever fucked-up reason He liked Adam. All Adam had to do was not blow it. *Do not fucking blow this, Freedman.* He took a deep breath and pressed OPEN.

The party was packed. It looked like the same crowd as The Hole, except now — instead of everyone crammed into a graffiti-sprayed, trash-strewn, gutted concrete building — they were crammed into a fancy apartment with expensive-looking furniture, art on the walls, and floor-to-ceiling bookshelves. Adam's house wasn't nearly as nice as this, but he suddenly felt homesick. For a moment, he wished everyone at the party would leave so he could curl up on the velvety couch and pull the soft white afghan over him.

Adam surveyed the crowd, but he didn't see the redhead.

"Hazel's not here." Casey was standing next to him. "Should I just give up and make out with Boy Casey?"

"Boy Casey's annoying," said Adam.

"I know," said Casey, "but he's hot."

"What are you guys talking about?" said June, Agnes beside her.

"Uh, nothing," said Casey. She looked around. "So, Adam, I bet some of the girls here are bi. Anyone you like?"

Adam was surprised. Back in Piedmont, on the phone, Casey had gone on and on about how she was going to hook him up with a hot New York girl, but once he got here it had never come up. He figured it had been all talk — just Casey loving the idea of herself as the cool older sister but not actually wanting to bother.

"Uh, maybe," said Adam.

"Let's go do a lap!" said Casey. She grabbed his arm and pulled him away.

"You really think someone here would hook up with me?" he said. Should he mention Redhead? But what if Casey knew her and didn't like her? What if she was like, *"That bitch? No."* Maybe Casey had someone else in mind for him. He'd talk to that girl, Redhead would watch, get jealous . . .

"Huh?" said Casey, distracted. "I only said that to get away from June and Agnes. We can*not* just hang around them all night." She was still in a bad mood.

"But is there someone you think I could hook up with?"

"Are you on crack? Everyone here is, like, *way* older than you. And *gay.*"

Adam hated Casey. Just because her life wasn't working out perfect didn't mean she had to be a bitch to him. He wanted to punch her in the face and go home.

"See that girl over there," said Casey, in a hushed voice. She nodded her head toward a short, stocky girl with a mullet. "She transitioned and then went back."

Adam didn't want to hear about someone's dumb transition again. He wanted to get drunk.

"Her name was Linda, and then she transitioned to 'Len' — got top surgery and went on T and everything — was a guy for like a year and a half, but then she, like, changed her, or his, mind and went back to being female. Now she just goes by 'L.' Isn't that crazy?"

"Who cares," said Adam.

"Everyone enjoying themselves here?" A girl with short hair, wearing a purple Lycra body suit, flounced in front of them.

"Totally!" said Casey. "Thanks for having us!"

The girl swiveled her head and bit her finger, looking across the room. "Ooooh! That boy is *fine.*" And she flounced off again.

"Carlisle, he's such a little faggot . . ." said Casey.

"You're just saying that 'cause that's what Schuyler said," said Adam.

"What?"

"That's what Schuyler said today, that that Carlisle boy or girl or whatever is 'such a little faggot.' You're a follower. You copy everything everyone does and it's pathetic." Adam almost never got this mad at Casey. He felt like he was drunk, even though he just wanted to be drunk.

"You're an *asshole,*" said Casey. "Go find your own fucking life, then. You think I want you hanging around me all the time? Talk about pathetic. What are you even *doing* here? At least I *belong* here!"

Adam's face turned red.

"You wish," he said. "You're just obsessed with everyone here."

"Go the fuck home, Adam. I can't believe you thought you would *get a girl* here. That is so sad."

"Hey, cutie." It was Hazel.

"Oh! Hey!" said Casey, suddenly beaming. Like she wasn't in the middle of a fight. Like she was filled with the fabulous spirit of life and always had been.

Hazel was holding two drinks; she handed one to Casey.

"You look hot," said Hazel, looking Casey up and down. Then she cocked her head at Adam. "I'm Hazel."

*Yeah. I met you, like, two hours ago.*

"I'm —" Adam started to say, but Casey interrupted him.

"That's just my little brother. I don't know why he's here."

Hazel looked away from Adam, instantly bored. She went back to giving Casey that stupid loaded gaze, and Casey went back to lapping it up.

"I really wanna fuck you tonight," said Hazel.

"I want you to," said Casey.

*Did they completely not care that he was standing right next to them?*

"I wanna fuck you while people watch," continued Hazel.

"I want you to fuck me while people watch," said Casey.

"I'm out," said Adam.

"Good," said Casey, not even looking at him.

"Why was your brother here?" Adam heard Hazel asking as he walked toward the door. He kept walking before he could hear Casey's answer. He got to the door. He stopped.

*No.*

*He was not gonna bail.*

*He was not some pussy.*

*Maybe nothing would happen with that girl, but he had to know that he fucking tried.*

*She was somewhere in this apartment, and no matter what he was gonna force himself to talk to her.*

*Fuck Casey, fuck Hazel, fuck Boy Casey, fuck June, fuck Agnes,* *fuck Mom, fuck Dad — he was not going home until he knew that he <u>tried</u>.*

Adam whipped around. Headed straight for the liquor table. Threw some ice in a cup. Filled it to the brim with vodka. Took a swig. Felt a lot better.

He saw Casey and Hazel talking where he'd left them and didn't give a shit if they saw he was still here. In five minutes he'd be talking to Redhead and what could they do then?

*"Adam, I thought you were leaving?"*

*"Um, I'm in the middle of a conversation? Do you mind?"*

Adam rotated his head a slow 180 degrees, scanning the party for the redhead like a superhero with "infrared-head" vision. *"Infrared-head." Ha-ha. That was funny. He was funny!*

He spotted her. Standing by the window. Talking to some girl. He imagined his vision like in *Terminator 2,* targeting in on her, giving him all the necessary stats. Everything was coded in fluorescent green. He was moving in. Nothing could stop him. He started walking toward the window. Took another swig of vodka. But how? How would he get her attention? What do they do in the movies? On TV? They're walking down the school hallway, they bump into each other, the girl drops her books, and the boy picks them up, something like that; he was getting closer, two inches away — DECISION! DECISION! Alarms were going off, he had to act now — *now!!!*

Adam threw his drink on the redhead.

Redhead and her friend stared at him. Redhead slowly started to brush the vodka and ice off her shirt. Adam stood there and watched.

"Um . . ." she said.

Adam broke into action.

"I'm so sorry, I'm so sorry," he said. He looked around and saw a stack of colored napkins on the liquor table. He ran over, grabbed a handful, ran back, and handed them to Redhead. "I am so, so sorry."

"Why did you . . . ?"

"I, um, I tripped, it was this rug, I —"

"You didn't trip," said the friend. "You just . . . walked over here and threw your drink on her."

"I . . ."

Redhead stared at him, but it wasn't mean. Just intensely curious.

"I wanted to talk to you," said Adam.

Redhead and her friend burst out laughing.

"That is the dumbest thing I've ever heard," said Redhead. And then, "I love it."

"Who *are* you?" said the friend.

"I'm, um, Adam."

"I'm Gillian," said Redhead. They shook hands.

"I'm Claire," said the friend. She and Adam shook hands too.

"So what do you wanna talk about?" said Gillian, grinning. She had that smile like she'd had when he saw her marching. *It was actually happening — this was actually happening.*

"Uh, I don't know," said Adam.

"You are fascinating," said Gillian. She stared at him with a delighted, amused look.

"Well . . . who do you know here . . . the usual . . ." said Claire.

"Um, I know Carlisle," said Adam. "And Boy Casey, I mean, Casey — the boy."

"Uh-huh . . ." said Gillian. She looked as if she was going to start laughing again, but it was a nice laugh. She liked him! "I don't really know Carlisle. We came with our friends Jackie and Nadia . . ."

But why did she like him? Why wasn't she totally weirded out by this twerp teenage boy at the party? She must think he's trans. Like Calypso had. Why else would she like him unless she thought he was trans? This was happening; he couldn't blow this. If she

found out he wasn't trans, this would all fall apart. It couldn't —
*he could not fuck this up.*

"Yeah, I came here with some of my other trans-guy friends,"
said Adam.

Gillian and Claire both nodded, smiling. Completely unfazed.

"That's cool . . ." said Gillian.

"I'm gonna go get a drink," said Claire. She raised her eyebrows
at Gillian and left.

Gillian smiled at Adam and rolled her eyes. "All my friends are
in couples. Claire's been with her girlfriend for, like, three years,
and Jackie and Nadia are at eight months. Whenever we go out
they try to turn me into a project."

Adam blushed. He took a sip of his vodka, but there was nothing left in the cup and he swallowed air. Gillian noticed and gave
him that amused look again.

"Here, have some of mine." She poured some of her drink into
his glass. *She wanted to share spit!*

"Thanks!" said Adam.

There was an awkward pause.

"So," she said, "um, what do you do . . . ?"

"I, um, I go to college."

"Uh-huh, what college?"

"Uh, Berkeley. But I'm visiting my sister for the summer. We
live in Bushwick."

"I live in Fort Greene," said Gillian. "There was, like, a mass
exodus of a bunch of us from Smith. I live with Claire and her
girlfriend, Lauren. Never live with a couple. I mean, I love Claire,
but it's kind of hell on earth."

"I live with my sister and a girl who's totally in love with her,
but it's, like, not reciprocated. If you want to imagine something
worse."

"I don't know . . . at least then everyone's kind of miserable. For
me, it's, like: The couple cooking dinner! The couple snuggled up

to a movie! The couple coming home from a night out, tipsy and in love! Me alone in my room, eating a salami sandwich in secret."

"I eat liverwurst in secret!" said Adam.

Gillian laughed. "Wait, why do you eat it in secret? Are your roommates vegan, too?"

"Uh, no, I just . . . thought I should eat it in secret."

Gillian laughed even harder. She smiled that smile at Adam. He felt like the funniest, cutest boy alive.

"Yeah," said Gillian. "Even if I knew they weren't totally grossed out by meat, I think I'd still lock my door. Eating alone in my room is not something I want people to know I'm doing. It's like masturbating or something."

Adam felt his cheeks go red.

"Should we get refills?" said Gillian.

"Sure!" said Adam.

They walked over to the liquor table, and Adam saw Casey and Hazel staring at him. Casey leaned in and said something to Hazel. What was she doing? He could not let her come over here. Boy Casey approached them. Good, he would keep them busy.

"So . . . I know what you were drinking, since it's all over my shirt," said Gillian. "At least you didn't mix with cranberry."

"I'm so sorry about that," said Adam, "that was completely retard — I mean stupid."

Gillian handed him a drink. "I don't care," she said.

"Pour it on me to get even! Seriously!" said Adam. He handed her back the cup and stretched his arms out, presenting his chest.

Gillian laughed. She dunked her finger in the drink and poked it on his chest, leaving a little wet dot on the white T-shirt. She looked down at her own chest. "I should actually go to the bathroom and try to clean up some more real quick." She looked up at him and smiled. "Don't go anywhere."

"I won't," he said.

Gillian walked away. Adam looked down at his chest and ran his finger across the wet spot. He could feel his heart underneath.

"*Who* was that?"

Casey was in front of him.

"Her name's Gillian."

"And . . . ?"

"I like her," said Adam.

"Does she know how old you are?"

"No. I told her I went to Berkeley for college, and if she asks, I'm gonna say I'm twenty, and if you tell her I'm not, I swear to god I will tell Mom and Dad everything." And he meant it. For the first time, he actually meant it.

Casey scoffed. But she knew he was serious. "Fine," she said. "We'll see how long that lasts . . . I'm leaving with Hazel." And Casey walked away.

Gillian came back.

"Hey," she said. "I just talked to Claire and Jackie and Nadia, and they're all going home to be boring lesbians. I was gonna go with them . . ."

Adam's heart sunk. He imagined himself falling through the floor, crashing through every story of the building, through the concrete foundation, into a grave of dirt.

"Unless, I don't know . . . were you gonna stay?" Gillian continued.

"Oh, sure!" said Adam. "If you were . . ."

"Cool," said Gillian. She took a sip of her drink.

. . .

For the rest of the night, Adam stayed in that wonderful, floaty drunk cloud where everything was funny and he didn't feel self-conscious. They talked about what it was like to move to New York, and Adam told Gillian about accidentally ending up in the

Bronx on the way to Mags Mumford's house to stuff envelopes, and Gillian told Adam how when she first moved here she was supposed to meet her mom's friend for lunch at the Guggenheim and somehow, she still wasn't entirely sure how, ended up on the ferry to Governors Island. It turned out they both used to be obsessed with the candied nuts sold in the carts on the streets, but then both ended up eating too many and now the burnt sugar smell made them nauseous.

At one point a really drunk girl stumbled up to Adam and Gillian and started talking about her cat. Like out of nowhere.

"My cat knows where I am tonight. And my cat does not care for it."

The girl rambled for at least ten minutes about how she needed to find a proper cat-sitter, and Adam and Gillian tried not to laugh and nodded along, exchanging little glances with each other. When the drunk person staggered off, Adam was almost disappointed. He loved their little unspoken looks. Talking without talking was the best kind.

Then Adam had started to feel a little dizzy, and he panicked that he was getting too drunk and was going to suddenly confess everything or have to throw up, and his life would be over, but Gillian noticed and she got them both water and pretzels and acted like it was no big deal, and soon he was back to feeling good-drunk. And then everyone had started climbing out of this window and up the fire escape, so Adam and Gillian had just shrugged and followed. The next thing he knew they were crowded onto the rooftop, and he and Gillian were pressed close, leaning over the edge, staring out at the endless glittering city, and for a moment he had felt as if he were flying, soaring over everything. Then Carlisle had freaked and was shouting that there were too many people on the roof and everyone had to get back inside right now, and they had all booed and hissed but cheerfully climbed down and into the apartment.

Sometimes Gillian asked him a question that made him nervous. Like, who else he knew here and how he knew them. He pointed out Boy Casey and said he knew him because Boy Casey was dating his sister. He found that the closer he stuck to the truth, the less anxious he got. He had always been really shitty at lying. It just made him so uncomfortable. At one point June and Agnes walked over, and Adam was terrified June was going to say, "Hi, Adam-who's-a-real-boy-not-a-trans-boy," but of course she didn't. She just said, "We're leaving," and they left. Adam and Gillian talked a little about the rally, but not about gay marriage or anything, only about how the hot dog vendor guys were selling cold bottled water for four dollars each and how messed up that was, but how they also both agreed that when stuff was expensive, for some reason it always tasted better.

Mainly they laughed. At stupid stuff. Half the time Adam didn't even know why they were laughing and he didn't think Gillian did either, and neither of them cared.

Around 2:00 A.M. the party started to dwindle. Only a handful of people were left.

"I guess we should get going," said Gillian. "You're taking the subway back to Bushwick?"

"Yeah," said Adam.

"You wanna walk together?" said Gillian.

"Sure." *Keep it casual, keep it casual.*

"Cool. Do you need to say goodbye to anyone?"

"Oh, um . . ." Adam paused. He looked over and saw Boy Casey standing in a corner with three other guys Adam didn't know.

"Those are your friends?" asked Gillian.

*Sure, why not.*

"Yeah, uh, be right back," said Adam.

Adam hustled over to the group. They saw him coming, and Adam watched as their expressions morphed from relaxed banter to *What the fuck does this guy want?*

"Just, uh, wanted to say bye. So, bye," said Adam. And he spun around before anyone had a chance to respond.

. . .

Out on the street, it was warm and dark and disturbingly quiet. Adam and Gillian headed down the block. He was nervous. Where did this go from here? It had been so perfect up in the hazy colorful bubble of the apartment. But now what? Did he try to kiss her? What if she backed away in horror, thought they were only friends? That wasn't possible. She liked him. He knew she liked him. Didn't she?

Gillian was talking about the drunk girl. "Oh my god, it's embarrassing enough to go up to some strangers at a party and start talking about your ex or something—but your *cat?*"

"'My cat knows where I am tonight. And my cat does not care for it,'" said Adam, mimicking the girl's nasally voice.

Gillian laughed. "That was perfect! You're so cute."

Adam blushed. He was glad Gillian couldn't see his face in the dark. He saw the glowing green bulb of the subway station at the end of the block. He had approximately two and a half minutes to figure out what he was going to do when they got there. He thought about an essay question on his American lit final. "What does the green light in *The Great Gatsby* represent?" He had left it blank.

They were there. They paused outside the entrance. Gillian looked so beautiful in the streetlight.

"I'm gonna get on the uptown to transfer to the express to Atlantic," said Gillian.

Adam looked over at the name of the subway they were at: 77TH STREET STATION. He had no idea how to get home.

"I'm, um . . . ?"

"You're taking the downtown to the L to Bushwick," said Gillian, laughing.

"Right," said Adam.

They smiled nervously at each other. God, he loved her smile.

"So . . . you wanna hang out again?" said Gillian.

"Yes!" said Adam. *Good lord, could he possibly have said yes any faster? Keep it cool, keep it casual.* "Um, let me get your number."

They took out their phones and exchanged numbers.

"Just so you know," Gillian said, putting her phone back in her pocket. "I've, um . . . Wait, I don't want this to come out wrong."

Adam's heart was racing. *Did she know? Had she figured it out?*

"I've never, um, dated a trans guy before. I mean, like, I've only ever had girlfriends. But I think I'm open. I mean, I am open. I just . . . thought I should tell you."

"Um, that's OK," said Adam. "I . . . haven't dated that much either."

"Really?" said Gillian. She sounded genuinely surprised.

"I'm kind of . . . shy," he said. *Fuck! Why did he just say that?*

"I know," said Gillian. "It's sweet." She leaned in and kissed him on the lips. Then stood back and looked at him. Adam's whole body was tingling. He leaned in and kissed her. They opened their mouths.

. . .

Adam collapsed on the subway seat as the doors closed. *"Be careful of the closing doors. This is a Brooklyn Bridge–bound Six train. The next stop is Sixty-Eighth Street, Hunter College."* The train jostled and sped off as Adam leaned his head against the window, closed his eyes, and replayed the kiss in his mind.

. . .

Adam turned his keys in the two different locks and creaked open the door to the apartment. The living room was dark and still. He imagined running through all the rooms, flipping on all the lights, blasting music, and jumping up and down, screaming as loud as he could. But then he heard crying coming from June's room. A soft, kittenish cry. He took a few steps to the center of the living room and peered over toward her door. The door was open and through the shadows he made out a dark lump, hunched on the mattress. Adam took another step toward her door — he should *probably* console her — but the dark lump rose up and shut the door before he could come any closer. And then it was quiet.

Adam turned and looked over toward Ethan's room. Ethan's door was cracked, a slice of bright light. His door was almost always closed, so Adam knew this gesture meant he wanted to talk. Adam felt a flush of warmth. Ethan would never *say* he wanted to talk or come into Adam's room the way Casey might barge in and demand sympathy — but Ethan wanted to, and the cracked door was his way of letting Adam know. Adam hoped Ethan's date had gone well, that Ethan wanted to tell Adam all about it, and then Adam could tell Ethan about Gillian — minus the pretending to be trans — and they would both punch each other in the shoulder and look up the girls on Facebook, and Ethan would be really impressed by how pretty Gillian was. God, she was so pretty. Adam replayed the kiss quickly in his mind. Then walked over to Ethan's door.

*\*Tap\**

Adam knocked lightly enough so it wouldn't push the cracked door open.

"Hey, it's Adam," he said, staring at the door.

"Hey, man, come in." Ethan's voice was quiet.

Adam walked into the room. Ethan was slouched in his computer chair, eyes on his monitor. The Rachel movie was on the screen.

"How was . . . the date?" said Adam, sitting down on Ethan's bed. He pretended not to notice the Rachel movie.

"Sucked," said Ethan.

"What happened?"

Ethan continued staring at the screen.

"Don't really wanna talk about it."

Adam nodded. Sometimes wanting to talk just meant having someone there. He thought about the silent glances with Gillian at the party. When you talked without talking, it was as if your brains were touching. Adam felt a shiver of electricity in his body. He looked around Ethan's room. The special gray-and-white-lined button-down shirt Ethan had bought for the date was crumpled on the floor in the corner. *Depressing.* But any depression Adam might feel was muted. Gillian was like a buffer inside his body. Nothing could touch him. He was safe from sadness. Ethan swiveled around in his chair. His face looked drawn. Raw around the eyes. Adam wondered if Ethan had finally cried.

"What about you? How was your night?" said Ethan.

"It was OK . . ." said Adam. He didn't want to act too happy. "I met a girl . . ."

"She a redhead?"

Adam nodded. And then he couldn't help it — he looked down at his lap and broke into a silly, sheepish grin.

"That's awesome, man," said Ethan. But his voice was hollow. "So give me the details."

"Um, her name's Gillian." *Gillian.* Adam felt like he owned the name. Like it was a word only he knew the definition of.

"Gillian," said Ethan. "So she's cute?"

Adam nodded. The kiss replayed in his mind.

"You deserve it, buddy," said Ethan.

Adam felt a pinch of guilt. He kind of felt like he was going to start crying. In front of Ethan? Are you kidding? He tilted his head back and stared at the ceiling, so on the chance any tears dared to form, they would absorb back into his eyes.

"I lied to her about my age," said Adam. *And something else,* inside his head.

"How old is she?" said Ethan.

Adam brought his head back down. He ran his hands across his face and through his hair, secretly rubbing away any potential wetness. "I'm not sure . . . How old are you when you graduate college?"

"I don't know, never went to college. Twenty-one? Twenty-two?" said Ethan. "Look, I wouldn't worry about it. It's not a huge age difference, and since it's just a summer thing she never has to know. Besides, you're really mature for seventeen."

Adam smiled. Ethan thought he was mature.

"You think so?" said Adam — then immediately felt embarrassed for asking Ethan to repeat it.

Ethan nodded. But he wasn't smiling. "I was a fucking wreck at seventeen," he said. Ethan turned in his chair and stared at Rachel, frozen on the monitor. He adjusted some things with the color, and the image flickered.

*What had gone wrong on Ethan's date? And what had actually happened between him and Rachel?* Suddenly, Adam was dying to know. *Needed* to know. He imagined that if he just sat there, very still, without making a noise, Ethan would start talking. He would tell him everything. All the questions Adam ever had about Ethan would be answered. From start to finish.

Ethan spun around in his chair. "Anyway," he said, "I should get back to work. Congrats on the girl. That's really awesome." His voice was cold.

Adam stood up. "Thanks, um, yeah, I'm really sorry about . . ."

"Whatever," said Ethan. He turned back to his computer. "I never should have gone. I was rightfully punished."

Adam walked out into the dark front room and closed the door. He thought Ethan was being a little dramatic. *"Rightfully punished*? This wasn't *Lord of the Rings*. It was weird, but for the first time, Adam felt ... cooler than Ethan. His happiness made him powerful. But as soon as he acknowledged this, he felt weaker than ever. He could not lose this. He replayed the kiss in his mind. Bliss. *But she thinks — eh.* He would worry about that later. He reached into his jeans pocket for his cell phone. Maybe she had texted? *"I can't stop replaying the kiss either."*

Adam's phone read: Text (2) His heart jumped. One was from gillian and one was from Casey.

Gillian: Just got home and woke up roommate's cat. It did not care for it. Adam grinned as the tingling feeling flooded into him.

What should he text back? Something else about the cat? Something about his roommates? *Just got home. Both roommates want to commit suicide. I do not care for it.* He stared at his phone, trying to think of what to type.

Just got home too! Erased it. Boring. And then: Feed it some of your salami sandwich. He pressed SEND before he could stop himself and then stared at his message, mortified. But then, right away, new message! His heart leapt again.

Gillian: Just did! Currently cleaning up cat puke. Strangely, liverwurst came up as well.

Adam laughed out loud. Then looked around. No one was watching. Just him in the dark in the glow of the phone. He checked Casey's message.

Casey: I'M SORRY. I was a total dick. Forgive me? Also, sleeping at Hazel's. THINK I'M IN LOVE.

Adam texted back: No big deal. I was a shit too. Then he wrote, THINK I'M IN LOVE TOO, but immediately erased it. Writing it made him terrified that he was jinxing it. Also, he wasn't convinced that his phone wouldn't somehow end up sending it to Gillian instead. He shuddered.

Adam made his way back to his bedroom. June still locked in her room, Ethan in his. He wished Casey were coming home. He felt close to her. Not like the sad people in this apartment. He and Casey were brother and sister, the cool ones whose nights had gone well. The people who things work out for. This was what he wanted to be.

# Chapter 8

IT WAS TUESDAY night, and Adam and Gillian had a date for tomorrow day. Everything had been planned by text. The idea of calling Gillian was terrifying, and fortunately she didn't seem to need to call Adam either. He was still replaying their kiss at the Seventy-Seventh Street subway stop twenty to thirty times a day, and Gillian's existence had become an amalgamation of that six-second memory plus the font of the name gillian as it showed up on his cell phone. It was going to be really weird seeing her in real life again.

Gillian had suggested they go to this exhibit called *Bodies,* which was a bunch of dead humans preserved in chemicals with their skin stripped away so you could see all their muscles and organs inside. It sounded awesome. Adam had immediately texted back: cool! But then, a couple hours later, Gillian sent another text saying: just realized bodies might be weird 4 u? or not? sorry if i wasn't thinking. we can totally do something else. Adam hadn't known what she was talking about, but then some subconscious part of his brain flashed an image of Boy Casey standing in the shadowy living room with his scarred, weird-looking chest. Gillian thought Adam's body looked like that. Adam had texted back: no, it's fine! But the anxiety over "the trans lie," which he'd been trying to ignore, had reared up again, and by Tuesday night it was all he could think about.

Casey always said, "Trans guys *are* real guys." So if that was true, then by the symmetric property, shouldn't the reverse be true too? Was it really a lie? I mean, yes. It was a lie. But how big of a lie? Adam wanted to run to Gillian's apartment, bust open her door, and yell: *"I'm not really trans! I'm only seventeen! But I think I love you!"* And she would laugh and smile and tell him it was OK, and they would fall onto her bed and have sex. He wanted to tell her so badly. But he couldn't. *"What the fuck are you talking about? Are you crazy? Get the fuck away from me!"* So the lie stayed inside him, a trapped gnat, buzzing between his rib cage and brain.

Meanwhile, the latest around the apartment was that "the Jews" had left a giant refrigerator on the landing, blocking the front door so it would only open a crack, and you had to squeeze through to get in and out. Adam and June had managed to push the thing a couple inches forward but couldn't do much more without completely blocking the neighbor's entrance. The only space for the refrigerator to go was down the stairs, which required some sort of hand truck. And even that seemed scary to manage. June was in an uproar over the whole thing. Agnes was apparently done, and June now channeled all her energy into ranting about the "selfish fucking Jews."

"I should call and threaten to get a lawyer! That's what I should do! It's a fire hazard. You guys do know it's a legal fire hazard, don't you? Guess we'll all just have to burn to death and then they'll be sorry. Or not!"

June paced up and down the living room in front of Adam and Casey, who were hanging out on the futon, Adam watching TV and Casey messing around on her laptop.

"Plus the bathtub drain!" June continued. "I mean, it's only been, what, a *month and a half*? That's a legal hazard too! We all probably have some horrible bacterial infection from the cesspool! I've been feeling sick!"

"Yeah, we should call and tell them we're gonna get a lawyer," said Casey. Her eyes didn't move from her computer. She was on Hazel's Facebook page. Casey was either talking to Hazel on the phone, talking about Hazel, or staring at Hazel's Facebook page. Mention of Boy Casey had been scarce since Saturday night.

"It's not like I haven't called them fifteen fucking times already," said June. "It's pathetic. It's *illegal.*"

Ethan padded out of his room toward the kitchen. He looked like shit. His clothes were rumpled, and there were bags under his eyes.

"Hey, um, Ethan?" said June. "Would you mind giving the Jews — I mean, the landlords — a call if you get a chance? I mean, I hate to say it, but I really think this is gonna mean a lot more coming from a man. That's just the way those fucking assholes roll."

"Get Adam to do it," said Ethan. He poured himself some grapefruit juice.

"Adam sounds like a girl," said June.

Adam gave June the finger. But then he felt a spark. Sounding like a girl, if you were pretending to be trans, was a good thing. As soon as Adam thought this, though, his mind doubled back. *He could not keep pretending.* The whole thing was ridiculous. Absurd. He needed to tell Gillian the truth on their date. He would just say he had been nervous, everyone at the party was gay, and he panicked. *"I'm not trans. I'm seventeen years old."* If she really liked him, she shouldn't care, right?

Of course she would care! Gillian didn't want to date some dork teenage boy. She didn't even want to date a *boy* at all. She'd say, *"Uh. Wow. OK. Look, I'm sorry, but . . . I can't do this."* And she'd walk away. Walk away! He absolutely could not tell her.

No, he had to tell her. She was going to find out eventually: there was no way around it, if they ever got to make out — have sex! — which was the *whole point,* right? So he had to tell her. But maybe if he didn't tell her right away . . . just waited a little bit longer . . . made sure she really, *really* liked him, so she wouldn't care if he wasn't trans, was only seventeen, because by then she would like him so much it wouldn't matter what he was. Yes, the right thing to do was continue to pretend for as long as he needed until he was absolutely sure she liked him enough.

No. He had to tell her, and he had to do it tomorrow. Everyone knows the longer you tell a lie, the worse it gets. And, besides, what was he supposed to do — just *never* make out with her? Once they started doing anything, she would "discover" the truth — the poking, protruding penis, *"Hi!"* — and then she would *really* hate him, she would stare in horror, she would gag and throw up, she would spit in his face. He had to tell her.

There was no way in hell he could tell her.

Adam felt his brain wheeze with exhaustion. *Tell her. Don't tell her.* The world's worst tennis match on eternal replay.

"Please, Ethan?" said June.

"Yeah, yeah, I'll do it," said Ethan. He shuffled back to his room with his glass of juice.

"God, and all I want right now is to take a fucking bath!" said June, staring up at the ceiling, as if she were actually addressing God. Despite the drain situation, June had become obsessed with taking baths. She would empty the dirty water from the tub cup by cup into the toilet, scrub it down with Ajax, take a three-hour bath while everyone else held their pee, and then leave the tub full of her grimy water. No one complained though, since taking baths seemed to be the only thing that gave her any remote pleasure.

June heaved another sigh and retreated to her room.

*What did "pretending to be trans" even mean, anyway,* thought Adam. Besides the obvious, that Adam had a dick and trans guys didn't. Adam tried to recall the interactions he'd had with Boy Casey and Jimmy. What made those guys different? Boy Casey talked about being trans all the time, but Jimmy never did. Adam wouldn't have even known Jimmy was trans if he hadn't seen his

ID. And there was something about Jimmy that made it seem like bringing up his trans-ness was *not* OK. Like Jimmy would just stare at you and say, *"What the hiz-ell you talkin' about?"* Adam wished Casey was still dating Boy Casey so he could gather more information. This Hazel girl was useless to him. He needed Boy Casey back in the picture *now*.

"What's going on with Boy Casey?" Adam asked, turning his head from the television.

Casey continued staring at her laptop. "I dunno. Catching herpes from someone."

"You still gonna see him?"

"Not really in the mood to get herpes right now . . ."

"Hazel could have herpes."

"Hazel does *not* have herpes. Anyway, we have safe sex."

"Safe sex? With a girl? What is that?"

Adam felt weird about how personal they were suddenly getting, but now he needed to know this stuff.

"Safe sex is important for lesbians *too*," said Casey. She shut her laptop and turned to Adam. She was revving up for a lecture. *Good.*

"There's dental dams, latex gloves, condoms for toys . . . and you should always boil."

"Boil what?"

"Your dildo, if you're using one."

"You do all that stuff?"

Casey gave Adam a weird look. She wasn't used to him being so nosy. He needed to be careful. Back off a little.

"Or whatever," he added. Eyes back on the TV.

"Well, I *have* . . ." said Casey, instantly wanting the attention back. "With Hazel, it's . . . different."

"Why do you like Hazel so much?" said Adam. "Boy Casey wasn't that bad . . ."

"You hated Boy Casey! Hazel is just . . ." Casey paused to stare into space as if she was conjuring Hazel's perfect image. "I just really like her . . . Did you know she got sixteen hundred on her SATs? When she was nine, she, like, built her own computer."

Adam thought about how Casey always had to dumb herself down around Boy Casey. It wasn't that Boy Casey was stupid, just that Casey was clearly smarter than him and this was apparent in any conversation. Probably the thing that annoyed Adam the most about Boy Casey — more than his self-centeredness — was that he *thought* he was just as smart as Casey when he obviously wasn't. Adam was pretty sure Boy Casey even thought he was *smarter* than Casey — which was just another example of him being less smart. Adam would never admit it to Casey, but she was pretty much the smartest person he knew.

"Her favorite authors are Philip K. Dick and Donna Haraway," said Casey, still on Hazel. "She identifies as a cyborg."

"She what?"

"Hazel identifies as a . . . never mind." Casey turned back to her computer.

"Well . . . I actually didn't think Boy Casey was that bad," said Adam. "He was kinda cool." The trans lie paled in comparison to this one.

Casey shrugged.

Adam's eyes returned to the television — an old *Friends* rerun. He tried focusing on the show, but his brain just started volleying back and forth again. *Tell her. Don't tell her.* Everything each character said seemed to steer him violently in one direction or the other.

Adam turned off the TV and walked into the bathroom. He shut the door and stared at himself in the mirror. He remembered the scary thing that had happened just five days ago, the night before the rally. That would never happen again. He had Gillian now. He had a good fucking thing in his life, and he had to hold

on to it at any cost. The thing had happened when he'd realized he
had nothing. Was nothing. Did you really need another person to
make you who you were? Yes.

Adam leaned in close to the mirror and examined his skin.
God, it was a fucking mess, as usual. Not "pizza face" disastrous
like Raphael at school, who might as well just commit suicide,
but pretty bad. Adam had three zits on his forehead under his
bangs — thank god for bangs — one zit in the crevice of the side
of his nose, and one to the left of his chin. His hands reached up to
squeeze the chin one, but he knew that would only make it worse.
*Fuck it* — he didn't care, he needed to get rid of it, and he needed
to get rid of it now.

*Squeeze*

*Argh!* A million times worse. Adam lathered on soap and furiously scrubbed at his face. *Ugh. Whatever.* There was nothing he
could do. He'd had zits when he met Gillian on Saturday, so she
wouldn't be surprised. Just unfortunately reminded.

"Whoa, sorry, dude." Ethan opened the door to the bathroom.

Adam reached for his toothbrush to pretend as if he were doing
something other than squeezing his zits.

"You nervous about your date?" said Ethan. "I always stare at
myself in the mirror for at least five hours the day before a date."

"Yeah . . ." said Adam. He put the toothbrush down.

Ethan leaned against the doorjamb. "Gillian. Did you guys
make out?"

Adam was touched Ethan remembered her name. "Yeah, we
kissed," he said. The kiss replayed in his mind.

"Well, that's good," said Ethan. "At least you don't have to
worry about that hurdle. Now you can just go up and kiss her the
moment you see her."

Adam's face went white.

"Don't be scared!" said Ethan. "Seriously, it's in the bag. This girl likes you. You guys already hung out, so she wouldn't have made the date if she didn't like you. You're in a top-notch position here. Not that you don't still have to play it cool, but . . ."

"Wait," said Adam. He felt hot and panicked. "How do I . . . play it cool?" The moment from last Saturday night of feeling cooler than Ethan had long passed, and Adam suddenly, desperately needed his advice. Ethan with his perfect clothes and chill attitude and hot ex-girlfriend. Ethan! Ethan would tell him how to make everything right.

Ethan sauntered into the bathroom and sat on the edge of the tub. Adam closed the toilet lid and sat down, too.

"OK, well, here's the thing," said Ethan. "Girls are strange, mysterious creatures. Guys are simple. We kind of just let you know how we feel. But girls have to play by this crazy set of rules where — OK, you know how in middle school, if you had a problem with another dude, you just punched him in the face?"

Adam thought about the time Colin had punched him in the face. And the time this kid Rodney had punched him in the face. And the time this kid Eric had punched him in the —

"Uh-huh," said Adam.

"Well, while that was going on, girls were having their own types of fights — but instead of fists, these fights were about secrets, and backstabbing, and rumors, and lies, and calling up your best friend from someone else's phone, whispering, 'You're a whore,' and hanging up. You know?"

Adam nodded.

"That shit doesn't just go away when you grow up and know better. It burrows into your brain and makes you crazy."

Adam wasn't entirely sure where Ethan was going with this.

"What I'm saying is it's just more convoluted with girls. And while there's something kind of sexy about all that mystery, it's also kind of sad." Ethan stared at Adam with fixed, intense eyes.

"So, what do I . . . do?" asked Adam.

"Just stay sensitive," said Ethan. "Because the moment you start to feel exposed — that's the moment she's exposed too. And that's what love is . . . when someone reaches inside you, through all the blood and nasty guts — they don't give a shit how messy their hand gets — and then they pull out this perfect *thing,* and that thing is the real you."

Adam nodded again. He wondered whether Ethan was going to get to the part about how to "play it cool."

Ethan stood up and stretched like he was about to leave.

"I just gotta figure out how to not be so nervous," said Adam quickly, not wanting Ethan to go.

"You'll be fine," said Ethan. "Trust me. Once you're in it, it will just all be happening and you'll know what to do." Ethan stood back and looked Adam over. "Now are you gonna shave first or what? 'Cause that high school–mustache look is not cool."

Adam ran his finger across the bristle on his upper lip. His cheeks and chin were still infuriatingly smooth, no matter how many times he'd dragged the razor over them.

"You can use my electric razor," said Ethan. "I'll switch out the blade for you. I've seen those shitty drugstore razors you use."

"Cool, thanks," said Adam. He had never used an electric razor before. His dad had one, but he'd always been too embarrassed to ask to borrow it.

"You're gonna need a good shirt, too," said Ethan, eyeing Adam's grubby T-shirt. "Hold up." Ethan ran into his room and came back with a faded blue flannel. "It's Steven Alan," he said, handing it to Adam.

"Thanks," said Adam. He put his arms through the soft flannel and buttoned up over his T-shirt. The flannel smelled like fresh detergent.

"Nice," said Ethan. He looked up at Adam's hair. "Now product." Ethan grabbed a small black tub of some stuff off the sink counter, dug his fingers in, and mussed it into Adam's bangs.

Adam felt that tingling feeling again, like with the stewardess on the airplane when he was eight. Ethan concentrated on Adam's hair, separating strands into perfectly messy clumps. Adam stood very still, not wanting Ethan to stop.

"All right," said Ethan, standing back to admire his work, "that looks good." He twisted Adam around to face the mirror.

Adam couldn't help smiling. For like the first time ever, he actually liked how he looked.

...

Adam lay in bed. It was midnight. His date with Gillian was in exactly eleven hours. Eleven hours to decide whether or not he was going to tell her.

If he decided *not* to tell her, it was very possible she would ask him questions about being trans, in which case he needed to be prepared to answer those questions. He couldn't just respond with, *"Oh, actually I'm not trans."* He needed to be able to consistently pretend to be trans until the right moment came to tell her he wasn't.

But what sort of questions would Gillian ask?

*"Why did you decide to be trans?"*

*"I just always felt like a boy inside."*

Well, at least that was true. *What else, what else ...* Adam's mind was blank. He dragged his laptop onto the bed, clicked on his sister's Facebook profile, and then clicked on Boy Casey's. *Shit.* It was private. The only thing Adam could remember from when he'd seen it before was "ABOUT ME: I'm an artist."

Adam and Gillian weren't Facebook friends yet, but if they became them, he could always adjust his info as needed. Or maybe he'd just say he doesn't "do" Facebook. Yeah, that was cooler anyway. He didn't have to worry about her searching for him on the Internet either. When you typed "Adam Freedman" into Google, about five million other people popped up first. He once scrolled through fifty-nine pages of entries before finding his name on a list for a Claremont kids' doubles tennis tournament from three years ago. There wasn't even a picture.

Adam clicked over to Google and typed in "trans guy." The first search entry was a *Wikipedia* page.

A trans man, trans guy, FTM is a transsexual or transgender man: a person who was assigned a female gender identity at birth, but who feels that this is not an accurate or complete description of themselves and consequently identifies as male.

*Duh.* This wasn't helpful. Adam noticed a YouTube video and clicked on that. A guy with shaggy blond hair wearing a hooded sweatshirt sat on a bed. He was talking about how he'd just hung out with his cousin, a "bio guy."

> *"I hadn't seen him since we were, like, ten, and we're both twenty-one now. At first, I couldn't stop thinking about it, just how unfair it is he got to be born with a penis, and I didn't. And wondering if he thought less of me. But once we started talking about it, he was pretty awesome. He said he has mad respect for trans men, because we've had to struggle, and he even said he's actually wondered what it's like to have a vagina. . . . He was just really open. I told him how it's just unbearable sometimes . . . having the wrong part down there."*

Adam's hand reached into his boxers and over his penis.

> *"Like when I'm having sex with my girlfriend — my fiancée — and I want to ejaculate, but I can't . . ."*

The guy's name was Luke Trevor. He looked completely like a real guy. Adam never would have thought he was trans. He clicked on another luketrevor video. The title was T-Shot Day, and it showed Luke about to inject himself with T.

*"I'm finally beginning to dig how I look. More like a man and not a little tween anymore."*

Luke plunged the syringe into his thigh and Adam winced.

*"My dose is one hundred milligrams a week. Half a cc."*

Adam grabbed a magazine and pen off the floor. He flipped open to a page and wrote in the margin: "100 mg a week. Half a cc." *"How much T do you take?"*

YouTube had dozens of luketrevor videos. Adam clicked on Becoming Me: Music Video. A song played over a series of shots of Luke: As a little kid. As a teenager on a BMX bike. In a hospital bed after surgery. Hanging out with friends. Standing on a cliff, arms raised in the air. Adam paused the video on the cliff shot. Luke was shirtless and his chest looked like Boy Casey's had. Curved scars underneath lopsided nipples. If Adam made out with Gillian, he would have to keep his shirt on. *Make out with Gillian.* Adam's heart sped up, and he replayed the subway-stop kiss. The video ended with white letters on a black screen: AGAINST ALL ODDS: JUST BE YOU.

Adam continued clicking on luketrevor videos. He was utterly entranced. Before he knew it, two hours had gone by. There were videos of Luke and his friend Alex — also a trans guy. Luke getting a piggyback ride from Alex, or Alex pretending to have anal sex with Luke. There was a video from Luke's birthday: "What's up from Kansas City! It's my birthday. That's all. Just wanted to capture the moment . . ." Videos of Luke's mother and grandmother, both avoiding looking into the camera, Luke talking about how much he loves them. A video of Luke telling his "coming out" story — how he'd tried to pee standing up as a little kid and his babysitter freaked and told his parents. Adam wrote down "tried peeing standing up" on his magazine.

Then the videos took a dark turn. There was one posted by someone named donttrustluketrevor, a static picture of a freeway overpass. The video was silent, and over the image of the freeway, little boxes of text popped up and then disappeared: "Luke Trevor is a fraud" . . . "a phony" . . . "a scammer" . . . "a traitor." Adam felt an eerie chill. He liked Luke Trevor. Why was somebody saying all this stuff? . . . Who *was* Luke Trevor?

Adam clicked on a video from only three weeks ago, titled Think You Know Me? Think Again. Luke was facing the camera, shirtless. His blond hair was slicked back, and he was wearing sunglasses. It kind of looked like he was going bald.

> *"I just need to say that there's a lot more to me than Luke Trevor. A lot of people are angry because their penis pump kits aren't working, but what people don't understand is that —"*

*What was he talking about?* Adam wrote "penis pump kit" on his magazine.

> *"— if there's a problem with your pump kit, then you need to take it up with the manufacturer, not me. I agreed to promote it, but that's where my involvement ends. I know there are a lot of people who hate me, but you know what? They don't know the slightest thing about me. There's a lot more to life than the Internet, so just because you saw me on YouTube, don't assume —"*

Adam clicked the video off. He was starting to feel nauseous. It was 2:37 A.M. and he needed to get to sleep. He'd gotten so involved in Luke Trevor's life, he'd barely accumulated any useful information. Adam clicked on one more video titled Metoidioplasty vs. Phalloplasty by Luke's friend Alex.

Unlike Luke, you could kind of tell that pudgy Alex used to be a girl. He sat on a living-room couch.

*"So I've finally decided what kind of bottom surgery I want. I'm going to go with the metoidioplasty. It just makes the most sense for me right now. And I can always get a phalloplasty later on if I want."*

Adam remembered a conversation Casey and June had had once.
*"Has he had bottom surgery?"*
*"No! Most trans guys don't."*
Apparently Casey did *not* know everything about trans guys. Adam wrote "decided to go with metoidioplasty." His eyes were closing and opening in that heavy, sleep-bleary way. He read over his list:

> 100 mg a week. Half a cc.
> tried peeing standing up
> penis pump kit
> decided to go with metoidioplasty

He tried to run the words through his brain like he did when he was cramming for a test. *100mgaweek.Halfacc.triedpeeingstandingup.penispumpkit.decided to go with metoidioplasty.*

His eyes were really closing. His head was a hundred pounds. He read through the list one more time, then did it once from memory. Then he ripped the page out of the magazine, got out of bed, stumbled into the bathroom, shredded the page into pieces, and flushed them down the toilet.

Adam got back in bed, crawling into his sleeping bag. And as he finally allowed himself to close his eyes, he saw the phrases *100 mg a week. Half a cc. Peeing standing up. Penis pump kit. Metoidioplasty* appear in little text boxes over an image of Gillian's face.

# Chapter 9

THE DATE. Adam woke with a start. He looked at his cell phone: 8:59 A.M. His alarm would be going off in exactly one minute. It was uncanny the way he'd woken up on his own, predicting the time. It must mean something. He checked the phone again, but there was no text from Gillian. Why would she text? They were seeing each other in two hours.

Adam got up and went to the bathroom. Ethan — who went to bed around 5:00 A.M. and rose around 2:00 P.M. — had left his electric razor out for Adam to use. He'd also placed the hair-product stuff right next to it: Bumble and bumble. Adam turned the razor on and stared at it buzzing. He brought it closer, and then even closer to his upper lip, his hand trembling a little, terrified he would slip and get a gash in his face and have to tell Gillian his mom had died so he couldn't make it. But once he pressed it to his skin, it stopped being scary. It felt smooth and effective. When he finished, there was only one small pinhead of blood. He dabbed it with his finger and put it on his tongue.

After showering, Adam wrapped a towel around his waist and dug into the hair product the way Ethan had and tried to muss it into his bangs. He closed his eyes and imagined Ethan was doing it. Back in his room, he got dressed in his Diesel jeans and a black T-shirt with Ethan's blue flannel over it. He buttoned up the flannel slowly. *Tell her. Don't tell her.* He laced up his white Adidas extra tight. Ethan had said: "Once you're in it, it will just all be happening and you'll know what to do." His mind flashed to walking to the subway with Gillian, the warm dark air, the glowing green subway bulb. "You're so cute . . ." she had said. *Gillian.* In just forty-nine minutes he was going to see Gillian! A wave of anticipation swelled in his chest and crashed with an elated spray.

. . .

Adam took the L to Union Square, transferred to the 4 downtown, and got off at Fulton. The address was 11 Fulton Street.

Outside the station, though it was a random Wednesday, the streets were dizzy with people. South Street Seaport was apparently some sort of tourist destination because vendors selling I ♥ NY shirts, and Statue of Liberty models were everywhere, shoving American flags in Adam's face as he tried to get his bearings. He had no idea which way to walk. It was even hotter than usual surrounded by all these people. Adam felt the hair product dripping onto his forehead and down the side of his nose. The T-shirt plus flannel combination was killing him. His entire chest was dense with sweat.

Adam checked his phone: 10:48. He could not risk being late and plowed through the people in a direction he prayed was right. He pulled the collar of his black T-shirt up from underneath Ethan's flannel and wiped the hair product off his face. BODIES. There it was! The same image from the website: a skin-stripped, muscle-and-bones guy sitting in the position of that famous sculpture *The Thinker.* And then he saw her — standing under the poster, looking at her phone. Was he late? Adam quickly checked his phone again: 10:52. No, she was just looking at her phone to look busy. Like he does. Like everyone does. Adam was filled with love for every single person on earth. He walked closer. Gillian's red hair was in a short, blunt ponytail and her lips pouted out, looking serious. She was wearing a tight, low-cut blue-and-white striped tank top and short black cutoffs. Smooth bare legs. Adam felt so instantly turned on, he wanted to take a photo of her, be transported back to his bedroom, beat off to the photo, and then be transported back to this moment so he could talk to her like a normal person and not the crazed sex addict that he was. Gillian looked up and smiled at him. He hustled over.

"OK," she said. "So this might be kind of weird, but I just feel like since it *exists,* I should see it, you know?"

"Totally," said Adam.

They went inside the museum, where everything was quiet and the air chilly. Gillian wrapped her arms around herself, and Adam imagined that they were his arms. Tickets were twenty dollars.

"Sorry it's so expensive," said Gillian. "I'm paying 'cause it was my idea."

"No," said Adam, pulling out his wallet. "Let me get this." He took out two twenties and shoved them under the partition before Gillian could get her money out.

"No," said Gillian. And she shoved her twenties into the pocket of Adam's flannel.

"No," said Adam, and he took the twenties out and put them in Gillian's shorts pocket but tried to do it so it wasn't like he was feeling her up.

"No," said Gillian, and she put the twenties in Adam's jeans pocket, and her hand near his crotch gave him an instant hard-on and his mind wiped out for five seconds.

"No, seriously," he said. And handed her twenties back to her, earnest.

"Fine," Gillian said. And she smiled, rolling her eyes.

A large group of people speaking French bustled past.

"I have to go to the bathroom first," said Gillian.

"Cool," said Adam.

They walked over to the bathrooms, where there were two signs next to the men's and women's rooms. Gillian stopped to read the signs, so Adam did too. The sign over the women's room read: *"Women use the bathroom more frequently than men for several reasons, such as drinking more liquid and having smaller bladders."* The sign over the men's room read: *"Throughout your life, you will eliminate more than 45,000 liters of urine. That could fill a small swimming pool."*

"Right," said Gillian. "Of course the women's sign is all about how women are different from men, and the men's sign gets to be this interesting universal fact. So annoying."

"Yeah," said Adam.

"Be right back," said Gillian.

Adam nodded and waited. He didn't have to go. He looked over at the entrance to the exhibition hall where another quote was painted in bold letters on the wall.

*"I consist of body and soul in the words of a child. And why shouldn't we speak like children? But the enlightened, the knowledgeable would say, I am body through and through, nothing more, and the soul is just a word for something on the body." — Nietzsche*

Gillian came back and they entered the exhibit, which was filled with dozens of stripped-raw human figures. From what Adam could tell, this was going to be awesome, and he got that excited, antsy feeling like when his family would pull into the parking lot of Great America and he'd see the tops of the roller coasters. The first human they walked over to was made entirely from an intricate lace of arteries and veins. It wasn't even clear how the whole thing managed to stand up.

"Wow," said Gillian, "it's so beautiful."

Adam examined it closer and felt his own arteries and veins

light up inside him, as if suddenly made fluorescent. His whole body felt delicate and weak. He twitched.

As they made their way through the hall, things got progressively more bizarre. At first the figures just stood there, upright and respectable. *"I am Skeleton Man." "I am Muscle Man."* Like 3D models from Adam's biology textbook. But as Adam and Gillian turned the corner, they ran into a figure lurched over, holding out a clump of entrails strung from his abdomen, a gaping-mouthed horror-movie psycho offering his guts to you.

"Jesus," said Adam.

"I think I may have picked the most unsexy date possible," said Gillian. She looked at Adam apologetically.

"No, it's cool!" said Adam.

"You're not totally turned off?" said Gillian.

Adam shook his head and smiled.

"Good," said Gillian. And she took his hand. And Adam got hard. Adam could be submerged in a pool of diarrhea and if Gillian touched him, he would still get hard.

They walked into the next room where "muscle 'n' organs" figures were manipulated into positions as if they were skateboarding, running with a football, and one just sort of awkwardly "reaching for the stars." Something about these position-molded figures made Adam feel . . . off. Like it gave them silly personalities or something. He supposed these were cooler to look at, but the break-dancing skin-stripped man made him uncomfortable. Adam wondered if Gillian felt the same way but was nervous to say anything. He didn't want them to disagree.

"Look," said Gillian, "have you noticed how they all have blue eyes?" Little glass eyes were fixed into the figures' muscly sockets. "I heard there's, like, this controversy that all the figures were actually Asian prisoners or something from China, who may have not given consent. And then they give them blue eyes. Amazing."

"What?" said Adam. "That's fucked up . . ." He was distracted by the sudden sensation that he could smell the muscles through the glass.

They wandered through the rest of the rooms, examining blackened, cancerous intestines, sea anemone–like glands, and trails of spinal nerves spreading out from brains. Adam noticed a group of teenagers being led around by a teacher. Summer school? The teens were loud and messy, saying things like, "Oooh, that's nasty," or "I'm hungry." Adam felt cool and above them. He was on a date. He was twenty years old and on a date.

"Hey, see those kids," whispered Gillian. "*Three* of them are wearing Jack Skellington *Nightmare Before Christmas* T-shirts. It's like they planned it."

"For who?" said Adam. "The dead bodies? 'Oh, cool, you're one of us.'"

Gillian laughed.

One of the girls made eye contact with Adam, blushed, and looked away. Adam blushed too.

"That teenage girl totally just checked you out," said Gillian.

"What? No, she didn't," said Adam.

"She's cute," said Gillian. "God, I'm such a pervert."

The next gallery was divided into two halves. Painted on one side of the wall was a woman symbol and on the other, a male symbol. A muscle 'n' bones man and a muscle 'n' bones woman stood watch, representing for each side. Adam noticed that the muscle 'n' bones woman had large eyelashes affixed to her glass eyes. Beneath the figures were display cases with disembodied genitals.

"How come everyone's crammed around the female display, but no one's looking at the male?" Gillian asked.

It was true. Adam didn't want them to go over and look at the male display, either. He felt embarrassed.

"It's crowded in here," he said.

Gillian's expression shifted.

"Yeah, let's get out of here," she said, smiling. And she took his hand and led him out.

The exhibit was over. Adam and Gillian stood in front of a round table scattered with pencils and little booklets titled *Impressions*.

"Let's see what people wrote!" said Gillian. She seemed more excited by this than she had by anything in the exhibit.

They hunkered down at the table and opened one of the booklets. They were sitting so close, the hairs on their arms touched.

"*Needs places to sit,*'" said Gillian, reading an entry out loud. "*My legs hurt.*' This is amazing."

Adam read the next one. "*Human beings are all the same. Everything we fight over — countries, religion, beliefs, ideas, money — is not real. What a sadness that we kill one another and hate one another.*'"

"Mm-hmm," said Gillian, with a conciliatory smile. She read the next one: "*The maker of these awesome bodies is Jehovah. Psalms 83:18. The person responsible for disease, sickness, and death is Adam. Genesis 2:17, 3:6.*'" Gillian pinched Adam. "Ooooh, Adam! Is it true?"

Adam laughed.

Then there was an awkward pause.

*Why?*

"Oh," said Gillian. "Are you or is your family . . . ?" She had an anxious smile.

"Oh, no," said Adam. "We're, like, Jewish, but not really. I'm nothing."

"Cool," said Gillian, relaxed. "I'm nothing too."

They went back to scanning the entries.

"You know what I've always actually thought . . ." Gillian said.

"Yeah?" said Adam.

"That we're part alien. Humans are. I mean, I believe in evolution and everything, but there's just something inexplicably *weird* about us. You know?"

Adam nodded. He did.

. . .

Adam and Gillian walked out of the calm, air-conditioned museum into the blazing chaos of South Street Seaport. They weren't holding hands, but they were walking close together. *Now what?*

"So . . . you wanna get something to eat?" said Gillian.

"Yeah!" said Adam, grateful.

They headed in a random direction. Adam was nervous. Inside the museum there was always some display or something to talk about. And at the party they had been drunk, and when you're drunk there's always something to talk about. But now, strolling along sober, his mind grasped for something to say. They had been silent for about eight seconds, otherwise known as fifty years. The awkwardness was shredding up his insides. He saw a movie poster on a building wall that read: *Lady in the Water — a film by M. Night Shyamalan.*

"God, that looks horrible," he said.

"M. Night Shyamalan," said Gillian. "I'm kind of obsessed with M. Night Shyamalan."

"Because his name is M. Night Shyamalan?"

"Yes!" said Gillian, turning to Adam with a grin.

"His ads always say 'a film by M. Night Shyamalan,' like, bigger than anyone else's ever do," said Adam.

"I know! Oh my god, did you see *The Village*?"

"Wait, which one was that — ?"

"OK, imagine a bunch of silly people who don't like the color red and take turns putting on a bird costume and going out of bounds for medicines — cut to: 'End. A film by M. Night Shya-malan.'"

"'Coming soon,'" said Adam, "'*M. Night Shyamalan* — a film by M. Night Shyamalan.'"

Gillian laughed.

And then, maybe because he had seen those *Nightmare Before Christmas* T-shirts, Adam started singing the words "M. Night Shyamalan," to the tune of "This Is Halloween."

"*M. Night Shyam-a-lan, M. Night Shyam-a-lan.*"

Gillian joined in. "*M. Night Shyam-a-lan, M. Night Shyam-a-lan.*" Then they just started laughing again. Gillian gave Adam that same amused look she had when they'd first met at the party.

"I'm, like, delighted by you," she said.

Adam blushed.

"You're really quiet and don't talk much, but then you'll just come out with this totally weird thing. I mean, in a really good way."

People often told Adam he was quiet. Which was strange to him. His thoughts were so loud, it felt as if he were talking all the time.

"I like you," said Gillian.

"Me too," said Adam. "I mean, I like *you*. Not myself."

Gillian laughed again.

"Should we get some pizza?" said Adam. They were in front of a Famous Original Ray's.

"Yeah, in a second," said Gillian. She grabbed Adam by the sides of his flannel and pulled him over into the alley behind the pizza place. Gillian leaned herself up against the brick wall and pulled Adam against her. They opened their mouths, and their tongues jammed into each other. Gillian's hands went under the back of Adam's shirt. His dick was fully hard, and he thought he might lose it. Why did this feel so unbelievably good? Gillian tugged him closer. He needed to hide his erection. He did *not* want her to think he was "packing." *God.* He adjusted his hips away from her.

Gillian moved her hands up onto Adam's neck and in his hair. He let his fingers hover near the low neckline of her striped tank top. His fingertips grazed the seam and soft, smooth skin underneath.

"That's OK," she said, smiling, and brought his hands up over her breasts. He could feel her nipples, hard and poking out under the fabric. If he came in his pants, he would never forgive himself.

A man shuffled down the alley in front of them, glancing over. Gillian and Adam giggled and dropped their hands to their sides.

"Should we go get pizza?" said Gillian.

"Yeah," said Adam. He adjusted his pants, willing his hard-on to go down.

They walked into the pizza place, holding hands.

"It's weird being publicly affectionate with a guy," said Gillian. "It's like no one really cares."

"Yeah?" said Adam. He needed to start saying more than "yeah."

*You're really quiet,* she had said.

"I mean, you know how it is with two girls," continued Gillian. "Guys always leer at you like you're putting on a show for them, or people act like you're making some big political statement and give you 'the smile' to let you know they're cool and they approve. So annoying."

"Yeah, my sister talks about that," said Adam. She did. One of Casey's favorite rants was about people who thought they were extra special because they were nice and friendly to gay people. "You don't get *bonus* points for not treating gay people like shit."

"That's so cool your sister's queer too," said Gillian.

"Uh, yeah," said Adam. He was starting to feel hot again. *Tell her/Don't tell her* reared up in his mind, but he shoved it away. He noticed a *Street Fighter II* game in the corner. "Hey, wanna play?"

"Yeah! I love *Street Fighter.*"

Adam dug out some quarters and hit TWO PLAYER. He picked Vega, and Gillian picked Fei Long.

*Damn.* Gillian KO'd him after, like, five seconds. Round Two. No mercy. Adam knew all the special moves — he did a Sky High Claw, then a Rainbow Suplex off a Wall Bounce, but Gillian hit him with a Flame Kick. *Fuck.* KO'd again!

"Ha!" said Gillian. She looked thrilled.

"Wow, you're really good," said Adam.

"I know," she said. "I don't even know what I'm doing. I just hit as many buttons as fast as I can, and I always win."

They bought slices and sat across from each other in one of the booths. Gillian took a napkin and spread it out on top of her slice. She pressed her fingertips down on the pizza, and the napkin turned translucent.

"Just ignore that I'm doing this," she said. Gillian lifted the grease-soaked napkin up and rolled it into a ball inside another napkin. Her feet kicked Adam's feet under the table. He kicked back and she grinned. She had three dimples — two on the left and one on the right. He loved her smile so much, it felt like being impaled on a metal fence.

Adam folded his pizza in half and crammed a bite in his mouth. The melted cheese and sweet basil tomato sauce dripped out of the flour-dusted crust. Delicious.

Gillian took a triangle bite off the end. "So . . ." she said. "Um . . . what's Berkeley like?"

"It's OK," said Adam. He quickly tried to chew and swallow the massive wad in his mouth so he could talk. He didn't hang out in Berkeley that much, but every now and then he and Brad went to Telegraph Avenue to walk around and buy dumb shit like herbal cigarettes and weed patches that Adam then threw away so his mom wouldn't find them. "There are a lot of hippies." *Wait, what if she likes hippies?*

"Ugh!" said Gillian. "I hate hippies. I swear I got scabies from my hippie roommate junior year. I mean — not that I have scabies anymore. Actually, it probably wasn't even scabies." Gillian's face was red. "But, yeah," she said, "Smith is basically made up of lesbians and straight hippie girls. I don't know which is worse."

"Definitely hippies," said Adam. He was starting to feel awkward. Not nervous awkward like before. Just . . . awkward awkward. He worried Gillian could tell because she started talking really fast.

"Yeah, it's kind of weird, like, having graduated, everyone figuring out what we're going to 'do,' you know? I mean, some people always knew. Like my friend Jackie just started med school at NYU, and, like, she's just really dedicated. It's really cool. I just wanted to move to New York and was lucky to get this part-time job at the Met — only because my mom's friend works there. I wasn't even an art history major. I was women's studies." Gillian rolled her eyes. "Yes, I majored in women's studies."

"That's cool," said Adam. He took another bite of pizza so he wouldn't have to say something else.

"It is not 'cool,'" said Gillian. "I mean, it wasn't horrible, I don't regret it — well, maybe I do — but I mean, it was fine, it's good, it's just definitely not *cool*. It would be cool if I were, like, a guy or a straight girl, maybe — but, you know, instead it's basically like, 'Hi, I'm gay and I majored in being gay.'" Gillian paused. "It's a little '*M. Night Shyamalan* — a film by M. Night Shyamalan.'"

Adam laughed. "But not all women are gay!" he said.

*And . . . you're not, right?*

Gillian rolled her eyes again. "You know what I mean. So, anyway, now that I have my degree in being gay, I'm kind of, like . . . still not sure what I want to do, you know? I actually really like the job at the Met. I get to work in this climate-controlled library underneath the museum where they have all these really old, rare books. I make these custom boxes out of this special acid-free blue cardboard to store them in. I love old books. The leather covers and tassels. You know? And a lot of them have illustrations inside. I don't know why they don't do that anymore. My great-aunt had this old illustrated copy of *Gulliver's Travels.* I used to go to her house every day after school. And now being at the Met sort of reminds me of her." Gillian paused and looked down. "I'm too nostalgic." She had that serious look, like she'd had when Adam had seen her waiting in front of the museum. He loved that look, too. He loved every single thing about her. Gillian took a small bite of pizza and chewed fast. "Anyway, um, so what's your major?"

Casey's major was biology. "Biology," said Adam.

"Really?! That's so cool!"

"Yeah." *Stop saying "yeah."*

"Wow . . . why didn't you say so in the museum? Do you have, like, a focus?"

"No . . . no focus."

"But you want to be a biologist?"

"Yeah."

"That's really cool."

"Yeah."

Adam's pizza was finished. He picked up his napkin and began quietly ripping it into tiny pieces. He was really hot. He wished he could take his flannel off. No one spoke for about six seconds.

"But, um, so you like Berkeley?" said Gillian. "I mean, apart from the hippies? My friend Andrea from high school goes there. Andrea Salzberg. Do you know her?"

Adam realized that when Gillian had asked him what Berkeley was like, she had meant the college, not the city. He didn't know anything about the college. Why had he told her he went there?

"Uh, I don't think so."

"I feel like I know a lot of people who went to Berkeley . . . What about Corinne Poggi?"

"No."

"Derek ... what's his last name ... Sorensen. Do you know him?"

"Uh, no."

"Um ... oh! My friend Kiley Quinn — from middle school."

He couldn't just keep saying "no."

"Yeah."

"You know Kiley?!"

"Uh, yeah."

"That's so funny! What's she like now? I haven't seen her in years."

"She's ... cool."

"Yeah? Like how?"

"I don't know."

There was a long, cold pause. Adam looked at his hands. Little pieces of napkin were sticking to his sweat-covered palms. He wiped his hands on his pants. He hated lying. He hated it, he hated it, he hated it.

"Is something wrong?" said Gillian.

Adam didn't respond.

*Say something!*

"No," he said.

"No?" said Gillian.

Silence.

Silence.

Gillian looked down. "I think I'm ... gonna go," she said. Her voice was hollow. She picked up her grease napkin ball and put it on top of her unfinished pizza.

Adam's heart was beating wild. It was all crashing down. He was ruining it. It was ruined. He needed to say something, but the only thing running through his brain was *100mgaweek.halfacc.penispumpkit.metoidioplasty.* What could he do? He needed to save it. How could he save it? *Just tell her! Just tell her!*

Gillian stood up and went to throw her plate in the trash. Her face was expressionless.

"I — I don't go to Berkeley," said Adam.

"What?" said Gillian.

Adam was silent.

"What do you mean?" she said. She stayed poised at the trash can.

"I don't go to college."

Gillian said nothing.

"I . . . I live at home . . . in Piedmont."

"You live with your parents?"

"Yeah," said Adam.

Gillian's face shifted. It didn't look mean anymore. Just curious.

"It was really stupid to lie . . ." said Adam.

"It's OK . . ." said Gillian, cautiously.

And then she smiled. She smiled! Those dimples. Adam was so relieved, he thought he might cry. Gillian sat back down at the table.

"I mean, I'm kind of mad you lied," Gillian said, "but I also kind of understand . . ."

She understood! He was going to tell her. He was going to tell her everything. *This was it.* He was going to do it. He could feel the flood at the back of his throat, bursting to be let out. Just do it — *now.*

"I'm so sorry," said Adam. "It was really, really stupid to lie. It just happened and then I couldn't take it back. Kind of like when I threw that drink. Anyway, so here's the thing. I'm actually —"

"My friend Aiden lied to his girlfriend at first too," Gillian interrupted.

*Aiden?*

Gillian blushed. "I mean, not that *we're* . . ."

*What was going on?*

"He's trans too," she said, looking down at the word *trans*.

"Oh," said Adam.

"He started out at Smith but was so fucked up over gender stuff that he dropped out after a year and moved back home and started transition. He didn't want to deal with being in college — especially *Smith* — while he was going through all that, so he just worked jobs and lived at home. Also so his mom could take care of him during surgery. He wants to start college again now and is kind of ashamed since he's twenty-two and the rest of us are all done." Gillian smiled at Adam. Adam smiled weakly back.

"Anyway," she continued, "so he hooked up with this girl and lied and told her he had graduated college, and then when it turned out it was going to be a real thing — like, they kept hanging out and ended up really liking each other — he had to come clean. It's kind of funny, she knew he was trans the whole time and was totally cool with it, but the big 'coming out' was telling her he'd dropped out of school and lived at home. We, like, processed how he was going to tell her a million times on the phone together. Anyway, I'm rambling. I guess what I'm saying is, I get it. And I think being who you are, being trans is . . . really brave."

Adam nodded. He felt as if cement had been poured into the shape of his body and hardened cold.

"So are you planning to go to college?" continued Gillian.

Adam nodded slowly.

"How old are you, anyway?"

This was it. His last chance. *Tell her.*

"Twenty-two," said Adam.

"Cool," said Gillian, "me too."

· · ·

Adam walked up the stairs of 206 Scholes Street. He and Gillian had kissed goodbye, and the kiss had made him want to collapse on top of her and sink his entire body into hers, but he couldn't be happy. They'd made plans for Friday night, but instead of feeling overjoyed, he felt terrified, sick. He could feel the lie seeping through his insides, like a toxic oil spill. He liked Gillian so much. He liked her more than he'd even known it was possible to like someone. He rammed his fists into his eye sockets. He hated himself.

"My father is one of the most powerful attorneys in the country."

Adam opened the door to Ethan on the phone. Judging by the way June was hovering next to him, Adam was pretty sure he was on with the Hasidic landlords.

"Yeah. If that refrigerator isn't gone by tomorrow morning, and someone isn't here to fix the bathtub by Friday, you will be hearing from him."

Ethan's voice was cold and measured. June hopped around like a boxer.

"Thank you." Ethan closed his cell. "They said it'll be done. It better be, since my dad's just an immigration law professor."

"Sweet," said June. "The Jews are going down! They may not understand *please,* but they sure as fuck understand *lawyer.*"

"Hey," said Ethan, looking at Adam, "how was the date?"

"It was . . . good," said Adam.

Casey looked up from her book on the couch. "You went on a date? With who? That girl from Carlisle's party?"

Adam nodded.

"What was a straight girl even doing there?" said Casey, glancing at June, who promptly wrinkled her nose.

"She's bi," said Adam.

Casey smirked. "Well . . ." she said, "what happened? Does she still think you're twenty?"

"Twenty-two," said Adam.

Everyone burst out laughing.

"It's not funny!" he said.

"Aww," said Ethan. "We're just playing. . . . It's a little funny."

"Why does this girl like you?" said June. And Adam knew she wasn't even trying to be mean — just genuinely curious.

"Adam's awesome," said Ethan. "Why wouldn't she like him?"

"Seriously though," said Casey, and she placed her book down on the coffee table. *A Cyborg Manifesto* by Donna Haraway. "She really believes you're twenty-two? I mean, I'm not trying to be an asshole or anything, but you kind of barely look seventeen."

"Shut up," said Adam. He picked up a Netflix sleeve off the TV and pretended to be absorbed in the synopsis. *The Apartment.* Some movie from the '60s Ethan had ordered that had been sitting there for weeks.

"So she thinks Adam's a little older than he is," said Ethan. "So what. It's not like age really means anything. My parents are thirteen years apart."

*That's not the lie I'm worried about,* thought Adam. He was suddenly scared he might start crying.

"Yeah, I guess," said Casey. "I just can't believe if I meet this girl, I have to pretend Adam's older than me. Being the older sibling is a crucial part of my identity!"

"Yeah, being middle is a crucial part of mine," said June. Then everyone got kind of silent and awkward. Ethan had had a brother, but he had died when Ethan was a kid. He'd never told them how.

"She's really cool and we like each other," said Adam. "That's all." And he turned around, went into his closet-room, and shut the door.

Inside, he fell to his knees and punched at his mattress, willing himself not to cry. He reached into his back pocket and pulled out the *Bodies* pamphlet. Held it lovingly, then crumpled it into a ball and threw it across the room. *Gillian.* She liked him. He was the luckiest, luckiest, luckiest person in the entire world. He was totally fucked.

# Chapter 10

IT WAS LATE Friday afternoon. Tonight Adam was going to meet Gillian at her apartment at 7:00 P.M., and then they were going out to dinner with some of her friends. Gillian had texted: Is it too soon for that? Followed quickly by: I just want to see you and I forgot about these dinner plans and it would be cool to bring you. Adam had texted it was fine, great, even though it made him feel as if his throat were puffing up and his hands had started stinging and gone numb. More people to lie to.

Meanwhile, the hallway refrigerator had been swiftly removed after Ethan's lawyer-threatening phone call, and someone was supposedly coming today to fix the clogged bathtub.

"I have a plan," said June. She turned down the TV and faced Adam and Casey, slumped in their usual positions on the futon. June's eyes were wild and shiny, and Adam wondered if she was gaining weight. She was wearing a tank top, and her stomach spilled out over the top of her jeans — her bellybutton stretched into a winking gash.

"A plan for what?" said Casey, not lifting her eyes from her book. She had finished *A Cyborg Manifesto* and moved on to *Neuromancer* — another one of Hazel's recommendations.

"A plan for the Jews of course!" said June. For a moment, Adam thought June had a plan to kill them. Or at least trip them on their way into the apartment with a shoelace nailed to the door frame.

"Uh-huh?" said Casey, still not looking up. Adam knew she wasn't listening. It was a surprise Casey heard June at all. When Casey was reading, nothing got through to her. She became dead to everything outside the book. It was an attribute their mom liked to brag about all the time.

"We put out all the Jewish items we can — that menorah you bought, whatever old Jewish holiday cards any of us can find. Adam" — June jerked her head toward Adam, suddenly needing him — "what Jewish stuff do you have?"

"I don't have anything Jewish," said Adam.

"Well, *look*," said June. "We'll put out all the Jewish stuff, they'll realize we're serious Jews, and then they'll love us and we'll never have to worry about them fucking us over again!"

"But we're not serious Jews," said Adam.

Casey, head down, turned the page of her book.

"Speak for yourself!" said June, flouncing around. "I can say the Hanukkah prayer. *Baruch atah Adonai . . .*" and she continued reciting it as she went into her room to look for "Jewish stuff."

June had had to take on a second job. The comic shop barely paid anything, and she'd already had to borrow money from Ethan to pay last month's rent. So now she was a medical research subject. A "guinea pig," she called it. Adam wasn't sure what the medical research she was loaning her body to was, but it entailed her leaving a giant jug of her urine in the bathroom and keeping a "mood chart," for which she was always asking everyone to help her rate her mood on a scale of one to ten.

"Only you know what your mood is," Casey had said. "We only know how you *act*." And June had looked crestfallen, like Casey knowing her mood had been the one slight glimmer of intimacy she was hoping they could share.

Adam listened to June reciting the Hanukkah prayer over and over in her room as she rooted around. He was pretty sure she was pathetically trying to impress Casey with it. Casey, who, if you clapped in front of her face right now, wouldn't notice. The apartment felt heavy with loneliness.

Casey looked at her watch. "Shit!" she said. "It's four-thirty! I'm meeting Hazel at seven! Fuck!"

"But you have, like, over two hours," said Adam. *I'm meeting Gillian at seven,* he thought.

"Uh, *yeah,* and I'm totally not ready," said Casey. She looked forlornly back at her book. "God, and I really wanted to finish this so I could talk to Hazel about it. She's so fast. She reads, like, a book a day. I'm so dumb and slow."

If Casey was dumb, Adam was brain-dead.

"She sent me the itinerary for our date on iCal," continued Casey. "Wanna hear it?" and before Adam could respond, she said, "First we're meeting at South Fourth and Bedford and having a romantic sunset walk over the Williamsburg Bridge. Then I'm going with her to get her tattoo worked on — the one in binary code on her wrist. I'm not allowed to tell anyone what it means. Then we're getting dinner in Chinatown at a special place where she knows the waiters. Then we're getting strawberry gelato at this other special place on the Lower East Side."

Adam noticed June, cast in dark shadow, standing completely still in her bedroom door frame, clutching the heavy gold menorah.

"And then," continued Casey, "there's a surprise! She won't tell me what it is. I have to get ready!" And she bolted up.

Casey was making Adam nervous. He should be getting ready, too. He went into his room and started rifling through his clothes. Ugh, he hated everything he owned. A few weeks ago when he'd bought his Ethan Diesel jeans, he'd tried to buy some shirts that seemed Ethanesque too, but now that he'd worn a *real* Ethan shirt, they all seemed horrible and like they were from Kmart. Adam went and knocked on Ethan's door.

"What's up?" Ethan was still in his pajamas.

"Hey, um, I'm going out with Gillian tonight, and, um, I was wondering if I could borrow that shirt again?"

"What?!" said Ethan.

"Oh, uh, I don't —"

"You can*not* wear the same shirt to your second date," continued Ethan. "Get in here — let's try on some other ones."

Adam walked into Ethan's room. The Rachel movie was still on his computer screen. Didn't he ever just get *sick* of it? Adam was sick of it, and he hadn't even seen the whole thing. Ethan took a shirt off a hanger in his closet and held it up to Adam. It was the special gray-with-thin-white-lines button-down he'd bought for his date with the Film Forum girl.

"This is Patrik Ervell for Opening Ceremony," said Ethan.

"It's what?" said Adam.

"A designer," said Ethan. "It's better without an undershirt. Try it on."

Adam felt shy taking his shirt off in front of Ethan. He didn't know why. He and Brad were shirtless together all the time. He lifted his T-shirt over his head, and Ethan turned his back to Adam to do something on the computer. Adam felt his nipples get hard. He quickly buttoned up the shirt.

"Sweet," said Ethan, turning around. "That's the one."

Back in the front room, Casey was putting on a fashion show for June as June cut out Stars of David from yellow construction paper and pasted them on the wall.

"Yeah, that's what Roxanne said Schuyler said," said June. "Whatever."

"*Auh!*" said Casey. "I am *not* a tranny chaser!" She seemed extremely pleased that this had been said about her.

"I think Schuyler's just in love with Boy Casey," said June.

"Hold on, let me try another shirt," said Casey, and she darted into her room.

*Tranny chaser?* This seemed like something Adam should be aware of.

"What are you guys talking about?" he asked June, casual. June slapped another glue stick–smeared Star of David on the wall.

"You know, 'cause Casey dated Boy Casey and now she's dating Hazel, two trans people in a row."

"What? Hazel is trans?" said Adam. Was *everybody* fucking trans?

"Yeah," said June.

Casey walked back into the room wearing a sheer tank top and probably a push-up bra.

"Hazel is trans?" Adam asked her.

Casey rolled her eyes. "Yes. What do you think of this shirt, June?"

"So how come you guys always call her 'her'?" said Adam. "I thought you were supposed to call trans people 'him.'"

"Not if they're trans *women*," said Casey.

Adam was completely confused. He'd thought Hazel was just a butch lesbian — butch like Sam was butch, with short hair and cargo pants and . . .

"But I thought —"

"She was born a boy, transitioned to being a girl, is attracted to girls, so she's a trans dyke," said Casey, fast and exasperated, like it was the most obvious thing in the world.

"I think I liked the other shirt better," said June.

"Really?" said Casey. "Is this one too slutty? Hazel told me she likes slutty. She calls me her slutty teenage college girl."

"I liked the other one," said June.

"I'm gonna wear this one," said Casey. "But I think I'm gonna wear a skirt, too." Casey turned around, went back in her bedroom, and shut the door.

The buzzer rang.

"It's them!" said June. "It's them! I'm not even ready! How does everything look?"

June ran to the bookshelf, adjusted the menorah, and then ran to open the door, almost slipping on a Star of David on the way. As she opened the front door, Adam saw her smile fall.

"You have clogged bathtub?" A short Hispanic guy in grubby clothes carrying some sort of suction machine walked into the room.

. . .

Adam took the G train from the Broadway stop to the Hoyt-Schermerhorn stop to get to Gillian's apartment in Fort Greene. As the subway sped along, he glanced around at the other passengers, replayed making out with Gillian in the pizza shop alley, and managed for moments at a time to forget the lie. But whether he was thinking about it or not, it was always there. Like a ringing in your head you don't realize is so loud until you plug your ears.

Adam exited the station. Gillian was at 488 Atlantic Avenue, apartment #2. He glanced around and saw Atlantic Avenue about a block away. He checked his reflection on the back of his phone. Then the time: 6:22. As usual, he had been terrified of being late and somehow calculated it would take an hour to travel seven subway stops. Actually, it was more a precaution. There could have been an emergency and they would have had to stop, and Adam would have been trapped underground with no cell phone signal, no way of contacting Gillian, who would just be waiting, waiting and realizing that she didn't even really like Adam all that much, now that she was annoyed with him for being late and had time to think things over. Definitely better to be obscenely early and kill forty minutes. He started in the direction of Atlantic Avenue but then thought better of it. Gillian, getting dressed for the date, peers out the window and sees Adam, pacing up and down the street below.

Adam walked down Livingston. He wondered what Kelsey Winslow was doing right now. Waiting in her bedroom for Matt to climb up that tree like a fool. *"My dad says I'm killing the tree."* Adam imagined Matt at the top of the branches, swaying slightly in the breeze, about to clamber through the window when — *snap!* The branch breaks and Matt comes crashing down, cracking his skull open on the concrete in a bloody sprawl. East Bay Prep would build a memorial water fountain for him like they did for that girl Amy Kirkland, who had died of Graves' disease, RIP 1992. Adam didn't like drinking from that fountain. It always made him feel like he was catching Graves' disease. Whatever that was.

It was only 6:27. *Jesus.* Adam started to worry he was going to show up at Gillian's with giant pit stains if he kept walking. He ducked into an air-conditioned Duane Reade and headed toward the back. Stared at the magazines, picked up a *GQ*, opened it, stared at an article — "How to Have Sex in the Car" — but couldn't concentrate enough to read. Maybe Kelsey and Matt were fucking right now. Just slippery slamming, ramming into each other on her bed. *"Oh, Matt, you feel so good! Harder!"* Why did he keep thinking about Kelsey? He had walked around the block before her house 500,000 years ago. He had barely even thought about her since he got to New York; she meant nothing to him. But now she felt eerily close. Like she was breathing on him. They all were. They knew who he really was, and it was inevitable that soon Gillian would too.

*"Oh, yeah, I — I'm not trans. I'm actually seventeen —"*
*"You're __what__?? Oh my god. Get away from me!"*
The most amazing, wonderful thing that had ever happened in

his life, and probably ever would, had revealed itself to be a sick, convoluted prank that he had masochistically constructed to humiliate himself. *"What the fuck is wrong with you?"* Everyone at EBP exploded in laughter. Brad was coming to New York in two weeks. *God.* He needed to fucking fix this before Brad got here. Get rid of Gillian. Pretend it never happened. Just let Brad see his lame, boring life at the apartment and say, *"Yeah, my life sucks, so what?"* He needed to go home. He needed to leave this Duane Reade, get on the subway, go to the airport, get on a plane, and go the fuck home. Real home. Piedmont home. And then quietly kill himself.

But as soon as Adam thought this, as soon as he acknowledged that committing suicide was indeed a real-life possibility he had at his disposal, he felt better. Euphoric almost, with a recharged desire to live. He slammed the magazine shut and felt a shock of that wild, unhinged video-game feeling he'd had the first night in New York. *"Prepare to meet your greatest challenge ever"* ran through his mind like a booming TV Xbox commercial. He loved Gillian. *I LOVE GILLIAN!* he screamed to himself. And he whipped around and marched out of the Duane Reade. *He was going in.*

...

Adam rang Gillian's bell.

"Just a second!" came through the intercom. Then a buzzing noise and he pushed the front door open.

Gillian's face was flushed. She was wearing a really low-cut V-neck T-shirt, and a silver necklace of a little bird hung across her exposed skin. Her lips were wet with fresh lipstick. God, she looked sexy.

"Sorry I'm rushed," she said. "I got home from work kind of late, and I sort of had to hurry." She led him into her room, which was bright and colorful; there was music playing. Adam felt so nervous, all he could hear was the song.

*"Jolene! Jolene! Jolene, Joe-leeeeeeeene."*

Gillian fussed around with something on the top of her dresser. "Just a doodad. I like doodads . . ." She handed Adam a tiny porcelain elephant with a proud raised trunk, which he examined with intense interest.

"Cool."

Gillian fumbled with the music, louder, then softer.

"OK, so tonight you're going to meet Claire and Lauren — you already met Claire at the party — they're my roommates, and then also Jackie and Nadia — they're a couple too. This girl Kate might come, I hope she doesn't, but she might. I don't like her."

That Gillian was acting so nervous made Adam feel calm. She was nervous because she liked him.

"Do you want a beer?" she said.

"Sure."

Gillian left and Adam looked around the room. Box set of *My So-Called Life.* Framed postcard of a yellow-on-blue painting that said: OOF. Soccer trophies. Everything seemed to buzz with color. He felt as if he was in a Disney movie and wouldn't be surprised if all the objects suddenly jumped to life and started singing and dancing. The I ♥ NY mug by the bed singing, *"Jolene! Jolene!"* to the bashful lamp, swinging her lampshade tassels.

Gillian came back with the beers. Amstel Light. Adam took a long swig, and as he swallowed, he could feel the trans lie — which had previously coated all his internal organs, lined the underside of his skin — begin to wash away. Just disappear. For the first time, he was certain there was a solution to his problem. A specific failsafe way to make this work. He wasn't sure what the solution was, but he was positive it was there. So positive the truth of it felt like a tangible thing he could hold. Gillian leaned in and kissed him. They tumbled onto the bed.

"We probably shouldn't . . ." she said. She grinned at Adam and played with the collar of his shirt. "We have to leave in, like, ten minutes, and I'm not going to want to stop if we start."

The way she said this made Adam's dick throb. He rolled over onto his stomach.

Gillian brushed her red hair behind her ears. "So . . . what did you do today?"

"Looked for Jewish stuff," said Adam.

Gillian broke out laughing. "What?"

Adam beamed. When he made her laugh, it felt as if he were the only person that could do that. "Well, I told you about my roommate June, right?"

They laid their heads against Gillian's pillows, and Adam told her all about June and the Jews and the cesspool bathtub and the cut-out Stars of David and June's horror-movie silhouette with the menorah in the door frame and the disappointing plumber. He did June's shrill, anxious voice and Casey's bored-unless-talking-about-Hazel voice, and Gillian laughed and played with Adam's shirt and gave him the amused look, and Adam felt as if he were transforming, right in front of her, in front of all the watching objects in the room, into the perfect version of himself.

"I just like you so much," said Gillian.

*I love you,* thought Adam.

"I like you too," he said.

"I love your hair . . ." Gillian pulled on Adam's bangs. "And your eyes . . . and your nose . . . I'm really attracted to you."

They leaned in and started kissing again.

"I have something to admit . . ." said Gillian, breaking away for a moment. She put her hand over Adam's shirt, on his chest. Adam clenched his perfect pecs. He was perfect.

"Yeah?" he asked.

"I kind of have this fetish . . ."

Adam put his hands under Gillian's shirt. Nothing was so soft. Nothing was so smooth.

"A fetish?" he said.

"Yeah . . ." said Gillian. She paused. "A Jew fetish."

Adam laughed and they kissed again.

"You are Jewish, right?" said Gillian.

"Well, actually I'm . . . yeah. I'm Jewish," said Adam.

"I've always been obsessed with Jews," said Gillian. "When I was nine, for Christmas, I asked my mom for Hanukkah nuts."

"Hanukkah nuts? I don't think there's such a thing as Hanukkah nuts."

"I don't think there is either. I think maybe my mom just knew I wished we celebrated Hanukkah so she got me regular nuts and told me they were Hanukkah nuts. And then I brought this tin to school asking everyone if they wanted some of my Hanukkah nuts."

Now they were both laughing and kissing, and needing to stop kissing to laugh.

"Too bad you weren't friends with June," said Adam. "I'm sure she would have been happy to cut you out some Stars of David."

"I'm scared of June," said Gillian.

"Me too," said Adam.

And Gillian laughed and rolled on top of him, and they almost fell off the bed.

Someone knocked on the door.

"Be there in a minute!" said Gillian. She stood up, her face bright red. "Is my face red?" she asked Adam.

Adam nodded. Her face always got red. He loved it.

"Great, they're totally going to make fun of me . . ." Then she smiled and leaned down and pressed her lips to Adam's. "I don't care."

. . .

Adam, Gillian, Claire, and Lauren sat on the C train heading into the city. The train was old and rickety and kept jerking at random moments. Adam liked the newer trains that ran smooth and had electronic boards informing you where you were and where you were going. With these old trains and the garbled announcer's voice, it was impossible not to get lost. Adam didn't have to worry about that with Gillian's group, though. He was just following.

"Kate's not coming, is she?" said Gillian.

"Of course she's coming," said Claire.

"Do you think Nadia ever cheats on Jackie with her?" said Lauren. "I mean, she definitely hangs out with her more than her."

Adam was having trouble keeping track of who was who. Everyone was "her." He could barely even keep Claire and Lauren straight. They looked identical. They both had black plastic glasses and bleached-blond hair and were wearing tight baseball tees. One blue, one green. He wondered if when they couldn't be together it was useful to masturbate in front of a mirror.

"Kate's still in love with Nadia, and Nadia loves the attention," said Claire. "Can you imagine Nadia giving up hanging out with someone who worships her? Yeah, right."

Adam had always wondered about the whole gay masturbation thing. If you have the body parts you're fantasizing about, couldn't you just touch your own and pretend they were someone else's? Like when he sat on his hand to make it numb before jerking off. Being attracted to vaginas and having the option to touch one *whenever you wanted*. He felt wildly jealous. Something about it just must not work.

"Nadia and Kate are best friends," said Gillian to Adam, trying to include him in the conversation. "They call each other 'nonsexual life partners' and even have matching rings."

"That's weird," said Adam.

"Nadia really wants to go to Bound after," said Lauren.

"Should we?" said Claire. "Do you want to?"

"Oh god . . ." said Gillian. "Really?"

"You've never been! You have to go!" said Claire. "Come on, we should go. It's only fun if we all go. We have to all go."

Gillian gave Adam a nervous look. "Would you totally hate it if we stopped by this play party?"

Adam didn't know what a play party was.

"Yeah, sounds great!" he said.

"It's not going to be, like ... a problem, is it?" Gillian asked Claire.

"Huh? What would the problem be?" said Claire.

"Like, 'Women Only,'" said Lauren. She gave Claire a look.

"Oh!" said Claire, and she blushed and gave Adam this really big awkward smile.

"I'm sure it's fine," said Lauren. She flicked Claire in the shoulder with her index finger, and Claire put her head in her hands to cover her face.

"Bound is totally cool with trans folks," Lauren continued, looking at Adam.

"Cool," said Gillian.

"Cool," said Adam.

"They just don't want, like, nasty bio straight men getting off on lesbians, you know?" said Lauren.

"Ugh. So repulsive," said Gillian.

Everyone sat in silence for a moment.

"When did you ... How old were you ... when you transitioned?" Claire asked Adam.

"Seventeen," said Adam.

"Cool," said Claire.

Gillian took Adam's hand and squeezed it.

"Wow, that's really young," said Lauren. "Your parents must be really cool."

And then, Adam had no idea where this came from, but he found himself saying: "I'm kind of fucked up over gender stuff. I don't really like to talk about it."

And everyone nodded as if he'd just said the most serious, profound statement they'd ever heard.

"Word," said Lauren. "My friend Chaz is trans. He doesn't like to talk about it either. That shit is private. People are always asking me, 'Has he had surgery? Does he have a penis?' It's like, 'Whoa, do people go around asking *you* about *your* genitals?' Didn't think so. Chaz just dissociates from what's down there. He doesn't want anyone going down there, not even a fucking doctor . . ."

And then Adam knew. He knew the solution. He knew how this was going to work. He would never tell Gillian the truth, and she would never be able to touch him. He would be so fucked up over gender stuff, he would never want to talk about it, and he would never let her take off his clothes. A pang hit his heart. But it was the only way. This was how they could be together. Maybe it would mean wearing three pairs of briefs to keep his dick in check, but so be it. And he would still have his hands and his mouth, and he could still touch Gillian all over her body, in every way possible, and make her feel good and maybe even make her come, and he knew it was worth it — there was no question in his mind this was worth it.

. . .

"But the truth is I'm just a big nerd."

They were seated at a loud Mexican restaurant, drinking salt-rimmed margaritas and eating greasy chips and salsa. The girl named Nadia had been talking pretty much nonstop since they got there, mainly about what a nerd she was. Nadia was gorgeous — long black hair, huge blue eyes with dark eye shadow, delicate features, and from what Adam could tell, under her tight, lacy black dress, a perfect body. There was no way this girl ever was or ever could be a nerd. Claire and Lauren, yes. Nadia, no.

"It's really funny, like, all my clients, my regulars, they have this huge fantasy of me over the phone, and they have no idea what a giant nerd I really am. It's kind of hilarious. They have no idea I'm doing it for my writing."

"Is our food ever gonna get here?" said the butch girl named Kate.

"What do you do, Adam?" asked Jackie. Jackie was butch, too, and black.

*You're black,* thought Adam.

"I'm, uh, applying to colleges," he said.

Gillian smiled at him.

"I live in Piedmont . . . Northern California. I'm staying with my sister for the summer. She's at Columbia."

The waitress came by and dropped off their food along with a second round of margaritas.

"About fucking time," said Kate.

Everyone started comparing dishes and giving one another little samples of each.

"The truth is I actually kind of suck at it," said Nadia.

"That one time I watched you do it, you were horrible," said Kate. Adam had noticed that Kate was always either complaining about something or insulting Nadia. He thought about June, always complimenting Casey. When you like someone, you either compliment them all the time or insult them all the time.

"They only hired me because I'm white," said Nadia. "Because I have a white voice."

"What the fuck?" said Lauren.

"Seriously," said Nadia. "It's really fucked up. When I went for the audition, it was like me and seven black girls, and the first thing they told us was that when the client asks what you look like, you have to say you're white. It's, like, a rule."

"God, no wonder I have race paranoia," said Jackie.

"What's race paranoia?" said Adam. He felt comfortable addressing Jackie because she had talked to him. *"What do you do, Adam?"* Kate and Nadia he was scared of.

"It's when you think everything has to do with the oppression of black people," said Jackie.

"I think everything has to do with the oppression of gay people," said Gillian.

"My mom thinks everything has to do with the oppression of women," said Claire. "She's, like, still stuck on *The Feminine Mystique*."

Everyone laughed.

Adam tried to think of something to chime in with. He wanted to show Gillian he could get along with her friends.

"Another rule is no masturbating," said Nadia.

"What? Ew!" said Claire.

"Well, it's not crazy, actually," continued Nadia. "I mean, you're spinning these erotic tales, sometimes you can get really caught up in your own story. I've found myself, like, venturing down there without even noticing."

"How much longer do you feel like you need to do this?" said Jackie.

"The worst rule, though," said Nadia, "is that you're not allowed to ever hang up on the guy. No matter how disturbing the call might get — well, unless they bring up children, then you have to report them or something. Rape's cool though. In general, only they can hang up on you."

"The time I watched you, you got hung up on like eight times in a row," said Kate, laughing.

"Everyone gets hung up on," said Nadia. "Guys will, like, get themselves right on the verge, call up, hear a girl say 'hi,' then come and hang up."

Adam had done that, once. Something told him this wasn't the thing to chime in with.

"You know who I heard is doing *real* sex work," said Claire. "*Heather.*"

"No . . ." said Gillian. "Oh my god."

"I thought I heard Heather was straight now and, like, pregnant," said Lauren.

"What?!" said Gillian.

"Wait, no, I'm thinking of that girl she worked with, Finley."

"Finley was always straight," said Gillian. "Nobody believed she was gay for a second. God, Finley was lame."

"As I was saying," said Claire, "apparently Heather's, like, a junkie and has sex with femme girls in front of guys for money. I'm not sure if she does stuff to them or not. Her name on Craigslist is 'Sage.'"

"How do you know this?" asked Nadia.

"That's so . . . sad," said Gillian.

"*Not* surprised," said Kate.

"Wait, *who* is Heather?" asked Jackie.

"You never knew about *Heather?*" said Lauren.

"It was freshman year," said Claire, "before you came."

"Do we really need to go into Heather?" said Gillian. Her face was getting red.

"Tell the Heather story! Tell the Heather story!" said Claire.

"Adam, Gillian hasn't told you the Heather story?" asked Lauren.

Adam looked at Gillian and raised his eyebrow.

Gillian covered her face with her hands. "*Gahhh!* OK! I'll tell it! Jesus." Gillian took her hands away. She looked embarrassed but also kind of thrilled. She took a swig of her margarita. "OK, so I'm a freshman at Smith, and there's this girl named Heather who works at this coffee shop near campus, and I'm, like, obsessed with her. I mean, I just thought she was like the hottest thing on earth. She had this choppy black hair and a lip pierce, which I thought was incredibly cool."

"And, like, the worst skin ever," said Kate.

"Whatever, I thought she was really hot. I mean, I guess she's, like, a prostitute now, but —"

"Sex worker," said Nadia.

"She kind of looked like Tegan from Tegan and Sara, so that was probably a big part of it."

"That was all of it," said Claire.

"Wouldn't that mean she also looked like Sara?" said Jackie.

"No, they look different. Sara's hotter," said Kate.

"Tegan's hotter," said Gillian.

"Sara," said Lauren.

"Tegan," said Claire.

The waitress came back up to the table. She paused by Adam. "What are you doing here?" she said.

*Did she just ask . . . ?*

"We're doing great, thanks!" said Gillian.

"Another margarita," said Kate.

"Me too," said Jackie.

Adam wanted another one, too, but was worried he was getting too drunk. The waitress walked away.

"Ah, me too," he called after her.

"Anyway!" continued Gillian. "So, I'm pretty much living at the coffee shop — like, I do all my homework there and just kind of pathetically eavesdrop on any conversation Heather is having. And one day, at the beginning of winter break, she's, like, telling this guy how she just broke up with her girlfriend and needs to move out of their place immediately but doesn't have anywhere to go."

Gillian was addressing the whole table, but her eyes shifted to Adam every few seconds.

"And my heart starts racing, and before I know it, I go over and I'm like, 'Hey, I uh, I have a place if you need one.'"

Everyone at the table laughed really loudly. Adam wasn't sure what was funny yet but laughed along with them.

"'I have half a dorm room!'" said Claire.

"Let me tell it!" said Gillian. "Yes, I had half a dorm room. My roommate was away for two weeks for Christmas break, but I sort of led Heather to believe she was gone for good and that it wasn't exactly a dorm room, but . . . 'off-campus housing.'"

"Are you insane?" said Jackie.

"Yes, I'm completely crazy," said Gillian. "So the next thing I know, Heather, this girl I'm beyond obsessed with, is moving *all* her stuff, like including furniture, into my dorm room on top of my roommate's stuff. And she's, like, sleeping in the bed across from me. Can you imagine? You have this crush on someone, and then all of a sudden they *live* in the same *room* as you."

"It's like Anne Frank," said Lauren.

"So, a week goes by, I still haven't worked up the guts to tell her I, like, like her, or whatever, when all of a sudden one day we're hanging out in the room, and my roommate leaves this message on the voice mail, being all, 'Hi, Gillian! It's Stacy! So I think I'm coming home early, see you tonight!' And me and Heather just kind of stare at each other for this totally loaded moment, and I'm like, 'You can share my bed.'"

The table erupted. This time Adam was laughing too.

"So she, like, spends one night in my bed. I whisper 'I like you' when we're falling asleep, but she doesn't respond, and I'm not even sure if she heard me —"

"She heard you," said Kate.

"And she moves out the next day and gets back with her girl-friend."

"Oh, man . . ." said Claire.

The laughter trickled out.

Gillian looked at Adam with her anxious eyes. He smiled big at her to let her know he liked the story. He did. She was crazy and stupid, just like him.

"And now she's eating pussy in front of old men for smack money," said Kate.

"I wonder how much she makes," said Nadia.

"Baby," said Jackie.

"I'm not gonna do it. I'm just curious. And besides, if I *did* do it, you would support me, right? I mean, it would be for my writing."

"Excuse me," Jackie called out to the waitress. "A round of Patrón shots?"

"So who's in for Bound?" said Claire.

"I thought we were going to Throb," said Kate.

"They changed their name — legal issues," said Nadia.

"Just watch me run into my cardiology professor," said Jackie.

"So what if you do? You're both *there,*" said Kate.

The waitress dropped off a platter of shots.

"Tequila was Heather's favorite drink," said Gillian, staring into her shot glass. "God, I really do hope she's OK . . ."

"To Heather!" said Claire, raising her shot.

"To Heather!"

"To Heather!"

"To Sage!" said Adam.

Everyone laughed really hard, and Adam couldn't help laughing too, even though it's corny to laugh at your own joke. He felt *good*.

They all downed their shots.

"I think I wanna actually play tonight," said Nadia, leaning in toward Jackie and gazing at her intensely. She was slurring her words. "I mean, with you and another butch. Double team."

Adam was feeling really drunk too. He looked at his sloppy plate of mashed-up enchiladas and mangled chile relleno.

"Let's talk about it on the way there," said Jackie. Jackie had had as much to drink as the rest of them but didn't seem drunk at all. Adam looked at Gillian.

"I'm, like, not looking to actually do anything," she said. "Unless you wanted . . ." He could tell she was really drunk, too.

"I bet you as soon as we walk in, Sling Girl will already be in position," said Claire.

"Every time we've gone, she's there, like, claiming the sling, spread-eagle, waiting for the first person to come up and stick something in her vagina," said Lauren.

"It must get cold, all aired out in the breeze like that, waiting for someone," said Claire.

Adam could feel himself getting hard. They were going to a sex party. *A sex party.* He felt simultaneously excited beyond belief and like turning to the side and retching onto the floor. There would be no way to keep his dick down at a place like that. He needed to go to the bathroom now and jerk off to try to wear himself out. He needed to do it twice.

"I'll be right back," he said to Gillian.

The men's room was locked so Adam leaned up against the wall, waiting. He'd only been there a moment when Kate flopped up against him. She was wasted.

"'Sup, dude," she said. Her breath was hot and sticky and smelled like tequila.

"Hey," he said.

"You like that? Me calling you 'dude'? I know you guys are really into that."

Adam was having trouble making out what Kate was saying. Her extreme drunkenness was making him feel even drunker too.

"But you know what?" Kate continued. "I don't buy it. Sorry. I just don't."

"OK," said Adam. He wished the person would get out of the bathroom already.

"Trans girls, yeah. That shit is real. But you guys — fuck that. You think I don't feel like a dude sometimes? What fucking dyke doesn't. Like I'm not sick of wearing sports bras and getting my fucking period? Are you kidding? But you guys are all, 'No, man, it's not about that, I'm just really a guy, I have a *boy* brain.' Whatever the fuck that means. You're a fucking trend, and everyone kisses your hairy asses for it and comes in their pants at the idea of 'giving you your shot.' But you're a girl. Sorry. That's just how I see you. Who the fuck likes being a woman? It's shit. And yeah, I'm jealous. You think I don't wanna fuck a girl with a giant clit? Get up in there. Actually be inside her? Fuck yes, I do. But does that make me a guy? I bet Gillian gets all into giving you head, treating your clit like some kind of cock, right? Bullshit."

The men's door opened and a little kid walked out, still buttoning his pants.

"Well, enjoy," said Kate, motioning toward the men's room as she walked into the women's. "The one good thing we women still have is a cleaner bathroom."

Adam walked into the men's room and locked the door. The smell of shit was overpowering, and there was piss all over the seat and floor. He tripped a little, too drunk to stand up straight, then unzipped his pants and took out his penis.

. . .

The gang walked down the street supposedly in the direction of Bound.

"How are we supposed to know what door it is if it's unmarked?" said Gillian.

"I'll remember," said Claire. "It's definitely on Houston. I'm just not sure of the cross streets; I'll remember it when I see it . . . I think."

The streets were getting emptier and darker the farther they walked. Adam was nervous, but Jackie and Kate basically looked like boys from far away, which made him feel safer. If they got attacked, it would be the three of them protecting everyone else. For now, he wanted to stay as far away from Kate as possible, though.

"It's just not really my thing," Jackie said to Nadia. They'd been having the same conversation since everyone left the restaurant. "I mean, I'm happy to go along and watch, but . . ."

"Well, it wasn't exactly *my* thing to spend all last weekend playing board games with your parents upstate," said Nadia.

They turned the corner and walking ahead of them was a man wearing a wig, miniskirt, fishnet stockings, and platform shoes. *Drag queen,* thought Adam.

"Or we could just follow her," said Lauren.

The drag queen entered a steel door in the middle of a brick building. The gang followed.

Inside was a short line of people and a woman taking money and stamping hands at a folding table. Behind the table, people entered through a drab black curtain. Adam got the sensation that he was back at EBP, buying his ticket for the annual school play.

"It's fifteen bucks," said Claire, looking at the group.

Adam took a twenty and ten from his wallet and tried to position himself in front of Gillian in the line.

"No," she said. "You always pay for everything."

"You bought my slice of pizza," he said, reminding her.

Gillian rolled her eyes and smiled. Adam noticed Kate rolling her eyes, too. He also noticed a large sign that read: WOMEN ONLY. The woman at the folding table had that snotty look that people in charge of letting other people in somewhere usually have.

Adam held out his money and was horrified to see his hand was trembling.

*Why had he thought he could get away with this?* The confident plan he had formed on the C train suddenly seemed wild, ludicrous.

The woman looked Adam up and down and sighed loudly.

"*Excuse me, women only,*" she was about to say. But before Adam could finish the thought, the woman had accepted his money and was stamping Gillian's and his hands.

The gang walked through the curtains.

"Oooh! Onion dip," said Claire. "I can't believe I'm still hungry, but I am."

"I'm not sure what I imagined when I thought 'sex party,'" Gillian whispered to Adam, "but it definitely involved some degree of people having, you know, 'sex.'"

Adam looked around the space. This was not the case with Bound. First of all, there was barely anyone there. And those who were here were a handful of unattractive older women in jeans, corsets, and running shoes, sitting on the couches by the entrance, hunkered over the onion dip and cubed salami. Only the drag queen in platforms wandered through the empty concrete main area, trailing her fingers along what looked like a children's backyard play castle and examining a wooden cross propped against the wall.

"Um, yeah, it's not exactly what I imagined either," said Adam.

"It will pick up," said Claire. "I bet Sling Girl's in the back. Let's go look."

Sure enough, as the gang moved — *like a school of fish,* thought Adam — toward the back of the room, they came upon an extremely fat woman in a pink princess dress splayed out in a sling. The dress was pushed up so that her vagina was completely exposed. Adam had never seen a real vagina, an actual real vagina in real life and not on his computer screen, before. And here he was, where it was totally appropriate to simply stand and stare at it. Instead of excitement, though, he felt a wash of sadness. He had fantasized that Gillian's would be the first he ever saw. A fear struck him that for the rest of his life, whenever he masturbated, this alien, sling-swinging, heavy-breathing vagina would be the only thing his brain could see.

"I can't believe I bothered to bring my dick," said Kate. She adjusted the backpack on her shoulders. "There isn't going to be anyone worth fucking here."

Kate said this loud enough for the fat Sling Girl to hear and Adam winced.

Another fat woman, wearing an office shirt and tie, who Adam recognized from the line at the entrance, sauntered up toward Sling Girl.

"Where's the pussy?" Office Woman said. And she started fluffing the girl's princess dress up and down.

Sling Girl made a cooing noise.

"Where's the pussy? Where's the pussy? Where's the pussy?" Office Woman continued in rapid fire between dress fluffs. She then reached into her bag and pulled out a Swiss Army knife. She popped the blade open and to Adam's horror began stroking the woman's vagina with it.

"There's the pussy . . . There's the pussy," she said.

Office Woman dropped the knife back in her bag, rolled up her sleeves, and pulled out a latex glove, which she snapped on her hand. She took out a bottle of some substance and poured it all over the gloved hand.

"Is the pussy ready?" Office Woman asked.

"Oh, the pussy's ready! The pussy is so ready," Sling Girl said.

The next thing Adam knew Office Woman had inserted her entire arm — up to the elbow — into the woman's vagina and was thrusting it in and out. He could see droplets of liquid spraying in the air as she thrusted.

"Oh yeah! You're fucking my hand!" Office Woman yelled. "Keep fucking it! Keep fucking it!"

"This is boring," said Nadia. She looked around. "Let's go back to the front and see if anyone hot has shown up."

The school of fish made its way back to the front, where a significant cluster of people was milling around.

"... It means fisting top. And black on the left is BDSM top. Those are just what's most important to me."

Adam couldn't see who was talking, but he recognized the voice.

"Well, I'm looking for a sub, so, if you wanna try out tonight."

The crowd shifted and Adam saw that it was Hazel. Two people behind her, he could see the corner of Casey's hair and shoulder.

*Fuck.*

Adam whipped around. "Hey, is there a bathroom here?" he said to Gillian.

*Please be in the back, please be in the back.*

"There's one in the back," said Claire.

Adam began fast strides toward the back of the room without answering.

He could *not* have Casey see him. There would be no way to explain.

CASEY: *"What are you doing here? You're a boy!"*
GILLIAN: *"Bound is totally cool with trans folks!"*
CASEY: *"Trans folks???"*

Adam felt on the verge of a heart attack. On the verge of an Ebola-like expulsion of all the liquids in his body from every opening.

*What could he do? What could he do? What could he do?*

He saw the bathrooms. A WOMEN sign on one door and on the door next to it a piece of paper with a handwritten *Women* sign taped over the MEN sign underneath.

*Give up. Give up. Give up,* a low voice chanted inside him.

And then he saw it. A little treasure chest on the floor between the two bathrooms. The sign above it read: FETISH WEAR AVAILABLE FOR USE IN THE BUILDING. PLEASE USE PROPER HYGIENE. RETURN HERE.

Adam fell to his knees and rummaged through the chest. He found a full head leather mask with only two eyeholes and a creepy *Silence of the Lambs* metal grid for the mouth. He pulled it on.

Ethan's shirt. Casey might recognize Ethan's shirt. He unbuttoned it as fast as he could and shoved it at the bottom of the fetish wear pile, praying no one would steal it. OK, could he go back like this? It was a sex party — it was fine to go shirtless, right? No! The trans chest. Gillian would be able to tell he didn't have a trans chest. Adam continued his frenzied rummaging until he found a leather vest that snapped up, covering the area around the nipples. He slid it on. Pulled off his shoes and socks as well, just to be safe, and hid them at the bottom of the chest. He stood up. Barefoot, leather vest, head encased in the menacing leather mask. It was kind of crazy . . . but he felt like a superhero.

Adam strode confidently back toward the front. He passed the cross propped against the wall and saw that Hazel, with a deliberate, focused look on her face, was whipping a naked girl spread out across it. The girl was hot, too. Creamy skin and the hint of a stubbly pink slit underneath her ass between her legs. Adam had to force himself to keep moving and not stare. He thought back to Boy Casey at The Hole making out on that disgusting couch with some random girl, Casey crying on her bed at home. Why did Casey always date these assholes? He tried to see if he could spot her but couldn't. He did see Gillian though, turning her head around, looking for him.

"Hi," he said.

Gillian jumped.

"It's me, Adam." His breath inside the mask made the already-sticky condensation worse.

Gillian looked him over. Then started laughing. "Why did you . . . ?"

"I just found this stuff and thought it would be funny. Hope I don't catch AIDS."

Gillian didn't laugh.

"I mean, I'm sure it's fine, I . . ."

Her face broke back into a smile. "You are so weird," she said.

A middle-aged woman in a bodice and combat boots began addressing the crowd.

"The Blowjob Contest will begin in fifteen minutes. Repeat: The Blowjob Contest is beginning in fifteen minutes."

"Don't know if you caught that," Gillian said to Adam, "but the Blowjob Contest is beginning in fifteen minutes."

"I thought it was ten, so now I'm just really confused," said Adam. He wasn't sure his joke worked behind the mask, but Gillian started laughing.

Gillian raised her finger. "I came expecting a Blowjob Contest, and god damn it I'm not leaving until . . ." She trailed off as they both kept laughing, Adam's mask now drenched inside.

Then he saw Casey. She was standing against the wall, alone, staring over at Hazel and the naked girl on the cross. Hazel was now fucking the girl with her hand from behind. The girl was moaning ridiculously loud, obviously fake. *God, shut up,* thought Adam. He was still nervous that even in his costume Casey might recognize him — sibling vibe was just like that — and it also occurred to him she could possibly recognize Gillian; Casey had seen her briefly at the party after the Gay Marriage Rally. He was about to take Gillian's hand and pull her somewhere else when Casey peeled herself off the wall and staggered directly toward Adam and Gillian, staring straight at Adam. Adam froze. Something in his body told him not to move. And then Casey stumbled away from them and over toward Hazel and Naked Girl. She was unbelievably drunk. Her path zigzagged in and out like a parody of a failed sobriety test. Adam had never seen her so drunk. He wanted to stop Casey from going over there, sock Hazel in the gut, put his arm around Casey, and take her home. His sister needed him.

"Do you know that girl?" said Gillian. She could tell he was staring. "She is *trashed*."

"No. Don't know her," said Adam, and he turned away from Casey, as if bored. He briefly imagined slicing his own head off with a machete. No wonder the world is full of crime. It really wasn't so difficult to become a bad person.

"Is that *Adam?*" said Nadia, loud.

"Shhh!" said Adam. "My name is Rölf." *Wherever the fuck that came from.*

The gang was all circled together again.

"You guys have to vote for me and Jackie in the Blowjob Contest," said Nadia.

Jackie squirmed. "I think the voting is just, like, how loud you clap?" she said.

"Oh, and, Kate, can we borrow your dick?" Nadia continued.

"What? No!" said Kate.

"I told you," said Jackie.

"Why not? It's not like it hasn't been inside me before," said Nadia.

"I've actually got mine, too. I'm packing it," said Claire. "You wouldn't mind, right?" she asked Lauren.

Lauren shrugged.

"Your dick is three inches long and lavender, so, no thank you," said Nadia. "I really wanna win this thing. Come on, Kate. I love your dick."

"I know you do," said Kate.

Things got loaded for a moment and no one spoke. Gillian rolled her eyes at Adam.

"What about you, Adam, I mean, Rölf. You got anything we can borrow?" It was the first time Nadia had spoken to Adam directly, and it felt as if she were poking with her dirty fingers at his internal organs. He didn't like her. It made him feel powerful, not liking this beautiful girl.

"No," he said.

He wanted to look over and see what was happening with Casey and Hazel, but didn't.

"Let's just forget it," said Jackie.

"Attention!" It was the bodice/combat boots woman again. "There *are* dildos available for those who need them for the Blowjob Contest. Please see me if you will be needing to borrow a dildo for the Blowjob Contest."

"Go over there!" Nadia said to Jackie.

"What? Just go over to her?"

"Yes! Now!"

Jackie slouched in the direction of the woman. Adam looked back over toward the cross, but Hazel, Naked Girl, and Casey were gone.

"Check it out," said Kate. She nodded toward a small crowd that had gathered around the drag queen who was on her hands and knees, her miniskirt pulled over her back, her fishnets around her ankles. She was wearing a black thong, and a woman with a buzz cut who looked about four feet tall was slapping the drag queen's ass with a black paddle.

Adam knew the drag queen was a man. There was no way he couldn't be. But when he looked at the thong area, it was as if there were nothing there. How was that possible?

"Do you think he's had, like . . . genital surgery?" he said to Gillian.

"Either that or bitch has one fierce tuck," said Nadia.

"Like when they push the penis way up inside the crack?" Gillian asked.

Kate grinned.

Adam really wished he could take his leather mask off. He felt like he couldn't breathe.

The Blowjob Contest was about to begin. Five teams lined up against the concrete wall. The boyish girls all had dildos hanging out from their pants or underwear. Jackie and Nadia took their place next to Hazel and Naked Girl. Adam still couldn't see Casey anywhere. He wondered if she had left. Maybe she was on the subway right now. He didn't like her alone on the subway at night in that short skirt and tight tank top. *She would be fine. She can take care of herself.* He hoped Hazel got mugged and murdered on the way home.

The bodice/combat boots woman blew a whistle from around her neck. Apparently she was the referee. The feminine girls dropped to their knees and went to work while the boyish girls leaned their heads back against the wall and performed expressions of intense pleasure.

Watching Jackie was painful. She was obviously miserable but trying to put on a good show for Nadia. Jackie bobbed her head up and down, saying, "Oh, yeah, uh-huh, yeah." The way she bobbed, her glasses kept slipping off, and she had to keep pushing them back up with her hand while she moaned.

The bodice woman blew her whistle again. The contest was over. How on earth were you supposed to judge a thing like this? It was all an act, and the dicks weren't even *real*. Adam felt like grabbing the whistle, blowing it, and addressing the crowd, *"Excuse me, yes, um, you're all COMPLETELY CRAZY."*

But there he was, barefoot, in his leather vest and fetish mask, pretending to be a transsexual. So be it.

The crowd clapped for each of the teams, and the bodice woman yelled, "The winner is ... Team Nadia and Jackie!" She handed them a cheap little kid's karate trophy with a bachelorette-party penis pop glued on. Nadia looked euphoric. Hazel looked pissed. *Good.*

The mask was killing Adam. He thought maybe he could take it off now that Casey was gone but didn't want to risk it. He squeezed Gillian's hand and told her he was going to the bathroom; he could at least take it off for a moment in there.

Adam stepped into the bathroom, which only had one stall and a small outside sink area. Someone was using the toilet. A large fart erupted from the stall and Adam cringed. Something about women farting was just so much grosser than men farting. He gagged a little behind his mask and was about to leave when he heard the person's voice. She was on the phone and it was Casey.

"Yeah, I just really wanna see you. I don't know, I miss you..."

He could tell she was trying not to sound as drunk as she was. Adam knew he should leave immediately. If she opened the door, it would be all over. But he had to find out what she said next.

"Yeah, come here.... It doesn't matter, just come now. OK.... I can't wait to see you. Bye!"

Adam was out the door. *Boy Casey*. She was bringing in Boy Casey.

Adam wondered if he could suggest to Gillian that the two of them leave. The thought of what would happen next — *Would they go back to her place? Would they make out? Would they...?* — made his chest clench up again.

"Hey." A girl was standing in front of him. She was pretty and dressed normal in jean shorts and a T-shirt, except for a spiked dog collar hanging loosely around her neck. Adam recognized it from the treasure chest.

"I'm just... I saw you when you first walked in," the girl continued, "and I thought you were really, really cute, and you look, like... really sexy in that mask, and I was wondering if... you wanted to play?"

Adam thought back to being a kid and how you would ask someone, "Do you want to play?" It had been the most normal question in the world, and then at some point, he couldn't remember when, it was something you would never dare say. It became, "Do you want to hang out?" But it wasn't just a change of words. It was an actual change of activity. Adam used to get so excited he would shake just thinking about going to Brad's house and play-ing Knights and Swords — this elaborate imaginary game they'd invented that used Brad's entire house and backyard as a playing field. But then at some point it became "hang out." And that's what they would do. Hang out and watch TV. Hang out and play video games. Their bodies hanging over various pieces of furniture.

Adam saw Gillian watching him and the girl. He couldn't read Gillian's expression, though. Which is why he loved her. Because sometimes, usually, he had no idea what she was thinking.

"Thanks for asking," he said to the girl (*god, that sounded ob-noxious — what was he supposed to say?*), "but I'm here with my girlfriend."

Gillian was definitely not his girlfriend, but Adam was feeling bold and cocky. This girl thought he was cute, thought he was sexy, and Gillian was watching, waiting for him. He was an object of desire.

"OK, cool," said the girl. "I mean if she wanted to join in . . . I'm sure she's really hot to be with you . . ."

Adam glanced at Gillian. He imagined kissing the two of them, two pairs of tits mashed against each other, Gillian's tongue in Dog Collar's mouth. His dick, which had been utterly unmoved by the Blowjob Contest, began pressing up against his jeans. He couldn't risk it. What if this girl just suddenly shoved her hand down his pants — *god, that would feel amazing* — but it was too risky. He needed to stay in control. He imagined his lie as a deli-cate caterpillar crawling between his cupped hands — any quick movement could crush it.

"Maybe next time," he said. And he walked back over to Gil-lian.

"Who was that?" she asked.

"Just some girl," he said. "She wanted to play, but I told her no." God, he was starting to sound like Brad.

"What?!" said Gillian, with a huge grin. She tried to get another look at the girl and linked her arm into Adam's. "You're my Rölf."

They headed back to the group. Jackie and Nadia were planning "the scene" they were supposed to perform for everyone as part of being winners. Nadia wanted Jackie to chase her around the castle, push over the cross, and then fuck Nadia on top of it with Nadia's own high-heeled shoe.

"It could also be kind of sexy if we just slipped out now and everyone wondered where we went," said Jackie.

"Balderdash and Settlers of Catan," said Nadia, apparently reminding Jackie of something.

"I guess we have to stay for their scene," said Gillian to Adam. "Then we can go. I really wanna get you home."

Adam's heart seized.

Jackie and Nadia's scene began with an announcement from Bodice Whistleblower. Everyone crowded around to watch. Jackie, as instructed, started chasing Nadia in and out of the castle. It looked like Jackie was dissociating in order to get through it. *The things one does for a beautiful girl,* thought Adam. Jackie probably thought she could never do better than Nadia. Looks-wise, she probably couldn't.

Hazel, still pouting over having lost the Blowjob Contest, watched the scene with arms folded and a judgmental look on her face. Her expression quickly changed, however, when Nadia grabbed Hazel's arm and pulled her into the center with her and Jackie.

*"Double team!"* Nadia screamed. Hazel flew into action, picking a stray whip off the ground and cracking it in the air while fist-bumping a bewildered Jackie.

Adam looked around for Casey and spotted her against the wall in the back, slumped over, still clearly wasted, her roving eyes tracking Hazel. He hoped Boy Casey would get here already.

And then in walked June. Blubbery, bull-nose-ringed June, wearing her baggy I'LL GO DOWN ON YOUR SISTER T-shirt. She looked around, nervously fingering one of the flyers that had been on the front table that everybody else had ignored.

*What the fuck was she doing here?*

Hazel and Jackie were pretending to kidnap and gag Nadia. Casey, spotting June, brightened and walked toward her. It was June she had called on the phone. Positioning himself behind Gillian, Adam stared as Casey threw her arms around June's neck and gave her a giant open-mouthed, drunk-as-fuck kiss. From the look of surprise on June's face, he knew it was the first. Casey backed off, and June stood there, glowing, with a cartoonishly goofy smile that stretched beyond the limits of her face. June took Casey's hands and leaned in to try to kiss her again, but instead Casey dragged June in the direction of the packed circle. She pushed through the three-deep crowd, right into the center where Jackie and Hazel were taking turns whipping Nadia's ass.

"Excuse me," said Nadia, uprighting herself and looking at Casey and June, "we're in the middle of a—"

"Rip my clothes off and fuck me," Casey said to June, ignoring Nadia. And June, with all the passion and pent-up desire that Hazel and Jackie couldn't even dream of attempting to emulate, threw herself on Casey, tearing at Casey's tank top and yanking down her skirt.

The crowd exploded.

"Let me get in there," said Hazel, swaggering forward.

But Casey stood up, looked Hazel in the eyes, and spat in her face. "Fuck off," she said.

The crowd was roaring; Bodice Whistleblower was going crazy on the whistle.

Adam knew he needed to get out of there now. Not only was he not about to watch his sister get naked and fucked (*those days have passed*), but he realized he could not have Gillian get a good look at Casey in the chance she ever saw a picture of her or met her in the future. It could already be too late, but he had to act now.

"This is boring," he whispered in Gillian's ear. "Let's just sneak out."

"Really?" said Gillian. She looked reluctant.

"Yeah, I wanna get you home," he said. *Who was he?*

Adam grabbed Gillian's hand and pulled her back to the treasure chest to trade out his clothes. He threw everything out of the chest, but while he found his shoes and socks, Ethan's shirt was gone.

"Fuck. My shirt," he said.

"You can't find it?" said Gillian.

"It was Patrik Ervell for Opening Ceremony."

"We could ask up front — they could make an announcement?"

"Fuck, should I just steal this vest?" said Adam.

"Just go shirtless; you're a guy," said Gillian.

"No . . ." said Adam.

"Right," said Gillian, quickly nodding. "Let's just go. Steal it!"

Adam tore off the face mask — *oh, sweet air!* — shoved on his shoes, and ran with Gillian through the main room toward the entrance, catching a glimpse of June hand-fucking Casey sprawled out on the cross. *Not very Jewish of her,* he thought.

They burst through the black curtains, into the front room, where the woman behind the foldout table stood up, saying, "Excuse me, I think that's one of ours, there's the 'B' for Bound, painted on —"

"'B' for 'Blow me!'" shouted Adam, and he and Gillian ran through the doors and into the night, pounding down the sidewalk, hand in hand, as fast as they could, careening around the corner, Adam's lungs burning, Gillian laughing, till they were finally far enough, and they stumbled, panting, and Adam took

Gillian in his arms and kissed her in the middle of the sparkling city.

. . .

Back at Gillian's apartment, Adam's heart had begun a quiet, consistent thumping. He was entering the unknown.

"Want another beer?" said Gillian, though they were still drunk from dinner. Adam thought back to Gillian offering him a beer when he'd first come to her apartment at the beginning of the evening. It was incomprehensible that it was the same day. He remembered how alive all the objects in the room had seemed. Now, in the shadows, they had gone to sleep.

Gillian came back with the beers, and they sat on her bed, sipping them, looking at each other with nervous smiles. Gillian was so beautiful. Adam wanted to lean in and start kissing her, but in the dark, silent room, he felt shy and hesitant. His eyes wandered to the framed photos on her bedside table. He picked one up. It was a prom photo — Gillian and another girl. It didn't quite look like Gillian though. Her hair was short and brown, and she was wearing a tux. She stood behind the other girl with her arms wrapped around her in classic prom pose. An eerie déjà vu feeling came over Adam. Like he swore he'd seen this photo before.

"This is really weird . . . but I feel like —"

Gillian snorted and took a slug of beer. "No, you're not crazy. You've probably seen it."

"What? Why?"

Gillian took the photo, stared at it for a moment, then placed it back on the table. "It was, like, in every newspaper in the country four years ago. There was an AP article."

"A what?"

Gillian inched in closer to Adam. Their legs were touching now. She lightly kicked at his foot.

"I grew up in this really small town in Oklahoma. And my girlfriend and I were, like, the only gay people. We got harassed a bunch, but it wasn't a huge deal until we tried to buy tickets for the prom and the administration told us we weren't allowed to go as a couple. It was completely fucked up. My parents were always really supportive though, and they got the ACLU involved, and there was like this whole public case against the school for discrimination. I was even on TV a couple times. I'm basically famous for being gay. I still get letters from teens saying like, 'You make me feel OK for being who I am. Thank you for literally saving my life.' It's pretty intense."

Adam realized where he'd seen the photo before. It had been cut out and taped, surrounded by various female celebrities, to Casey's bedroom wall.

"That's . . . weird," said Adam, smiling at Gillian, unsure how to react.

"Well, it *is* a little weird for me now," she said, kicking at his foot again. "I mean, dating you . . ."

"It is?"

"Well, *yeah*," she said, giving him a *duh* look. "But I just, I really like you. I think you're so sexy . . ."

Adam looked down at his beer and blushed.

"And I like that you're shy," she continued, "but then when you do say something, it's like the best thing ever. Like, you're totally weird — but not in that obnoxious way that 'weird' people are, where they're always trying to show off how 'wacky' they are. Your weirdness is like a hidden jewel."

Gillian leaned in and started kissing him. Her lips made Adam's body shiver with electricity. They fell back onto the bed. Gillian started to roll on top of Adam, but he knew if she did she would feel his dick, rock-hard in his pants. He pushed her over so that he was on top, on his hands and knees, leaning his head down to kiss her. His dick hovered, pointing straight out, about two inches above her.

"The thing is," Gillian said, running her hands under the vest across his skin, "I know I could never be with a bio guy. I'm just not attracted to them. I hope that's not, like, offensive . . . Aiden told me never to tell you that."

"That's . . . OK," said Adam. All he could feel was a mind-blotting hot core of pleasure at the tip of his dick.

Gillian pulled off her T-shirt and unhooked her bra, pushing them onto the floor. The streetlights glowed through the window on her two perfect tits with hard pink nipples. Adam dropped his head and slid his tongue across them.

Gillian started breathing heavy. "I don't see why it's so bad," she said, in between breaths, "liking you just how you are . . ."

She reached down and pulled her jeans off too. Her underwear was thin, and Adam could see a mat of dark hair underneath. He put his hand over the underwear, and it was soft and wet. Gillian breathed harder, opening her legs.

Adam inched back on his knees and slipped the underwear off. He cupped his hand over her again, and this time his fingers slid inside.

"Yes . . ." Gillian said softly.

He moved his fingers in and out, and then brought his head down and pressed his tongue against the slick pink flesh, poking out between the hair. *The clit,* he thought.

"Oh god . . ." said Gillian.

It tasted like sweat and saliva, and Adam kept pushing with his fingers and sliding with his tongue, praying that he was doing it right, which it seemed like he actually might be because Gillian's breaths were getting louder and faster, and he moved quicker and harder to match her, and soon it was all a frenzied blur of tongue and wet and clit and breaths and push, and then Gillian stopped and her legs stretched out and she gasped in a way that startled Adam and she tried to pull him on top of her, but he couldn't because his dick had never been so hard and huge in his entire life and was totally visible trying to jam its way out of his buttonhole jeans. He fell onto his side next to her.

Gillian leaned up and kissed him, smearing the wetness that was all over his face onto her own.

"You're really good at that," she said.

"Thanks," said Adam. His dick felt like a magnet, trying to get at any part of Gillian's body. He rolled over onto his stomach.

"I really want to do something to you . . ." said Gillian. "Make you come . . ."

Adam said nothing.

"I mean, whatever you're cool with," she said. "I totally get it if you don't want to . . . I mean . . . but I want to . . ."

Adam stayed silent. He wondered if Gillian could hear his heart.

"What do you usually do . . . ?" she asked.

"I don't know," whispered Adam.

"Do you like to use, like, a dick?" she asked.

Adam slowly nodded.

"I mean, I have one. Unless you brought one?"

Adam shook his head.

"Would you want to use mine? I really want to feel you fuck me like that."

Adam found himself nodding again.

Gillian grinned and leaned over the side of her bed, groping around underneath. She pulled something out of a box and showed it to Adam. A large, black rubber penis and the strappy thing it must go in. Sam had tripped when she put hers on.

"You can put it on in the bathroom," said Gillian. "I'll wait."

In the piercing fluorescent light of Gillian's tiny bathroom,

Adam stepped out of his jeans and boxer briefs. His dick, aimed straight at the ceiling, was the size of his forearm and purplish in color. Pre-come was smeared all over the head.

*Think, Freedman,* he said to himself. *Figure this out.*

The drag queen at Bound had looked like he didn't have a dick at all. *"Bitch has one fierce tuck." "Push it up into the crack."* Adam tried pushing his dick down and up against his balls but it was too hard and sprung back. Part of him knew he should just beat off, just get it over with. But he didn't want to. He didn't know how yet, but he wanted to come with Gillian. At least in the same room with her, looking at her, somehow.

*Think. Think. Think.*

Adam opened the medicine cupboard over the sink. He hadn't known why he did it, but as soon as he did, he saw the box of Band-Aids. He grabbed the box, quickly unwrapped a Band-Aid, and stuck it over his dick, pressing his dick flush up against his stomach. He would need a bunch of Band-Aids to get the job done and hurriedly started unwrapping and sticking until his dick was completely strapped to his stomach in a swathe of Band-Aids, only the head poking out by his bellybutton. He pulled his briefs up high over everything and then stepped into the strappy black thing, pushing the black rubber penis through the hole in the front. He could feel the base of the rubber penis pressing up against his dick and it felt good. He tugged the straps tight. He then stepped into his jeans, pulling them up high as well, buttoned the top button, and pushed the black rubber penis out through the lower open buttonholes.

*You can do this.*

Adam walked back into Gillian's shadowy room. He could see the dark mass of her lying on the bed. He felt terrified and silly with the black penis dangling out the front of his pants, but this was what she expected. This was the way it was supposed to be, right?

Gillian looked over at him, her eyes lowering to his crotch. She smiled.

"You look really hot," she said.

Adam climbed onto the bed and over Gillian. She was completely naked, and he had never seen anything so beautiful in his life. They started kissing, and her mouth still tasted and smelled like the amazing wetness below. His dick, which he hadn't thought could get any harder, strained against the layers of Band-Aids, briefs, and jeans.

Gillian reached down and ran her hand gently over the black penis.

"Oh, hold on," she said. And she leaned over and took a condom out of the drawer on her bedside table. "I just use these when I haven't remembered to boil . . . gross, sorry."

"Cool," said Adam. He ripped open the condom and, making sure the right side was facing up, slipped it over the black penis. The way he had practiced a million times alone in his room. As if practicing would get him closer to the moment of it happening.

"Put it in my mouth," said Gillian.

Adam inched on his knees over Gillian, and she took the black penis and put it in her mouth. She moved it in and out, licking the head and shaft.

Adam felt one of the Band-Aids break loose.

"I don't even think we need lube," she said. "I'm so turned on by you."

Gillian spread her legs wide around Adam. He moved back on his hands and knees, and taking the black penis in his hand, aimed it at her open, glistening hole.

*This is it. This is it.*

The black penis slid right in, and Adam moved his hips, pushing it in and out, but not too fast, for fear something would go wrong.

"You feel so good," said Gillian, and Adam moved a little

quicker. The head of his own dick was rubbing up against his stiff jeans and stomach, and the way it rubbed felt so amazing that he pushed even faster and sweat was dripping down his body and he could feel the Band-Aids breaking off, but he didn't give a fuck, and he rammed the black penis into Gillian harder and harder, and the friction felt so fucking good. *I'm doing it,* he thought. *I'm having sex, I'm actually having sex,* and in that instant his balls clenched up and come shot from his dick all over his pants.

"Ohhhh," he groaned; it felt like the come would never stop, an endless spewing of hot streams all over his stomach and jeans. *Fuck — it might show!* And Adam quickly grabbed the mug off Gillian's bedside table, and in pretending to miss taking a drink, spilled the water over his lap, masking any come that could have seeped through.

"Oops," he said, laughing. And Gillian, sitting up, laughed too.

"Give me some of that," she said, and took the mug and drank the rest. "That was great," she said, looking him in the eyes.

Adam grinned at the print on the mug in Gillian's hand, then looked back up at her, beaming.

"I love New York!" he said.

# Chapter 11

WITHIN TWO WEEKS, Adam had become the preeminent expert on anything and everything trans. He knew more than Casey. He was pretty sure he even knew more than Boy Casey. He was almost positive that if he were playing *Jeopardy!* and all the categories were Trans, he would go home with a million dollars. Every moment of his life that wasn't spent with Gillian was devoted to researching, memorizing, and internalizing all things trans.

He knew that a "packer" is what you call a soft, realistic-looking dildo that you wear in your underwear during everyday activity to have the feeling of a penis. He knew that testosterone could be delivered to the body three different ways; injectable (of which the dosage varies between 50 mg and 300 mg per injection, depending on the ester and regimen), transdermal (available in both patch or gel/cream form), and oral (though this method didn't always have all desired effects, such as cessation of menstruation). There was also research into a subcutaneous testosterone pellet, replaced every three to four months, though no one in the "community" — trans guys on the Internet — had tried this themselves.

Adam knew that Buck Angel was a famous trans man porn star and that many people enjoyed watching his videos where he is fucked in his vagina ("cockpit," "mancave"). Adam knew that some trans men were OK with being fucked in their vaginas, liked being fucked in their vaginas, but others were not and this area was off-limits (Adam was the off-limits type). He knew that gender identity and sexual orientation are *not* the same thing and that you could be straight and trans or gay and trans; you could be like Hazel — a girl who used to be a boy but now was a masculine butch lesbian. Sometimes when people transitioned, they found their orientation shifting as well. Adam, who had always been, and still only was attracted to women, was a "heteronormative" trans man.

He knew that True Spirit used to be the big trans conference everyone would go to and was where a bunch of community members got to meet for the first time (Adam never got a chance to go) but that it was over, and newer conferences like Philadelphia Trans-Health and Gender Odyssey were gaining popularity. Southern Comfort was also still going strong.

Adam, post-op on his chest (double-incision/bilateral mastectomy) but pre-op on the bottom, was well versed in all the options for FTM genital reconstruction surgery. There was metoidioplasty (cutting of ligaments and removal of tissue that releases the testosterone-enlarged clitoris), there was scrotoplasty (inserting testicular implants into the labia majora and joining the two labia to create a scrotal sac), and there was phalloplasty (the construction of a penis using donor skin from other areas of the body) of which there were several methods: pedicled pubic flap, pedicled groin flap, free tissue flap, forearm free flap. He was familiar with the risks and costs of a hysterectomy and how it is one of the few surgeries that trans men are able to have covered by insurance. He knew that if you were going to have surgery, you should absolutely — no *if*s, *and*s, or *butt*s — quit smoking.

He knew about body dysphoria, and lo-ho and no-ho, and why you should say "cisgendered" instead of "bio," and what it means to be "stealth."

Adam knew all these facts and spent hours boring them into his brain and looking up words like *pedicled* on www.medterms .com, not because he would spew them out at Gillian in moments of spastic trans panic, but because just knowing them made him feel safe. He acquired information like artillery. All these facts, meshed together inside him, formed a bulletproof vest. If Gillian or one of her friends *did* ask him about any of them, he would be ready. If he wanted to casually drop a reference into a conversation, he *would* be able to do that.

But while knowing these facts helped Adam feel secure, and the very physical act of researching and memorizing quelled his anxiety, they were ultimately not what made him able to sustain the lie. What he quickly realized, after the night he and Gillian first had sex and he knew there was no turning back, was that in order to lie effectively, he had to believe the lie himself.

And the thing was, there *were* elements of being trans that Adam related to. Trans people often saw transition as the start of their real life, their true life, rejecting who they were before — and this was exactly how Adam felt. The person he was back at EBP was dead to him. Fuck that loser! That wasn't the real him — *this* was, with Gillian. Gillian, who said, "You're so sexy," and "Your weirdness is like a hidden jewel," and who the other night had whispered in bed, "You're my sweet boyfriend."

And the way Adam treated his body around Gillian *was* the way a trans person might. He never took off his shirt or pants, and she knew never to ask him to. During his trans research, he had learned that trans guys who had not yet or did not want to have top surgery would often bind their breasts. The best method was an official "binder" — a tight, thin undergarment originally made for men with gynecomastia (larger-than-average male breast growth), but some trans men used ACE bandages, which they would tightly wrap around their breasts and safety-pin in place.

The community warned that ACE bandages were very dangerous and could restrict breathing or lead to fluid buildup or broken
ribs, but their mention had given Adam an idea. As a solution to
the problem of his erections, every time he hung out with Gillian,
he preemptively ACE-bandaged his penis up against his stomach,
so that when it got hard, it wouldn't stick out and was barely no-
ticeable under the layers of bandage, underwear, and jeans. When
he and Gillian had sex with the strap-on, the friction of his own
penis against his stomach still made him orgasm, but the bandages
were thick enough that they absorbed most of the come. *"I know I
could never be with a bio guy. I'm just not attracted to them."* That's
what she had said.

Of course, alone in his bed, Adam fantasized obsessively about
actually sticking his real penis inside Gillian. He had completely
forsaken Internet porn for the repeated fantasy of this singular
physical act. He would conjure exactly how the inside of her vagina felt on his fingers — slick and hot and slightly bumpy, but
supple — and enclose that mental sensation around his penis as he
made himself come, ejaculating into every crevice of her insides.
He thought about Luke Trevor and his YouTube videos about
wishing he could ejaculate inside his girlfriend when they had
sex, and Adam, sometimes despising with all his heart the black
rubber penis that he and Gillian always used, commiserated along
with him.

And out of these elements of truth, Adam constructed a reality
in his brain in which he was trans. A different *kind* of trans, an
Adam-only trans, but "trans" nonetheless. And if this was true,
then it wasn't really a lie, and it wasn't a deception, and what he
and Gillian had together was pure.

And in fact his being trans rarely even came up. She knew he
didn't like to talk about it, so it was almost always avoided or
hopped over in conversation, like a wobbly-looking stone when

trying to cross a creek. They talked about everything else. They would order Indian from the place around Gillian's corner, always getting the same thing — lamb tikka masala and vegetarian samosas — and they would report the latest with their roommates or tell each other about their families. Adam told Gillian how his mom was incapable of not squeezing at least one criticism into a conversation ("Sometimes in the middle of the day, I'll just randomly hear her voice in my head saying, 'Adam! Elbows!'"), and Gillian told him how her parents were the opposite, "aggressively supportive" ("They were, like, obsessed with me and my high school girlfriend; it's like they wanted to climb into bed with us") and how that was smothering in its own way. Then they would fold themselves up in Gillian's bed and watch a movie on her laptop, talking through the whole thing, making fun of it, or addressing the characters. Adam had never seen Gillian cry for real, but she cried easily during pretty much any movie. They once watched this teen movie about a girl moving away from home to go meet her true love or something, and Gillian had started bawling during the opening credits, just music over the girl packing up her childhood room, before anyone had even said anything. He'd made fun of her all night for doing that, and she would just laugh and punch him and say, "I hate you," with her giant dimpled smile.

Adam knew the trans thing was crazy. And hovering around him was always the understanding that *this cannot last,* but being with Gillian just made him feel so good all the time, that nothing else, nothing outside of being with her in the precious bubble of the present, really mattered at all.

He could tell that June was feeling something similar. Since the night of Bound when June had ravaged Casey with on-this-earth-unparalleled abandon, she and Casey appeared to be kind of ... dating. The "dating" consisted of Casey being in a weird, edgy mood all the time but sometimes sleeping in June's room,

and June walking around the apartment with a perpetual terrified smile that reminded Adam of a photo of his mom on Space
Mountain.

Adam and Ethan agreed that this dynamic was far more disturbing than anything that had come before.

"How do you think they have sex?" Ethan had asked Adam. "I
mean, not to traumatize you or anything—"

"Uh, a little late for that."

"But seriously, is it just, like, June worshipping Casey's body?
Like, I have this image of Casey just lying naked on her back while
June slowly trails her fingertips up and down over—"

"Aaah! Stop!"

"It's not like I *want* to imagine it! I can't *not!* It's compulsive! I
mean it's happening right there in the next room . . . whatever 'it'
is . . . OK, I'll stop."

Ethan was out of his funk, which had lingered following the
failed Film Forum date. He still spent every night tinkering away
on the Rachel movie, but he'd stopped talking about her out loud
as much.

"I think I might, like, actually try Internet dating," he said to
Adam. "There are some cute girls on there . . ."

"What? You don't have to Internet date! You're, like, every girl's
dream," Adam said. And then there was a weird silence when they
realized how awkward that sounded coming from Adam, and they
both started laughing.

"I'm shy!" Ethan said. "And, besides, not every guy just randomly runs into his fantasy girl at a party."

The way he said that made Adam blush with pride. That was
the way the story of *his* life went. The magical, charmed kind of
life. Ethan made him feel that way a lot.

The day after Bound and the First Sex with Gillian, Adam had
to tell Ethan he'd lost his shirt. At first he was nervous, but Ethan
hadn't seemed mad at all. He just gave Adam a perplexed look.

"Um, may I ask how?"

"Well, there was sort of this . . . 'play party'? Like kind of a sex party? And Gillian wanted to go, so —"

Ethan started laughing. "You know what, man? It's totally cool. I don't even need to know what happened."

"Really?"

"Just tell me — you and Gillian . . . ?"

Adam looked down and grinned.

"I knew it! First time? . . . Ever?"

Adam nodded.

"Well, the bad news is you *might* be obsessed with her for the rest of your life. But the good news is — what the fuck am I talking about, I think you're aware of what the good news is."

And then they both started laughing.

"The first time I had sex with Rachel, I was so freaked out to be actually doing it, all my limbs went numb and I could barely feel anything."

"I kind of had no idea what I was doing," said Adam. He tried to find a way to tell Ethan about it, without the details he couldn't share. "It's like . . . uncharted territory down there. There's all these, like, weird folds, and . . ."

"Yeah, I know what you mean," said Ethan. "It's like, 'Wait, have I just been rubbing the wrong part for the past ten minutes?'"

Adam had a horrified look on his face, and Ethan laughed even harder.

"Our stuff is so much more simple . . ." said Adam. "Although the first time I ever, like . . . came, I totally freaked out and thought it meant I had AIDS or something."

Ethan doubled over again.

"I was eleven and didn't realize stuff would come out, you know?"

"I hear you," said Ethan, trying to catch his breath. "Seriously though, man" — and he looked Adam in the eyes — "I'm happy for you."

People said those words a lot but usually because they were supposed to, and there would be a tinge of jealousy or competition or even a subtle reappraisal of oneself that trumped any happy feeling for the other person. This moment with Ethan was one of the rare instances when Adam knew the person truly, genuinely meant it.

*"The bad news is you might be obsessed with her for the rest of your life."* And the truth was Adam couldn't imagine feeling any other way. Life before Gillian was a cold, colorless wasteland through which he had pursued the meaningless business of being alive for god knows what reason. Really, what *was* the point of life if you didn't have this in it? He wasn't being dramatic. It was a legitimate question. And the notion that some other girl — some stranger, some Kelsey Winslow–like farce — could replace Gillian's role was absurd. There was no replacing Gillian; the thing itself was Gillian. It was what Ethan had said: *"The person whose world you always want to live in."*

Gillian had given Adam a mix CD, and every night he wasn't with her, he had a routine of listening through all twenty-one tracks in bed, in the sleeping bag, with his headphones on. The CD case cover said "Adam's New York Adventure" in typewriter print, and Gillian had cut out a construction paper New York City skyline and pasted it over a blue paper background. Little fake jewels were glued to the sky for stars.

Adam had never thought much about music before. The gang at EBP all listened to rap — T.I., 50 Cent, Eminem, Jay-Z, Nas. Adam thought some of it was cool, but he never cared enough to actually buy anything. Brad and Colin were always quoting Jay-Z, talking about being a nigga with ninety-nine problems like they *really* related to it. It was basically not acceptable to listen to anything other than rap though, and while Casey always had some girl band blasting out of her room, it never occurred to Adam to like what she was playing, only to yell at her to close her fucking door. Listening to Gillian's mix, however, made Adam want to run up to every person he saw and say, "Hold up, wait, did you know about this thing called *music?*"

Every track on the CD held a distinct secret message about him and Gillian. The mix began with the Lovin' Spoonful's "Summer in the City," and the song was jumpy and exciting and about how insanely hot it had been that fateful day of the Gay Marriage Rally. And when the guy sang about meeting on the rooftop, it was just so perfect because *they* had been on Carlisle's rooftop and it made Adam grin like a fool into the dark. Track 3 was Avril Lavigne's "How Does It Feel," and Adam imagined him and Gillian holding hands, walking through the *Bodies* exhibit, the muscles and skeleton men trailing them with their beady glass eyes. Track 7 was fast and catchy but slowed down in the middle, and when the band, Matt Pond PA, sang about the type of son one should want, it was referring to Adam's old life: his mom, his dad, Brad, EBP, and how they didn't understand him or want him for who he was the way Gillian did. Track 12 was Tegan and Sara — Gillian had said she was "in love" with Tegan — and the song was called "So Jealous" and was about Adam being jealous of this Tegan, but also jealous of anyone who had ever been with Gillian, or ever would be, and his stomach would clench at the thought. But then the track would switch, and it was Arcade Fire singing "Rebellion" about lies, lies, and the song was huge and magnificent, and Adam's emotions would soar and sweep because it was about how everything is a lie and everything is the truth, and sometimes there's no way to tell the difference because the world is a glorious, grand, fucked-up place and we're all in it together. Then track 18 was the Flaming Lips with "Do You Realize?" about floating in space, and it was him and Gillian fucking, the way it felt when everything disappeared except their tongues in each other's mouths and their bodies moving with the exact same rhythm. Track 21 was the last track, and in the empty space before the music began, Adam would feel the loneliness creeping up because soon the mix would be over and the deadly silence would follow, and he would be aware of his body in his bed in his room again. But then the music would start, and it was the Cars singing "Who's gonna drive you home," and it was so beautiful, but Adam would well with despair because they were singing about how the summer would end, and he was going to have to leave New York City — and as those last three minutes of the mix played, Adam would see himself flying alone at the back of an empty airplane through the icy, dark sky.

# Chapter 12

BRAD WAS ARRIVING late that afternoon.

Adam had told him to take the AirTrain to the Howard Beach A to Broadway Junction to the L to get to Bushwick, but he was almost positive Brad would get lost and show up hours late. He kind of liked the idea of Brad getting lost, truth be told.

Since it was the middle of the day and Casey, Ethan, and June were all at work, Gillian had come over to the apartment to hang out before Brad arrived. The two of them spent their time almost exclusively at Gillian's, though Gillian kept asking Adam when she was going to meet his sister. Adam had no interest in taking that particular risk, but Brad was a different story. Brad meeting Gillian — his hot, cool, older girlfriend — was imperative. Gillian meeting Brad, his dork teenage friend from Piedmont, was significantly less appealing. Adam had been vague about how old Brad was, just that he was younger than Adam and also still lived at home with his parents — not because of trans stuff like Adam, but just because Brad was a loser.

"So he's a bio guy?" Gillian had said.

"Yeah, cisgendered," Adam answered. "He actually doesn't know I'm trans."

He told her they'd met a couple years ago playing tennis at the club their parents both belonged to. Another truth-lie, since he and Brad did play tennis at The Claremont together all the time.

Adam and Gillian were curled on the futon watching *A Few Good Men*, which they'd discovered was a shared favorite. Gillian leaned against Adam's chest. She was wearing one of her really low-cut V-necks where he could see half her tits sticking out, especially from this angle. Since the beginning of the movie, his dick had been in a state of semi-hardness, wrapped against his stomach in the ACE bandage. As they watched, they talked back at the screen, laughing at Jack Nicholson being dramatic and loving it when anyone went into a fast, wordy "Aaron Sorkin rant," as Gillian called it.

Onscreen Tom Cruise and Demi Moore were in the middle of a frenzied work session surrounded by stacks of files and Chinese food.

"Why are work montages in movies always with Chinese food?" said Gillian.

"I think maybe it has to do with gesticulating with chopsticks?" said Adam.

"Yeah, like when you're struck with a genius idea, it's more effective to pause mid-chopstick in the air, rather than like with a forkful of hanging pasta."

Adam laughed.

"Also Jews love working, and Jews love Chinese food, so ..." said Gillian.

"You and your Jews!"

"You're my Jew."

Kevin Bacon was now pacing the courtroom. He turned and faced the jury, told them how Lieutenant Kaffee was going to try to pull off a little magic act, try to dazzle you with official-sounding terms like Code Red.

"The only reason this movie works is because the order has the cool-sounding name 'Code Red,'" said Adam. "Like, what if instead of 'Code Red,' the order was called ... 'the Helena 567 Blue Breakfront,' and they had to repeat that all the time? 'Did you

order the Helena 567 Blue Breakfront?' 'You're goddamn right I
ordered the Helena 567 Blue Breakfront!'"

Gillian hunched over laughing. He loved when he made her
laugh like that. Like she just couldn't take it and would stay doubled over, trying to collect herself. She sat back up.

"That was amazing." She moved back under Adam's arm.

"That was retarded," said Adam. Gillian didn't care when he
said "retarded." Sometimes she said it too.

Gillian just smiled at the movie. "Adam Freedman. I bet you get
into any college you want."

Adam chose not to correct her or mention his 2.6 grade point
average and abysmal score on the SATs. He shrugged.

"Of course, you're only applying to places in New York," said
Gillian. She turned to him with a fake-stern look.

"Of course," said Adam.

They didn't talk about it seriously, but the ongoing "joke" was
that Adam would return to Piedmont at the end of the summer,
get his shit together, apply to college in New York, and come back.

*I will,* he thought. *I'll finish my fucking last year of high school,
and I'll apply to every fucking college in New York so one of them has
to take me, and I'll come back for you — I will.*

Tom Cruise stared blankly at his chalkboard covered in Post-it
notes.

Gillian moved her hand in between Adam's legs. She knew she
was allowed to put her hand between his thighs but never on the
crotch and never, *ever* inside his pants. All this had been commu-
nicated silently through the moving of hands by other hands or
shifting of bodies out of the way. Once she had asked, "Have you
ever let anyone touch you?" And Adam had said, "No." It never
came up again.

The warmth and pressure of Gillian's hand against his thigh felt
so good, and Adam's dick got harder. He looked down at her tits
and her flat, smooth stomach exposed where her shirt had pushed

up. His whole body was buzzing with pleasure. As if she could tell, Gillian leaned over and pressed her face against his, her lips on his cheek.

"I love the way you smell," she said. "It's, like, narcotic."

Adam had completely lost interest in the movie. Some witness on the stand was listing off reasons why a marine might receive a Code Red. Gillian lay down on her back on the futon, and Adam climbed on top of her. He pushed his tongue inside her mouth. Moved his hands all over her big round tits.

"Take my clothes off," Gillian whispered.

Adam immediately unbuttoned Gillian's jeans and pulled them off, underwear and socks tugged along with them. Gillian took off her shirt and unhooked her bra. She lay utterly naked on the futon while Adam still had all his clothes on, even his shoes. As much as he wanted her to be able to touch him, there was something about this, him fully dressed, like he could get up and do anything he wanted at any moment, and her, pale white and vulnerable below him, that especially turned him on. He could tell it turned Gillian on too.

Gillian reached her hand down and spread her legs as she started rubbing her clit. She moved her middle finger up inside herself, then took it out and put it in her mouth.

"God, you make me so wet," she said.

Adam shoved three fingers inside her. His hand was thick and grubby. He curved his fingers up and pressed against the slightly raised G spot on the top toward the back. He'd learned about it on a trans message board.

"Fuck. Yes," said Gillian, breathing heavier. "Do it harder."

Adam thrust his hand in and out, Gillian getting wetter and wider, his fingers pulsing up against the spot.

"Oh god," said Gillian, "I wish you were packing — I want to feel your hard cock inside me."

"Tell me how much you want it."

"I want you to fuck me so bad, I'm such a slut, tell me what a whore I am for your big, hard dick."

"You're just a whore, you're just a slut that wants a dick rammed up inside you —"

*BANG* *BANG*

Someone was at the front door.

"Who is that?!" said Gillian, bolting up.

"Fuck!" said Adam. "Brad?" He looked at his watch. "He's not supposed to be here!"

"Help me!" said Gillian, scrambling on the ground for her clothes. Adam handed Gillian her bra.

*BANG* *BANG*

"Just a minute!" Adam shouted.

Gillian pulled on her clothes and gave Adam an *OK* nod. She was still barefoot, and her face was flushed and glowing. *Just-been-fucked face,* thought Adam.

Adam walked over to the door. His heart was racing. In the past couple weeks, he'd gotten so comfortable with the trans lie around her, he'd forgotten the intense anxiety it could cause. Introducing Gillian and Brad was a bold-ass move. It felt like crisis perched on a ledge, but in a perverse way, he wanted that feeling. A singular adrenaline rush that nothing else could elicit.

Adam opened the door. Brad had an annoyed look on his face, but his expression shifted when he noticed Gillian, hovering behind Adam.

"Hey, uh, what's up?" Brad said, straightening his posture, lidding his eyes, trying to appear attractive. Brad glanced at Adam with a look that said, *You're fucking kidding me. You got her?*

And in that instant Adam realized that his fantasy, the fantasy he'd had almost exactly two months ago on the first day they moved into the apartment, of Brad coming to visit and interrupting Adam having sex with his hot redheaded girlfriend, had come true. And with this realization came a shivering euphoria that the world was an indisputably magical place, possibly entirely crafted for and revolving around Adam. But there was also something almost scary about this revelation. Like God, with his bristly beard, was licking the back of Adam's neck.

"I thought you weren't coming till, like, five!" said Adam.

Brad trudged in and dropped his bags on the floor. "We got in early and I took a cab. I wasn't about to get on some AirTrain or whatever and five different subways. Why did you even tell me to do that? Freedman, making shit unnecessarily complicated since the second grade."

Brad grinned at Gillian, trying to give her his man-meat-on-a-stick smirk, but Gillian just returned with a bored look. Adam could tell she thought nothing of him. He was a flea to her. *"I would never date a bio guy. I'm just not attracted to them."*

"I like unnecessarily complicated," Gillian said. And gave Adam a kiss on the corner of his mouth.

The kiss made Adam blush, and Brad just stared at him. Brad stuck his pinkie finger in his ear like Adam knew he did when he was nervous.

"You guys should catch up," Gillian said, sauntering over to the couch to put on her shoes. "But we should all get together tomorrow night or something." And as she leaned over to do up her black Converse laces, her V-neck swooped down and her entire amazing rack was visible.

Adam and Brad watched, like neither of them could believe she was real.

. . .

After Gillian left, Adam and Brad walked over to Danny's Pizzeria on Bushwick to get slices.

"Damn, New York is dirty," said Brad, looking around. "Is that human shit?" He pointed to an especially vile pile, wet with chunks.

"Uh, that's dog shit," said Adam, "but I guess now I know what your shit looks like."

They each got two sausage and pepperoni slices and giant ice-filled cups of Coke and sat down at one of the little tables inside.

"It's hot here, too," said Brad. "Nasty hot. This city is giving me a rash on my balls." He reached down and scratched himself.

Adam wished he'd taken off his ACE bandage before they'd left. He'd forgotten.

The two of them chewed in silence for a moment. Adam waited for Brad to ask him everything about Gillian.

"So Fletcher dumped Alice and is hooking up with Sandy now," said Brad. "I knew he always wanted in on that. I figured I should fuck Alice, just to make it even, but I don't even want to. He told me she doesn't shave, so fuck that. I don't want some hairy-ass bush, you know what I'm saying? I'd let her give me head though . . ."

Adam watched Brad chewing and talking with his mouth open, pizza sauce smeared on his teeth.

"We're doing a guys-only camping trip when I get back," continued Brad. He dropped his pizza crust in his soda and left it to soak. "Just me, Fletcher, Colin, and Stephen. Return-to-the-earth kind of shit. We might even try to kill some animals to eat."

"How the fuck are you gonna kill some animals?" said Adam.

"We'll make spears and shit. And Stephen's dad knows how to make traps. Tahoe was fucking epic. One day all the guys got up super early and ditched the girls and went dirt biking by ourselves. Colin fell off and broke his arm. It was awesome."

Brad removed his soggy pizza crust from the Coke and dangled it in front of Adam's face. He knew wet bread made Adam gag. "Waaaaaaaaant some?"

"Ugh. Fuck off."

Brad retracted the mushy crust and slurped it up with relish.

*Why wasn't Brad asking him about Gillian?* It was like Brad was trying to prove that even though Adam had a hot-as-shit girl-friend, he was still the odd man out. Still the loser with no guy friends, which is what apparently *really* mattered. Adam could hear his inevitable return to EBP like muffled voices screaming at him through plate-glass doors.

"So what have you been *doing* here?" said Brad. "Like, aside from the girl, who do you hang out with?"

Adam shifted his position. The ACE bandage was killing him.

"My roommate Ethan, he's, like, twenty-one."

"Fag?"

"No! . . . And don't say 'fag.'"

"You're a fag for telling me not to say 'fag.' So is he gonna chill with us?"

Adam took out his cell phone. "Yeah, um, let me text him and see what he's up to." Adam had never randomly texted Ethan before. So what? He could do it. It wouldn't be weird. U around tonight? My dick friend is here. want 2 hang?

In the half minute it had taken Adam to text Ethan, Brad had already gotten involved in some text conversation of his own. Brad chuckled at the text, but Adam didn't ask what it said. Why did Brad hate him so much? Why wasn't he happy for Adam, telling him how amazing Gillian was, telling him how much he'd missed him this summer? Adam wanted to throw the table over, grab a chair, and wreck the entire pizza place. He could never win. He could never fucking win. His phone dinged in his pocket. It was Ethan.

can't. getting drinks with work people

"Well?" said Brad.

Ethan didn't give a shit about him.

"He has to work," said Adam. He felt like crying. He felt like a fucking pussy. He felt five seconds away from reaching into his pants, pulling out the ACE bandage, and throwing it on the floor. *"Oh, that? Just some random shit that got stuck in my jeans in the dryer."*

Brad's phone dinged. He looked at the message and grinned. Started texting a response like Adam wasn't even there. Like he wasn't sitting directly across from him.

"So guess what, Casey was dating this guy that used to be a girl," Adam found himself saying.

Brad looked up from his phone. "She what? Casey was dating a dude? I swore my dick would be the first that got in there."

"Shut up, that's my sister. So this guy, like, took hormones and shit and got surgery to turn himself into a guy."

"I don't get it."

"Like, she-males, from the Internet, chicks with dicks, but reversed."

"Huh?"

"That was Casey's boyfriend, this girl who took male hormones and got her tits cut off and now looks and acts like a guy."

Brad grimaced. "That is fucked up. Your sister's a straight-up freak. Who would want to have sex with that?"

"She's, like, obsessed with anybody transsexual. Apparently the clit, like, grows into a kind of mini-penis . . ."

"Ugh! Freedman, you're gonna make me retch."

Adam laughed. It was a sick, weird laugh, like his voice after sucking helium out of a balloon.

"Yeah, it's pretty nasty," said Adam.

"Hey, remember that *Freaks* video we rented when we were, like, nine?" said Brad. "Peeeeeenheads!"

Now Adam was laughing for real. "We hid the cover and told your mom it was a kids' movie about the circus!"

"I had nightmares about the worm guy in the bag for, like, two weeks."

"I know! You called me and you were like, 'Adam, every time I close my eyes, I see the worm guy.'"

"Shut up! You were scared of him too!"

Brad reached into his cup and threw some ice at Adam, and Adam threw some ice back, both of them really laughing.

"So what are we doing now, anyway?" said Brad, the laughter subsiding.

"I don't know . . . wanna watch *A Few Good Men*?" said Adam.

"That movie sucks. Sure."

They got up and walked back to the apartment.

. . .

Adam and Brad were sprawled on the futon, about halfway through the movie, when Ethan came home with two six-packs.

"I love this movie!" Ethan said. He dropped the beer — Coronas — on the coffee table and flopped down next to Brad. "What's up — I'm Ethan. You're Brad, right?"

Ethan slipped off the tie he wore to his job at Film Forum, tossed it over the arm of the futon, and undid the first few buttons of his shirt. He had stopped shaving recently, and the scruff around his face made him look cool and old. Ethan, returning from work, cracking open a beer. Adam could tell Brad was impressed, and he felt a rush of affection for Ethan. Ethan had blown off work friends. He had come for Adam.

Ethan handed Adam and Brad beers. "So, you just got in? What do you guys got planned? He's not gonna meet Gillian before I do, is he?"

"Yeah, I already met her," said Brad. "She's hot."

Adam took a slug of beer to hide his grin.

"Yeah, no shit," said Ethan. "I've seen her picture. Adam sucks, right?"

"Yeah," said Brad, laughing. "Fuck him."

"Dick."

"How'd you meet her, anyway?" said Brad. *Now he was interested.*

"At this party."

"She thinks Adam's twenty-two," said Ethan, laughing and spilling foamed beer on himself, the way Adam always did.

Brad turned to Adam. "You told her you were twenty-two?"

"Yeah."

"And she believed you? You look twelve."

"Eat a dick."

Brad turned to Ethan and said, "He looks twelve, right?"

"Adam has a youthful, boyish charm. But, yeah, I kind of see what you mean. Sorry, bro."

"See!" said Brad.

Ethan and Brad chuckled at each other.

"Whatever," said Adam. "She likes me."

"Joke's on us, right?" said Ethan.

"Oh, and you're nineteen, by the way," Adam said, knocking Brad with his beer.

"I'm only nineteen? Why do you get to be older than me?!"

"At least I made you older at all," said Adam. "I could have just said you were some nerdy teenager I was nice to out of pity." This was, essentially, what Adam had told Gillian.

"Fine, I'm nineteen. I can deal with that. So she got any hot friends?"

"Most of her friends are gay."

Ethan busted out laughing.

"What?" said Brad. "Why?"

"I dunno, they just are. She mainly dated girls before. I'm the first guy she's really into."

Brad's eyes bugged with jealousy.

"Dude, you look like you just dumped a load in your pants," Ethan said, laughing.

Brad turned red.

"I think some of her friends are bi," said Adam, "so you might get lucky. If you don't fuck up and start talking about your home-room teacher or lunch period or something."

"Well, what's my story? Come on, what's the lie I gotta tell?"

"This is rich," said Ethan. "You're totally gonna fuck it up."

"No, I won't!" said Brad. "I can lie! I'm a better liar than this dumb-ass."

"That 'dumb-ass' is trying to help you get twenty-two-year-old lesbian pussy," said Ethan. "So I'd shut the fuck up."

"All right. Word," said Brad. He took an awkward, overly conscious sip of beer. "So, what's my story?"

"We met playing tennis at the Claremont," said Adam. "You're nineteen, I'm twenty-two, and we just started rallying one day and kept meeting up after that. You graduated from EBP two years ago and are kind of a bum, living at home with your parents."

"This is supposed to help me get a girl? How about I went to Berkeley High? EBP's such a fag school."

"Try Allyson Academy where I went," said Ethan. "Talk about a fag school . . ."

"Anyway," continued Adam, "you're at home because you were really good at baseball — college recruiters were all into you. But then the summer after graduation, you got drunk one night and fucked up your arm in a car wreck — your best friend riding shot-gun almost died, and the guilt fucking kills you." Adam had no idea where this story was coming from, only that it was flowing from his mouth as if he were watching a movie on the insides of his eyes and just reporting what he saw. It was that easy. An image appeared, and he described it.

"So I'm a bum who lives at home and almost killed his best friend."

Ethan guffawed.

"The injured-best-friend thing is good for sympathy," said Adam, "makes you seem tragic. Trust me. Now you help take care of your grandma, who also lives at home with your folks —"

"Both my grandmas are dead."

"Your arm is better, and you've had some calls from colleges again, but you don't want to leave your grandma. Your mom is mean to her. Abuses her. You think she might be slowly trying to poison her."

"What?!"

Ethan had to spit his mouthful of beer into a leftover coffee mug.

"That shit's not that important though," said Adam, laughing. He felt silly, goofy. This was all just so stupid. But it was *fun*. He took a sip of his beer. "The main thing is, you want to stay until she dies, which could be any day — she's ninety-five — and then you're ready to play college ball and, fuck it, maybe even go pro. Also, you're in between girlfriends. But you and Sandy were super serious. Even talked about marriage. You're just kinda romantic like that. Also you got her pregnant, but you guys put the baby up for adoption, and every morning you pray to God that one day your son will try to contact you."

"You're fucking retarded," said Brad.

And now they were all laughing. Really laughing, the kind where it feels like you might actually injure yourself. Adam looked at Brad and Ethan, their bodies bobbing, beers sloshing in their hands. *My two best friends.* He felt *happy*.

"So what did you *actually* tell Gillian about me?" said Brad, catching his breath.

Adam felt a pang in his heart for Gillian but buried it.

"Well, maybe not *all* of that . . ."

Brad kicked his feet up on the coffee table, put his arms behind his head, and leaned back on the futon. "OK, so I'm nineteen, Claremont tennis, sick grandma, best friend car accident, what's my best friend's name?"

"Whatever, it doesn't matter," said Adam. "Marvin?"

"OK, Marvin. My best friend in the whole wide world, Marvin."

And they all busted out laughing again.

"You're coming out with us tomorrow too, right?" Brad said to Ethan. "So you can back me up and shit?"

"As much as I would love to witness this . . ." said Ethan. He took a swig of beer and kicked his feet up on the coffee table too. "I gotta say, I see some tragedy in the future."

"What? We can do it!" said Brad. "I can totally pull this off!"

Ethan raised his eyebrow in doubt and then turned to Adam.

"Just don't let this fool fuck up what you got going? OK?"

Adam loved Ethan. He fucking loved him.

"No shit," said Adam. And he and Ethan reached across Brad and clinked beers.

# Chapter 13

"LET'S PLAY PRETEND You Don't Know Me."

Gillian smiled big as she explained the game to Adam. Her flushed cheeks and her dimples and her huge blue eyes. "I run ahead and lean up against that wall, and as you pass, you pretend you're seeing me for the first time and try to imagine what you would think of me."

"OK," said Adam, "but I'm just gonna think you're beautiful."

"No!" said Gillian, blushing. "I mean, you have to try to imagine what you think my life is like — like what kind of person I am."

Gillian ran ahead. She, Adam, Brad, Nadia, Jackie, and Jackie's friend Lionel walked down the street toward the karaoke bar. It was sundown and the sky hung pink between the cracks in buildings. They were in Chinatown, and the trash-scattered sidewalks and restaurants with their bright red Chinese character signs and Peking ducks swinging in the windows made Adam feel cool and like he was showing Brad the *real* New York. They'd all met outside the subway station, and everyone was already drunk. Brad and Adam had finished a six-pack at the apartment before they'd left. Gillian and her gang appeared to have done something similar.

"Let's play it too!" Nadia said to Jackie, and she ran ahead and joined Gillian, reclining against a brick wall.

Jackie rolled her eyes at Adam, and he rolled them back. At first Adam was worried Brad would be disappointed there were more guys than girls hanging out (Jackie counted as a guy), but Brad was so enamored with Nadia, it didn't matter. That she was obviously with Jackie didn't faze him at all — that was almost part of it. "Lesbian pussy, here I come," he'd whispered to Adam, definitely too loud, when they'd first met up with everyone.

Part of the reason Adam had gotten so drunk was nerves — that Brad might actually blow his cover or Gillian might refer to something trans, even though she knew Adam was stealth with Brad and shouldn't. He had thought getting drunk would soothe him, make him chill out, and feel like everything was going to be fine, but instead it made the anxiety worse. He felt unhinged, not in control, his surroundings slippery and grease-covered. He wished Brad and he had just stayed home with Ethan. Ethan who knew the real him and the real Brad, and there were no lies; it was all just jokes and comfort, and Adam felt solid and safe. He never should have agreed to Brad hanging out with Gillian and her friends. Brad had seen Gillian; he knew she was hot — there was no reason for them to see each other again. But Brad had gotten so excited about meeting his own lesbian, and Gillian had said on the phone, "It's sweet seeing you with your friend, even if he's kind of a douche. I like watching you guys together," and Adam had felt trapped. Ethan had said, "I see some tragedy in the future," and as Adam recalled that now, it felt like an omen. He remembered that first night in New York, walking to the *L Word* party down Lorimer, sucking on the Cherry Bomb pop, and that fleeting second of elation when he'd known — he'd just known — everything would turn out right. Now, drunk and stumbling down this twisted alleyway, the sidewalk all buckled and cracked, he felt a murky insistence in his body that something, some thing he couldn't conceive of yet, was going to go horribly wrong.

"What did you think?" said Gillian. She ran back and grabbed

Adam's hand as they continued walking. She was so cute when she was drunk. Her voice got really high.

"I thought you looked Jewish," he said.

Gillian punched him.

"Prostitute?" Jackie was saying to Nadia.

Brad almost walked into a bus stop pole.

"Someone do me!" said Lionel. "Everyone do me!" and he ran ahead and posed against a building like Gillian and Nadia had.

Adam could tell Lionel was trans. He was short and his hands were tiny. He had hair on his face but in a patchy trans-guy way. His hips and butt swelled out of his Dickies. His voice was tranny nasal. Something about him just seemed like a fucking girl. And that stupid fucking name. Everyone on the Internet had names like that: Lionel, Elias, Aiden, Asher, Tucker, Tristan. Adam was sure Lionel passed to Brad — that wasn't a worry — the question was whether Jackie had told Lionel that Adam was trans and whether Lionel would start running his mouth. Gillian knew not to tell people, but Jackie's alliance was to Lionel, not Adam. I mean why was Lionel even here? *"Adam's this really cool trans guy; you guys should be friends."* Adam had caught Lionel looking at him, checking him for trans giveaways too.

The karaoke bar was empty when they arrived. Empty, except for one old Chinese man hunched at a table in the back who looked up with a cracked-tooth grin at Gillian and Nadia as if they had come there to meet him.

The gang packed themselves into one of the red booths while Jackie ordered a round of drinks. Nadia and Lionel pored over the thick karaoke song binder. The emptiness in the bar felt oppressive. Adam could not imagine anything more awkward than someone getting up and singing right now.

The bartender — a too-old-for-her-outfit Chinese lady — came over with the drinks. Adam watched Brad guzzle his whiskey, his teeth crunching the ice louder than any other sound in the bar.

"So, Brad," said Gillian, "you dating anyone?"

Brad glanced at Nadia, who was murmuring lyrics, psyching herself up to sing.

"I'm dating this girl Sandy," said Brad. He stuck his pinkie in his ear. "I mean, I *was* dating her, back in high school, at Berkeley High."

"You haven't dated her since high school?" said Gillian. She took a sip of her drink, giving Brad a weird look over the rim of her glass.

Brad's pinkie pulsed in and out of his ear. "Yeah. Not since my arm injury."

Adam leaned in, poised and ready to take over if this got any worse. Gillian was drunk. He had that on his side. Things were sloppy, confusing. Things could be explained as something else at a later time.

"Your arm injury?" said Jackie. "Can I ask what happened? I'm in med school, so . . ."

"Hey, Adam," said Lionel, "you wanna get in on this Backstreet Boys duet with me?"

"I hurt it playing baseball," said Brad. "I mean, in a car wreck on the way home from baseball practice."

"Uh, sure," said Adam to Lionel. He turned to Brad. "You just sprained it; it wasn't a big deal." He needed to reel Brad in — they weren't supposed to actually *use* that retarded story. What was wrong with Brad?

"'*Tell me why,*'" Lionel sang disturbingly loud. Lionel wasn't drinking, but he kind of seemed like he was on crack or something.

"Yeah, I just sprained it," said Brad. "Mainly it just hurts when it rains and shit, you know?"

Brad looked especially pleased with himself for having ad-libbed this detail.

"That could be cold agglutinins," said Jackie. "It's when antibodies cause red blood cells to clump together in low temperatures and can cause pain. Or your pain could just be the increased pressure from the temperature drop. That shouldn't happen with an old sprain though, only breaks."

"It might have actually been a break," said Brad, finger returned to his ear. "It was a while ago."

"Hey, Adam, you're from the Bay, right?" said Lionel. "I got my top done with Brownstein in Oakland, so I was there for a week last March."

"Word," said Adam.

"Pretty sick town. And Brownstein was the shit."

"How do you know Adam?" Jackie said to Brad.

"Tennis," said Brad, eyeing Adam.

"Are you sure about that?" said Gillian, laughing. "You look uncertain." Gillian looked at Adam.

"Who'd you go with?" said Lionel.

"Fischer," said Adam.

"Sweet. My friend Beaumont used her."

"What?" said Brad.

"Where I got my surgery, you know," Adam said, and he gave Brad a barely perceptible head nod. Then quietly, but catching Gillian's attention too, Adam said, "Appendix."

"Oh, yeah!" said Brad, acknowledging this must be part of some previous lie Adam had told: Adam's own tragic story involving an inflamed appendix and possible near death. Tragedy breeds sympathy. Brad kicked Adam under the table and grinned.

Gillian gave Adam a knowing look and then leaned over to Lionel. She gestured at Brad with her head. She was trying to tell him not to out Adam in front of Brad, but Lionel wasn't getting it.

"You're good at this," Brad said to Adam under his breath.

More people were coming into the club now, filling up the other red booths and thickening around the bar. Adam smiled. He *was* good at this. His whole body felt electrified, ready for whatever came at him next. He imagined his brain as a jigsaw puzzle of lies, everything fitting perfectly, a 1,000-piece Van Gogh painting.

"Hey, Nadia, can I get you another drink?" said Brad, noticing Nadia's empty glass.

"How old are you?" said Nadia.

"Nineteen."

"Last time I checked you had to be twenty-one to buy alcohol."

Jackie laughed as Brad turned red. She was amused by Brad's crush on her girlfriend.

"You know what I have no desire to ever do?" said Nadia, staring out as if in reverie.

"Yeah?" said Brad.

"Have sex with a man," said Nadia.

Jackie laughed really hard.

"Do you work out?" said Lionel to Adam. "You look awesome."

"Uh, a little," said Adam.

"I just don't like the idea of a guy fucking me. It's like he thinks he's getting something. Or getting away with something," continued Nadia.

"Yeah, I know what you mean," said Gillian. She caught herself on the last word and looked quickly at Adam. *It's different with you,* her expression said. *No problem, of course,* his expression said back.

"Don't knock it if you haven't tried it," said Brad with a lip-sneered smile.

"Oh, I've tried it," said Nadia.

"Yeah, I've been trying to lift a little, even though my doctor told me not to yet," said Lionel. "I'm just ready to get ripped. What's your dose?"

*Jesus, he would not give up.*

"I'm gonna sing a song!" said Gillian, jumping out of her seat. "Lionel, will you sing it with me?"

"Uh, sure, what are we singing?"

Gillian grabbed Lionel's hand and dragged him over toward the karaoke DJ. They stopped midway, and Gillian whispered something in Lionel's ear. Lionel nodded and looked at Brad.

"I'm buying a round of shots," said Adam. "Hey, Gillian, you guys want shots?"

"Thanks, baby," she said.

"Straight edge!" said Lionel, and he drew an X across his chest with his finger.

The music for Gillian and Lionel's song came on, and Lionel started in.

Adam strolled confidently up to the bar and slapped down Ethan's ID. Ethan had loaned it to him before they went out. He'd done that a few times. Adam loved using Ethan's ID.

"Five shots of whiskey," he said. "Jameson."

Ethan Karl Anderson from 90 Field Point Circle, Greenwich, Connecticut 06830, grinned back up at him and winked.

Adam looked around and realized the bar had become packed, buzzing with loud, rowdy hipsters, their gang a natural part of it.

"'You cry . . .'"

Adam's head turned to the karaoke stage, where Gillian was singing the cheery, '60s-sounding song. She was usually so nervous and bumbling, but now, smiling up at the lyrics on the screen, this perfectly pitched, startlingly bold music just rolled out of her mouth like it wasn't anything. He'd sometimes heard her singing softly along to music in the background but had no idea she was actually this good. Why hadn't she told him? Her voice was beautiful. All he wanted to do was stand there and listen to her.

"Whoooo!" someone cheered behind Adam.

Adam looked around and saw that people had stopped talking to step closer and watch her. Everyone could tell she was amazing. Adam's chest seized. She'd never even said she liked singing. Let alone that she was good at it. Adam felt a desperate, wild neediness. She was *really* good. A crowd had formed at the front of the stage. These people loved her. They wanted her. But she was *his,* right? She belonged to him. The separation between them seemed suddenly vast, insurmountable. Gillian and her talent on one side of the world, Adam on the other.

Gillian turned away from the screen, and her eyes met Adam's. She put her hand to her heart as she sang, and his body fluttered. She was his. He was the one she wanted. *You can't have her. You can't have her. You can't have her.* He flung these thoughts at the various patrons watching her.

Gillian handed the mic back to Lionel. His voice was embarrassing in contrast. Weak and strained. Tentative and pathetically hopeful.

Adam looked back at the booth. He could tell Brad was frustrated by the Nadia situation but, at the same time, fueled by some inexhaustible optimism, still hadn't given up. It was kind of hilarious actually, the way he kept that cocky grin on his face. Nadia and Jackie were clearly fucking with him, and Brad was just riding along, bouncing up and down with no seat belt in the back of their janky-ass car. It was sweet, his earnest perseverance in the face of pure shit.

When they were kids, he and Brad had been equals. Everything was after-school snacks and Knights and Swords for hours, chasing each other all over the house. And then in middle school that had stopped, and Brad's crude asshole side had emerged, which impressed Adam and made him fear Brad because, for some reason, Adam couldn't do it too. But watching Brad now, it all seemed so obvious. That asshole persona — what had always made Brad so cool and old and inherently *better* than Adam — was really just another dumb play sword for Brad to swing in front of himself.

Gillian and Lionel finished, and everyone in the bar whistled and applauded. Gillian's face went back to being bashful.

Another song came on, some aggressively rhythmic thing

Adam didn't recognize but that caused Jackie and Nadia to shriek and jump out of the booth.

"Oh my god, they have *Ani?!*" said Gillian, equally excited by whatever was playing.

Jackie and Nadia joined Gillian and Lionel onstage.

"Adam! Sing it with us!" Gillian called to him.

Adam reddened. *No way.* He shook his head.

"Please?"

*Oh god, please no.*

"Just this one!" she pleaded.

His gorgeous girlfriend. So Adam hustled over to the stage, where the four of them were singing.

"*'I cannot name this . . .'*"

Gillian grabbed Adam's hand, but he saw Brad looking awkward, left alone in the booth, so he broke free and ran and grabbed Brad's hand too.

"I'm not doing this shit alone," said Adam.

"Fucking kill you, Freedman," said Brad, but he was grinning, and they ran back on the stage, where the rest of them were really going at it, and Adam and Brad had no idea how this fucking song went, but they bounced up and down, and Nadia even threw her arm around Brad, and by the second time the chorus came on, Adam and Brad winged it and sang too, and soon they were just screaming along with whatever words they could, and Gillian kept kissing Adam, and Brad was doing his dumb-ass dance moves, and it was just so much fun — *it was fun, it was fun, it was fun.*

Adam looked at Gillian and at goofy Brad, and he thought of Ethan at home and his sister, Casey — Casey who had made all this possible! — and he was filled with such intense love for each of them, it felt like he wanted to cry or maybe laugh or some absurd expression of emotion he'd never performed before, but then Nadia was punching him in the shoulder and saying, "Shots!

Shots!" and so he got himself together and ran through the people back to the bar where the shots were waiting.

"That's you, honey?" said the bartender.

"Yes!" said Adam, and he cupped his hands around the shot glasses — balancing two on each side, one suspended in the middle — and carried them carefully back to the stage.

. . .

"You're sure?" said Gillian.

They were all standing outside the Canal Street subway deciding who was going where. Gillian was taking the C back to Fort Greene and wanted Adam to come home with her. She was drunk and had those loose, drunk eyes, looking him up and down, not caring how obvious it was she wanted him. It was so fucking sexy.

"I can't . . ." said Adam.

"Brad doesn't care, right, Brad?" Gillian said.

"Dude, I don't give a shit if you spend the night at her house — just give me your keys. I'd rather sleep in your bed than on that futon anyway."

Adam hesitated.

"I mean, don't make me twist your arm . . ." said Gillian. "God, I feel like some nympho girlfriend."

Brad gave Adam a look like, *What the hell is wrong with you?*

"Let's go-o-o-o-o," said Nadia, hanging off Jackie. "I'm sleepy. Wanna go home-home."

"It's just we told Ethan we'd hit that bar with him," said Adam. "Remember?"

This idea appealed to Brad, so he nodded his head. "Oh yeah, we did."

"We're gonna walk to the J," said Adam. He leaned in to kiss Gillian goodbye.

Gillian gave him a confused smile. He could tell she was hurt but trying to play it off. He wanted nothing more than to go home with her right now. But he couldn't. He wasn't wearing the ACE bandage. Wearing it around Brad made him want to kill himself so he hadn't. And he was too scared to go home with Gillian and into her bed without it.

"I'll call you tomorrow," he said.

"Yeah, yeah, I get it, boys' night out . . ."

Gillian and her friends headed down the subway steps, and Adam and Brad continued on the street.

"So is there a cool bar in your neighborhood that doesn't card?" asked Brad. "Somewhere you and Ethan usually hang? I'm feeling restless! You think he'll be up for it?"

"Sure!" said Adam absently. He was still thinking about Gillian. She thought he didn't want her.

"Dude, I'm texting Colin and telling him I hooked up with that Nadia girl. You'll back me up, right? I think he's lying about fucking some girl in San Francisco. I think he's still a virgin, actually." Brad's head swiveled to Adam. "You're fucking Gillian, right?"

"Um, duh," said Adam.

Brad threw some boxing punches into the air. "Man, I hope Ethan's up to go out. I'm feeling fuckin' *restless!*"

. . .

As soon as Adam opened the door to the apartment, he knew something was wrong. He could tell Brad sensed it too, the way his blathering abruptly trailed off.

Casey, June, and Ethan sat around the television, watching intensely. Casey looked like she had been crying.

"Quiet!" Casey said, as Brad shut the door. She hadn't seen Brad since he'd arrived in New York — hadn't seen him since she'd left for college a year ago actually — and this was apparently her way of greeting him. Brad didn't seem to notice or care. Things were as the two had left them.

"What's going on?" said Adam.

"Nelly Chua," said June, with a somber face. Then turned back to the television.

Adam and Brad sat on the floor to watch. It was a news channel, and a reporter was explaining how they'd found the body of a teenage girl that had been missing the past couple weeks.

*"A witness brought police to the site in Wyandanch, New York, where Nelly Chua was found hogtied and buried in a shallow grave."*

They cut to an image of somewhere in the woods. The way the reporter said "shallow grave" bothered Adam. As if they were trying to make it sound like a cool horror movie or something. But he guessed if the grave really was shallow, that's how you describe it.

The screen switched to an image of Nelly Chua's smiling face. She was really pretty. Casey started sobbing. The news did that thing where the reporter starts the whole story over from the beginning, *"We're here at the West Babylon, Suffolk County, police station, where three hours ago the two-week search for Nelly Chua came to an end . . ."*

"I hope they fucking die. I don't give a shit. I hope they get the fucking death penalty," said Casey.

"I hope they fucking die," echoed June.

Casey's phone, which was in her lap, rang. She answered it, jumping up from the couch. "Hey," she said in a soft, nervous voice.

"Hazel?" mouthed June.

Casey ignored June. She turned her back to everyone and paced while listening into the phone. She stopped and hovered by the entrance to the kitchen. "But you're OK?"

June watched Casey with the same intensity she'd previously been giving the television. Her fists were tight little balls under her stomach bulge.

"I just — thanks for calling me back," Casey continued. "I'm just, I'm just so upset and I — you're sure you're OK?" She started crying again. "I know . . . I know . . ."

"Shit. Did Casey, like, know this girl?" said Brad.

As Brad said this, Adam saw the words "transgender teenager murdered" on the screen, and he knew it wasn't that Casey knew her.

No one answered Brad. He hit Adam lightly on the knee and said in a low voice, "Wanna go back out? Should we ask Ethan?"

Adam glanced at Ethan. He was just watching the news, his face expressionless.

"Just hold up," said Adam. He had a horrible feeling in his stomach.

Casey closed her phone. "There's going to be a candlelight vigil at Union Square tomorrow night," she said to everyone.

"Are you going with Hazel?" said June.

"She's going with her friends. But of course I'm going."

Casey took her seat on the couch and resumed staring at the television. June put her hand on Casey's leg, but Casey moved away. Adam saw June lightly punch the offending hand with her other hand.

"So you knew this girl?" Brad asked Casey.

"No," Casey snapped.

Brad gave Adam an exaggerated "Jesus, what'd I do" look.

"It's just like Brandon Teena," said June. "The bathroom, everyone crowding in to see . . ."

Adam wondered if Gillian had found out yet. If she was going to call him the way Casey had called Hazel. It wouldn't be as intense for Gillian because this was a trans girl, like Hazel, not a trans guy, like Adam. But she still might call. The horrible pang came back in his stomach.

The murdered girl's mother was on the screen now, crying, *"I'm going to bury him in the prettiest dress I can find. With makeup."*

"It's *her*," Casey said to the television. *"Her."*

"Shut *up*," said Ethan. "Her mom obviously loves her."

Casey got really awkward and quiet. She looked into her lap and wiped at her wet nose.

Adam's phone dinged. gillian. His heart twitched, the way it always did when he got a text from her. The text read: just found out about Nelly. You? Are u OK? He texted back: yeah just found out too, watching on TV now . . . He added a sad-face emoticon and then quickly deleted it. He hit SEND and looked back up at the television. His stomach was killing him.

Someone was being interviewed. *"It's messed up, man. This is tragic, no other way to put it. It's tragic. He shouldn't have done that. Leading people to believe you're a girl when you aren't. Letting them have sex with you. But it's tragic."*

"Fucking asshole," said Casey. She looked back down at her phone.

Adam's phone dinged again, and Casey picked up hers, then set it down, disappointed.

Adam looked at Gillian's text: so fucked. He texted back: seriously. hope they get lethal injection. She texted back: wish u were in my bed. Adam texted back: me too.

*"Alex Marquez, John Hibbings, and Cesar Padilla have been taken into custody. Marquez and Hibbings are said to have engaged in sexual activity with Ricardo Chua, who dressed in women's clothes and went by the name Nelly."*

"God, can they get anything fucking right?" said Casey. Her nose was running again, and she rubbed at it with the collar of her T-shirt.

"It's OK," said June. "We'll go to the vigil tomorrow." She started to put her hand on Casey's shoulder, but Casey whipped away.

"Would you stop *fucking* touching me!"

June retracted her hand and stared at Casey with a smile that looked like a skeleton's.

Ethan turned the volume on the television up.

The three guys were shown with their hands cuffed behind their backs, shuffling down a corridor. The screen then cut to a younger school photo of Nelly with short hair, looking like a boy, and then back to the happy-girl photo.

"He tricked those guys into thinking he was a girl?" said Brad.

"She didn't *trick* anybody," said Casey.

Adam saw silent tears making their way down June's still creepily smiling face. He was pretty sure she wished she could go into her room and cry for real but didn't because that would seem disrespectful to Nelly. Her smile addressed the television.

"But they did it because they thought they were having sex with a girl," said Brad. "I mean, I'm not saying they should have killed her, just . . ."

*Oh god, shut up,* thought Adam.

Casey's eyes narrowed in on Brad. "They had sex with her because they wanted to. No one forced them. There's no reason she had to tell them she was trans."

Brad gave Casey a weirded-out look. "What kind of sex did they even have?"

"Oral and anal," said June softly.

"Look, if I let a girl blow me and then it turned out she had a dick —" said Brad.

"Adam, get your friend the fuck out of here," said Casey.

"Dude, just chill," said Adam.

"What? I'm serious. How'd she even hide that with anal? I'm not saying they should have killed her —"

"I'm *so* happy to hear you don't think she should have been brutally murdered," said Casey. "That's really noble of you."

"Look, all I'm saying," said Brad, "is you shouldn't pretend to be a girl and have sex with guys if you're a dude — you wouldn't understand, it's a straight-guy thing. That can really fuck you up."

"What, because it makes you scared you might be gay?" said Casey.

"Because a straight guy doesn't want to have sex with a man!" said Brad.

"Dude, just shut up," said Adam.

"What? You don't agree? You wouldn't care if a girl blew you and then it turned out she was a *guy?*"

"SHE WASN'T A FUCKING GUY!" screamed Casey.

"She had a PENIS!" Brad shouted back. "I don't care what she called herself. Adam, that would freak you out, right?"

"Just drop it," said Adam.

"I'm just saying, it's messed up to trick a straight guy like that, right, Adam? Come on, back me up, man!"

The truth was Adam knew it would totally freak him out. "Yeah, I guess she could have told them before —"

"I don't tell people before I hook up with them," said Ethan.

Everyone turned toward Ethan. His face was unreadable, blank. A moment of silence passed, and all they could hear was the television.

"What do you mean?" said Adam.

"That I'm trans. I've hooked up with people without telling them."

The first thing Adam felt was a hot wash of shame. Then an acute awareness of Brad sitting next to him. He looked away from Ethan, focused on the floor beneath the futon. There were layers of dust balls down there. He could feel his face burning. Adam looked up at Casey and June, but they were just watching him, curious. They already knew.

Brad started snickering nervously.

Adam looked back at Ethan. All he could see was Ethan as a girl. Naked, sitting in that chair.

"What?" said Ethan.

"Nothing," said Adam. He turned to watch the TV but comprehended nothing, only his brain rewinding back to the first day he met Ethan, all of them sitting around the empty apartment drinking beers, and re-envisioning that moment with the knowledge that Ethan was really a girl. His brain fast-forwarded to him and Ethan in the bathroom, Ethan loaning him his electric razor, but now in the memory Ethan was really a girl. Every interaction, every conversation he'd ever had with Ethan, raced through his brain, memories doubling up on top of other memories, but now with Ethan as trans, Ethan as a girl, Ethan with a vagina.

Ethan stood up, walked into his room, and shut the door.

"So glad you came to visit," Casey said to Brad.

"I asked you," Adam said to Casey.

She knew what he was talking about.

"He asked us not to tell you," she said.

June stood up and walked into her bedroom.

Casey stood up and walked into hers.

Adam went into the bathroom and sat on the toilet just in time as liquid shit poured out of his ass.

Outside, Brad changed the channel.

. . .

Adam lay on top of his sleeping bag, eyes pressed up against the solid hot black. He was coated in sweat. His phone lay on the mattress next to him. Gillian's last text: wish u were in my bed. He kept looking at it, thinking it would make him feel better, but instead it made him feel sick, made the nausea well up. And every time he closed his eyes, as hard as he tried not to, he saw Nelly, someone grabbing at her penis, hitting her over the head with a shovel — Ethan standing naked; Nelly in the grave, bloody face bashed in; Ethan with his legs spread, revealing a vagina. "There's all these weird folds," Adam had said to him, and his body jerked in humiliation, and he punched at the mattress and saw Nelly being fucked in the ass by one of the guys, her own penis getting hard, and then the shovel.

Adam opened his eyes and was back, trapped inside the thick black substance molded to every surface of his body. He thrashed around, wiping his sweat on the sheets.

*Just get some water and chill out, just get some water and chill out.*

He opened his door and walked into the living room toward the bathroom. The lump of Brad was on the futon. Sound asleep. Not a care in the world.

Adam softly padded past him. He opened the door to the bathroom and was about to walk in when he heard Brad chuckle behind him. Adam turned and looked at the dark, amorphous lump.

"So tell me, does Gillian have a dick or something, too? Is that what's going on?" said Brad. Then he chuckled again, shifted, and rolled onto his other side.

# Chapter 14

THE REST OF Brad's visit — five days — was something Adam forced himself to get through. They watched movies at the apartment. They ate pizza at Danny's Pizzeria. They took a tour of the Statue of Liberty because it was something to do, even though neither of them wanted to. They slept late. Till noon, sometimes 1:00 P.M. Both of them just waited for it to be over.

Brad tried to bring up Ethan a few times in a jokey way like, "Dude, so he actually has a pussy down there? That is so fucking weird!" but Adam ignored him and eventually Brad dropped it.

Adam and Ethan barely spoke. They'd see each other around the apartment and each turn the other way. Over and over Adam's brain kept replaying that moment:

*"What do you mean?"*
*"That I'm trans."*
*"What do you mean?"*
*"That I'm trans."*
*"What do you mean?"*
*"That I'm trans."*

All the things Adam had said to him, and what Ethan must have really been thinking. He had no idea who Ethan even was. He wished he had never met him.

A few days later, Rachel arrived.

The first time Adam saw her, she emerged from Ethan's room as if she had crawled out of his computer screen. The living, breathing flesh version of someone Adam realized up until now he hadn't really believed existed. She nodded at Adam, brushed a lock of dark hair out of her eyes, and went straight into the bathroom, head down. After that, she and Ethan were always either locked in his room or out. Why she was here, who had contacted who, what had happened, Adam didn't know. Only that something about their reunion had the haunted air of someone having given up.

The morning after the Nelly Chua night, Adam told Gillian he was going to hang with Brad for the rest of his trip. He couldn't be with the two of them together again. He just couldn't. And the thing was, when he thought about seeing Gillian, even just the two of them, the awful pains in his stomach returned. He had to bend over and clutch it, the cramps were so bad. He couldn't let her know he felt this way though. He had to pretend everything was normal, that Brad was just being a needy brat, so he texted her steadily every day — dumb stuff, like the weirdness of Caesar salad pizza or whether *Reversal of Fortune* was a movie worth watching. The occasional i miss u.

When Brad left, Adam knew their best friendship was over. That when Adam returned to EBP, they probably wouldn't be friends at all. Not with Brad, not with any of them. Eats Big Penis. Enjoys Black Pussy. In one and a half weeks, Adam's summer in New York would be over.

The idea. The precious little idea like an illegal firecracker, buried inside his body, waiting to be lit. That he could just get through the last year in Piedmont and then come back to New York, back to Gillian. This idea itched inside him, demanded to be paid attention to, to be thought out with actual reason and actual determination, rather than the vague, unrealistic generalized hope it had been given until now.

But if he was actually going to do this, if he was going to give this a chance as a possible future, a future where they were really, truly together — he knew he would have to tell her.

. . .

The minute Adam closed the door behind Brad, he pulled out his phone and called Gillian. His heart felt like a separate being from the rest of his body, the way it banged up against his chest, trying to break free and run somewhere, anywhere else, *Get me the fuck out of here!* He was going to do it. He was going to tell her tonight.

"Hey! Brad's gone! Wanna hang out?"

"Sure."

Adam suggested they hang at her place and watch a movie, but Gillian said Claire and Lauren were having Lauren's cousin and his girlfriend over for dinner, and she kind of wanted to get out of there.

"Why don't we hang at yours?" she said.

There was something slightly accusatory in the way she said it. Or maybe Adam was just paranoid.

"Let's hang at yours," she said again.

Adam paused. "Sure."

They hung up and Adam walked promptly into the bathroom to stare at himself in the mirror.

In three hours she would know, and his life would either be over or a version of bliss he couldn't yet comprehend.

By the time Gillian was supposed to arrive, it was dark out and Adam was posed on the futon by the table lamp's faint glow, reading and rereading page 61 of Casey's copy of *Grapes of Wrath*. It was kind of pointless to pretend to be reading since he was going to get up to buzz Gillian in and open the door anyway, but the act made him feel calm and serious, and fit the tone of what was about to happen more than some cracked-out reality TV show blasting in his face. Casey was at Hazel's (they were back together, sort of ); June was in her room, probably writing the pros and cons of various suicide methods; and Ethan and Rachel were out.

The doorbell buzzed, and Adam's heart lurched into action, attempting its panicked escape again.

*You don't have to tell her immediately,* he told himself. *Wait till the moment is right.*

"Hi!" he said, opening the door.

"Hey."

Adam leaned in to kiss Gillian and she kissed him back, but there was something stiff about her body. Or was there? Maybe she was always like that. It had been five days. The longest they'd been apart since they'd met. He'd grown used to imagining her face, and this real face, in its hyper-detail and space-filling three-dimensionality, looked alien.

"I brought this," she said, handing him a DVD of the Mark Wahlberg movie *Invincible* that was out in theaters. "It looks dumb, but Claire bought a bootleg copy in the subway, so."

"Cool!" said Adam.

He would tell her after the movie. They would get cozy and comfortable, and he would tell her when the movie was over. He hoped the movie had a happy, inspiring, man-who-beats-all-odds ending and *not* a bummed-out "life is sorrowful but we persevere regardless, I guess" ending. He needed to tell her while they were feeling happy and inspired and like anything in this crazy life was possible. Of course, the movie *was* called *Invincible* and starred Mark Wahlberg, so he was pretty sure things were on his side.

They settled onto the futon, and Adam waited for Gillian to snuggle up close to him, the way she usually did. But she stayed on her side, knees pulled up to her chin. He hadn't planned on them making out until he told her, but he'd thought they would at least cuddle. He was strapped up with the ACE bandage because even cuddling made him hard, and when he did tell her, it needed to come from his mouth and not some *Surprise!* penis poking out of his jeans.

The opening credits began with a crooning '70s song. Kids in bell-bottoms and puffy down vests ran through backyards and jumped up and down on rooftops, water towers in the background.

Adam picked up the DVD sleeve and scanned it: 104 minutes. Almost two hours. How was he going to get through this? His heart still knocked away inside him, though less aggressively now (no violent escape plan, just a mentally ill inmate compulsively rapping on his cell wall, *"Excuse me? May I please leave? I'd like to leave now"*). His stomach twitched and twisted with the awful pains as well. His body was falling apart and just fucking telling her was the only thing that could restore it to normal — 102 minutes to go.

"Hey, are you Gillian?"

June was standing before them.

"Yeah, hi," said Gillian. She reached out to shake June's hand.

"I've heard a lot about you," said June. "I mean, only good stuff. It's great to finally meet you."

"Oh, yeah, you too."

June smiled. It was the smile of a depressed person. The way Adam's aunt Susan always smiled. Like congratulating someone on getting engaged after you've just been diagnosed with brain cancer. But it was a kind smile. June really did seem sort of excited to meet Gillian. Adam felt a surprising brief glow inside himself. June cared about his life. He felt unbelievably sad for her. *I'm sorry,* he said inside his head.

"I just wanted to say," June continued, turning to Adam and lowering her voice. "That I'm sorry about the thing with Ethan . . ."

He wasn't sure why she was talking so soft, since Ethan wasn't even home.

"I mean, I think it was right to respect what he wanted . . . but it just sucked for you to find out like that, like we all shared some secret you couldn't know. It shouldn't have been like that."

"Thanks . . ." said Adam.

June nodded her head. "Really cool to meet you," she said again to Gillian, and walked back into her room. Music started playing.

"June's cool," said Gillian.

Adam could tell she felt guilty too, for all the times they'd trashed June just to have something to laugh about together.

"What was she talking about?" Gillian asked.

And Adam realized this was his in. It had to be. He would tell her about Ethan being trans, which would lead to: *"Speaking of being trans . . ."* A prickling sensation scattered over his skin as his intestines expertly formed a fisherman's knot. He pressed pause on the DVD, and Mark Wahlberg froze mid-sprint across the football tryouts field.

"Do you wanna go in my room?" said Adam. His voice cracked, nervously. God, he was so fucking obvious.

"Um, sure," said Gillian. "Is everything OK?"

"Yeah," he said. He tried to regain control of his voice and steady it. "Just better to tell you in private."

They walked into his room, and Adam turned on the swivel-head office lamp on the floor. Gillian slipped off her sandals and sat on the mattress. Adam shut the door and joined her.

"Well . . . ?" she said.

It occurred to Adam that maybe he should kiss her a little bit first. Something seemed off between them, and that wasn't the way it was supposed to be when he told her. Before he had been relying on the happy, inspiring end of the movie to set the mood, but now they had fast-forwarded to the moment of it happening, and it needed to feel right, but something about now just didn't feel right.

"I missed you," he said. He leaned over and put his hands on her bare knees, his lips on hers, but she didn't respond. He inched back and smiled, but Gillian's face stayed impassive.

"So what was June talking about?" said Gillian. Her voice was cold.

*Could it be possible she already knew?*

"Well, like, you know the night of Nelly Chua . . . ?"

Gillian nodded, her face now exhibiting the appropriate mixed emotion of sorrow and righteous anger. Why had he brought up Nelly Chua? That was not the mood he wanted to set. He tried to start over.

"Ethan and I were hella tight, and then I found out everyone knew he was trans except me; he was lying to me the whole time."

Gillian gave Adam a confused look. "Did he know you were?"

Adam paused. He stared down at his sheets. He could still see come stains in various spots where he'd been lazy cleaning up. Each of them, at the moment of ejaculation, in his imagination, had gone inside Gillian. She was going to despise him.

"It's not that I care that he is. Obviously. I'm just mad about how I found out. Like, he just announced it in front of all these other people who already knew, and it made me feel stupid."

A lie. Adam did care that Ethan used to be a girl. The truth was it changed everything.

"But did he know you were?"

That accusatory tone again. *She knew. Did she?*

"I mean, I understand if he had his reasons for not telling me at first. I think that completely makes sense, if someone —"

"So he didn't know you were trans?"

"No, um, he knew all about me."

Gillian wrapped her arms around her knees, the way she had on the futon. "So why would he care? That's weird."

"I know."

Adam needed to get this out. It was getting too convoluted.

"Well, you know," he continued, "I think everyone has their

own reasons for waiting to tell someone something like that, you know? Like, sometimes when you first meet someone, you know they think of you a certain way, and so you let them keep on thinking that, because you want them to like you, you know?"

"Yeah . . ." Gillian picked at her toenail. Every part of her body was gorgeous, but she picked her toenails, and they were always a jagged, blood-crusty mess.

"And you want to tell them, but then it just feels like the right moment never comes . . ."

"And it's kind of like, 'What's the point, maybe I should just keep it how it is,'" she said.

"Yeah, exactly!"

"Even though it feels superficial . . ."

"Yeah."

"Or sometimes it's like you don't want to have to tell the person, like you want them to know, you want them to just *ask*."

"Yes!" said Adam.

The front door to the apartment slammed shut. Footsteps toward Ethan's room. He and Rachel were home.

"Is that how you think Ethan felt about telling you?" said Gillian.

*What were they talking about?*

"Yeah, I think he was, you know, scared to tell me."

"Have you guys talked about it since you found out?"

"Not really."

"You should go talk to him."

"What?"

"Was that him coming home?"

"Uh, yeah, I think so."

"You should talk to him."

So the next thing Adam knew, instead of telling Gillian, he was walking out of his room and knocking on Ethan's closed door.

No response.

Faint music. Adam knocked a little harder.

Still no response. Adam knocked harder.

Ethan opened the door. "Fuck. Off." Then he closed it.

Adam stared at the closed door for a moment, then turned around and walked back to his room.

Gillian was sitting in the same position, picking at her toe. "What happened?" she said.

"Oh, it was fine. He was just in the middle of something."

Gillian didn't respond.

Adam needed to get back on the subject. He needed to do this and fucking do it tonight. But not with her cold like this. Why was she being like this? She had never been like this. He thought about Gillian laughing, Gillian with her rosy dimples, Gillian grabbing his T-shirt and opening her mouth as she kissed him. Why wasn't she like that? What was going on?

Adam scooted close to her and put his hand gently over her foot.

"You're gonna give yourself gangrene."

She didn't laugh.

He leaned in to kiss her, and she sort of kissed him back. But something was still wrong. He put his hands over her arms and pulled her down onto the bed, opened his mouth wider, tried to push his tongue deep in her mouth, the way she liked. She let him do it, but she just lay there. He put his hands under her shirt, tried to start breathing heavy, put his hand under her bra, his knee between her legs — she let him do all of it, but she didn't do it back: she was a rag doll, a corpse bride; she was dead.

"What's wrong?" he asked, barely above a whisper. He didn't want to know.

"I think I want to go home," she said. And she sat up, put her sandals on, and walked out of his room.

# Chapter 15

ADAM WOKE UP to bright sun, girl music, and Gillian and Jackie talking in the front seat. He was squeezed in the back of Jackie's car with Lionel and someone named Riverrun, and they had been driving all night, headed to the woods of Michigan for "Camp Trans."

The night Gillian had gotten up and left, Adam had lain on his mattress, staring into space, trying to figure out what was going on. *Why was she acting like this? What had changed? What was Gillian thinking?* The way he saw it, there were three possible explanations.

One: She knew he was lying about being trans and was furious, but wanted him to admit it before she brought it up.

Two: She had decided she was really gay and didn't want to be with a boy, trans or otherwise, but didn't know how to tell him.

Three: She just plain didn't like him anymore.

Adam had stayed up that night until 4:00 A.M. looking up information on the Internet about every college in New York City, how hard they were to get into and when their applications were due. Acting as if, despite everything, this was still the plan — and all he had to do was put it into action — was the only thing that made him feel better.

The next morning he had called Gillian and pretended the

weirdness had never happened. He rambled, "Did you know Hunter only counts math and critical reading SATs, and their average is only 1197? They have two deadlines for application — February 1st and September 15th — so I could conceivably start this spring! There's also Eugene Lang, but it's a little harder to get into, but not like NYU or anything. Brooklyn College is easier, but . . ." It was the first time he'd said anything about returning to New York not in the safe, jokey tone. And Gillian had said, "Yeah, that sounds great, cool; Lauren's friend Jessamine goes to Eugene Lang," and Adam had tried to make a joke about "What kind of name is Jessamine?" but Gillian ignored it and her voice was distant, off, still cold.

He'd clutched his phone and wished she would scream at him and tell him she hated him, but just tell him *why*. But instead she also acted as if everything was normal, even though it obviously wasn't, and she said she knew they didn't have much time before he had to leave New York, but Jackie and Lionel were going to Camp Trans for the weekend and it sounded fun and maybe they should go too? And because Adam was the North American authority on all things trans, he knew that Camp Trans was an annual grass-roots demonstration in the woods coinciding with the Michigan Womyn's Music Festival, protesting their policy, which doesn't allow trans women into the festival, and he said, "Yeah, of course, Camp Trans is really important," and had hung up more confused than ever.

Riverrun smelled god-awful. He was a shrimpy guy (trans, duh), dressed in rags held together by string, with feathers sticking out of his hair and dangling from his ears. He also had giant combat boots, which he'd taken off, and his raw feet soaked pungently in the sun, planted on the divider between the two front seats. Adam didn't know how Jackie or Gillian knew him, just that Jackie and Nadia had broken up, so there was a free seat in Jackie's car and Riverrun had taken it.

"But what they don't understand is that I'm just a little nelly boy, a fairy, like them," said Riverrun.

"Let's play the festie game," said Gillian.

"No . . ." said Lionel, emerging from sleep and putting his pillow over his head. "The festie game is triggering for me."

"But we have to play the festie game! It's part of it! And people might really ask us," said Gillian.

"What's the festie game?" said Adam.

Gillian turned around to look at him. "Oh. You're awake." Then she turned back.

Adam had thought once Gillian and Jackie picked him up in the car last night, everything would be fun and filled with the spirit of a road trip, and he and Gillian would be in the back together, cuddling and kissing. But he felt as if he were drowning, and now there were, like, a million other people there too. He wondered if they could feel the weirdness between him and Gillian.

"OK, you be the Camp Trans person, and I'll be the festie," Gillian said to Jackie.

"Yeah, yeah," said Jackie.

"Um, this is a festival for women-born-women, why can't you just accept that? Start your own festival if you want to." Gillian put on a high, whiny voice for the part.

"It's a festival for women," answered Jackie, who sounded bored. "By excluding trans women you're making a statement that trans women aren't women, which affects the policies of other women-only spaces like shelters and clinics, which are imperative to trans women's safety and health."

"It's just a *music* festival. *God.* And besides, I was raped — can't I have at least one safe space for one week out of the year where I know I won't have to see a penis? If I saw a trans woman in the shower, it could be really triggering for me."

"Trans women are not interested in flaunting themselves," Jackie droned on, "and plenty of women at the festival use very realistic strap-ons. This is about your own fear that trans women are really men. It's a harmless body part."

"I'm not saying they're men, but can't there be a place just for women-born-women? There *is* a difference; we've had different experiences growing up."

"All people have had different experiences growing up."

"But it's just one music festival! I totally support trans women; just let me have my one music festival! I wanna see Le Tigre!"

Gillian's voice had moved into a shrill singsong. She was really getting into her character. She was having *so much fun,* while completely ignoring Adam, squished in the back next to a "fairy" whose hairy, rotting-vegetables-at-the-bottom-of-a-garbage-bin armpits were now shoved in Adam's face as Riverrun expanded all his limbs across the back seat. For the first time, Adam felt hate toward Gillian.

. . .

Camp Trans was a sparse affair. A handful of mismatched tents lay scattered across a clearing of dry, yellowed grass. Campers in jean shorts and patchy, mohawked hair milled around.

Adam, Gillian, Jackie, Lionel, and Riverrun, sleeping bags and two tents strapped to their backs, headed toward the makeshift Welcome Tent. An attractive girl wearing a halter top and a cowboy hat jumped up to greet them, quickly launching into the rules and regulations of the camp.

"You can set your tents up anywhere you like. Camping spaces are designated as Non-sober with Sex, Non-sober with No Sex, Sober with Sex, and Sober with No Sex."

"A lot of people in the Sober with No Sex section?" joked Jackie.

"I don't know," said Cowboy Hat, "I'm in Non-sober with Sex," and her eyes swung over to Adam. Adam looked at Gillian, but she couldn't care less, was engrossed in a pamphlet about Lyme disease on the counter. *I'm gonna fucking cheat on you,* he thought. But he didn't even want to. All he wanted was Gillian.

Cowboy Hat trumpeted on. "Everyone needs to sign up for a work shift on the schedule. Welcome Tent slots are filled, but we could really, really use Waste Disposal." The way she said it, everyone pretty much had to put their name down under Waste Disposal, which was empty. Everyone except Jackie, who wrote her name in large capital letters under Medic Tent. Adam noticed "Casey Freedman" scrawled under Cooking. He knew she would be here. Casey had been chattering about Camp Trans for weeks, and when Adam had told her he was going as well with Gillian and her crew, Casey had balked.

"*You're* going to Camp Trans?"

"You know Gillian's bi, and she has a lot of trans friends; it's important to her."

"I know, it just feels like you're appropriating my entire life. . . . Well, at least I'll finally get to meet her."

Adam had been anxious, charged with adrenaline to negotiate this inevitable encounter. But now, here, he didn't even care. If Casey met Gillian and blurted something out, or Gillian said something or whatever, so be it. At least it would all be fucking over, and he could finally give up.

"What's this?" said Lionel. He was looking at a piece of paper tacked to the post of the Welcome Tent. Cowboy Hat laughed.

"That's just a little running contest between our lead organizer Hazel and her sub, Blaise, on who can bed more campers. Hazel's winning."

Casey was off in her own world of turmoil, anyway. No longer the special siblings that good things happen to, but the rejected ones, trailing pathetically after the objects of their desires, each following some sinister bread-crumb trail into the deep woods of Michigan, only to be told: *"No, I'm sorry. I just don't want you. What are you even doing here?"*

The gang trudged in the direction of the campsites to set up.

"Why are you being so weird and quiet?" Gillian said to Adam in that same cold, flat tone.

"I'm not," said Adam, staring ahead.

*Fuck you. Fuck. You.*

...

Everyone at Camp Trans, around twenty people, stood in a circle at the center of the clearing, holding hands.

"Jordan, 'he.'"

"Alyssa, 'she.'"

"Deirdre, 'she.'"

You were supposed to state your name and preferred gender pronoun. Clarification on gender was indeed necessary. Looking around at the group, it was as if a hatful of pronouns written on scraps of paper had been thrown into the air, each scrap, sometimes two, landing randomly on a person, regardless of what he or she looked like. Adam had gotten used to boyish girls turning out to be trans, the general rule that masculine = he and feminine = she, but here at Camp Trans it was a free-for-all. You couldn't be sure of anything, except that you were most likely wrong.

"Blaise, 'he or she.'"

"Jackie, 'she.'"

"Riverrun, 'ze.'"

"Adam, 'he.'"

Casey, who was three people in the circle down from Adam, looked at him with a stifled smirk. He stuck his tongue out at her (would've given the finger but didn't want to break the hand-holding circle), and then they both had to look at the ground to keep from laughing.

After the pronoun circle, Casey walked up to Adam and Gillian. Adam felt himself tense up. *Just let it happen. Just get it all fucking out there.*

"This is my sister, Casey," he said.

"Cool, great to meet you," said Gillian. She seemed barely interested. All those times: *"When do I get to meet your sister? When do I get to meet your sister?"* And now it was happening, and she didn't even give a shit.

"Fucking Camp Trans," said Casey, as if she'd been coming for years and was totally over the place.

"You look kind of familiar," said Gillian.

*Yeah, you watched her get fucked on a cross at Bound, bitch,* thought Adam. Bound. The night they first. A crashing sadness.

"Carlisle's party," said Casey. "Isn't that where you met Adam?"

"Oh, yeah," said Gillian.

"Casey," shouted Hazel. She was standing a few feet away, dressed in a black tank top and cut-off cargo pants, holding a bullhorn, looking impatient.

Casey's jaded affect instantly transformed into eager desire to please. She ran toward Hazel, shouting over her shoulder, "See you guys later." Hazel had already begun walking away before Casey reached her.

"The fat-phobia caucus is now taking place in zone four," Hazel shouted into her bullhorn. "Fat phobia. Zone four."

The great climactic moment of his sister and Gillian meeting had come and gone like nothing. Adam had a vision of himself on his hospital deathbed, a disgusting old man, his whole life having come and gone like nothing.

"Everyone's headed down to the swimmin' hole!" It was Lionel, running toward them in swim trunks and a T-shirt, carrying a towel.

"What about the fat-phobia caucus?" said Jackie. "I thought we were going to that?"

Jackie was kind of overweight, and Adam felt a flush of embarrassment for her.

"Yeah, that's happening," said Lionel. He glanced over at a

group of about four fat people and one skinny person sitting in a circle in the grass. "But if we don't go now, it'll get too cold for swimmin'. Don't you guys wanna go swimmin'?"

"Yeah, fuck it, let's go swimming," said Jackie.

They followed a group of Camp Transers carrying towels and inner tubes. The group walked along the dusty shoulder of the road, butted up next to a hill of forest and against the traffic of occasional cars driving through.

A girl carrying a long fluorescent orange noodle sidled up to Gillian. "There's room on this noodle for two," she said.

*Who the fuck was this bitch?*

Gillian laughed. "That is a nice-looking noodle."

"*Mi* noodle *es su* noodle."

*Was that supposed to be clever?*

The girl ran her fingers through her choppy brown hair and adjusted the noodle over her shoulders like it was one of those wooden planks with heavy pails of water on either end. She projected her chest out and flexed her arm muscles as if she were actually carrying some great heavy weight.

"I'm Erica, by the way."

"Gillian," said Gillian.

Erica didn't ask who Adam was, and Gillian didn't introduce him.

They got to "the Swimmin' Hole," which was a small, craggy cove inside the forest, leading out into a sprawling still lake. It had been sunny when they first arrived at the camp, but now the day had turned overcast, the horizon of the lake meshing seamlessly into the gray sky. Everyone acted like it was still the brightest, sunshiniest day, though, and began tearing off their clothes and running into the water, whooping and hollering.

Adam sat down on a rock, and Gillian sat next to him. Piece-of-shit-I-hope-you-burn-in-hell-Erica took off her tank top, sports bra, shorts, and underwear, with overly cavalier action. She stood, presenting her nakedness, as in, *Yeah, I'm straight-up naked now, you like?* She smiled at Gillian.

"You coming?"

Erica had tits. She had a vagina. And as Adam stared at her with seething hatred, he simultaneously imagined his penis inside her and the unconditional exquisite pleasure he would feel.

"In a bit," said Gillian.

It was just him and Gillian on the rock. The first time they'd (sort of) been alone since that night in his room. Neither of them spoke. The campers frolicked and splashed in the lake. Hit one another with noodles and jumped, four at a time, onto sinking inner tubes. The only other person not in the water was a man in a dress sitting higher up on the rocks, strumming a duct-taped acoustic guitar. The way he was sitting with the dress hiked up, you could see his full dick and balls hanging out, splayed across the rock like some reptile trying to warm its cold-blooded body.

*"It's not my fault you don't like that I'm wearing a dress,"* the man in the dress sang.

*She's the one that's being a bitch,* thought Adam. *She should speak first, not me.*

More silence passed.

"Well, this is awkward," said Gillian, and Adam wanted to strangle her and slam her head on the rock, because she said it coldly, not in a way he could actually respond to, not a sweet, "Hey? What's going on with us?," just a flat, toneless, "This is awkward," and it wasn't fair — how was he supposed to respond?

"Yeah," he said.

"I think I'm gonna go in," she said.

Most everyone in the water was naked. A few people were still wearing underwear or swim bottoms, but everyone was topless. Loose-hanging surgery scars on the trans guys, buds of breasts on girls you could tell used to be boys, low-hanging udders on lesbians who were probably, like June, politically opposed to wearing bras. All these fucked-up bodies that most people in the world would call repulsive but here were celebrated. The bodies were bodies, and they were made to have fun.

"Think I'm just gonna stay here," said Adam. If he didn't take his shirt off, it might be conspicuous. *"What's that trans guy's problem? Why's he being so precious? Just take it off, man. We're all brothers and sisters here."*

"Well, I'm going in," said Gillian. She stood up and, with her back facing Adam, took her clothes off.

He stared at the ground. It hurt too much to watch. He wanted her so badly. He loved her so helplessly. He looked up and she was already in the water. She'd kept her bra and underwear on. *Good,* he thought. As if that made a difference, as if it were a sign she was still his. Erica was making her way over. Doing that labored, wide-legged gait everyone's forced to do when trying to walk fast through water.

Gillian's slim, pale body, a will-o'-the-wisp in the midst of everything. Adam felt a pang of desire. Hers was the body the world at large wanted — whether it was to fuck or possess, they all wanted it. That was what she owned.

Gillian and Erica were now talking. Erica was clearly checking out Gillian's body, and Gillian was doing the same. He wondered if she was getting wet looking at Erica. If her clit was swelling up and getting hard the way it did.

*Fucking dykes,* Adam thought.

Maybe Gillian really was just gay. Just wanted to shove her mouth on another girl's cunt, and nothing else could really compare.

Erica put her hands around Gillian's waist.

*How could she just fucking let that happen? He was sitting right fucking there, watching it like a goddamn movie. Did she just not give a fucking shit?*

She was gay. She liked girls. She had experimented with Adam and decided, *"Eh, not for me."*

*"I just think I actually really need to be with a girl,"* she would finally tell him.

He thought about the stuffed folders she had shown him full of all the letters from all the gay teens across the world who had written her and e-mailed her after her prom story in the AP article came out. *"Thank you for literally saving my life"* and *"I know I don't know you, but I have a huge crush on you"* and *"I didn't know how to tell my parents, but I showed them the article and you told them for me. Thank you." "Thank you!"* They were all signed *"Thank you."* And he imagined Gillian and Erica, falling onto her bed, all the letters spread out across the sheets, like the million dollars cash in *Indecent Proposal,* and Gillian and Erica fucking, the letters flying around them like all those hundred-dollar bills.

He looked down. His white Adidas were caked in mud. The feeling that he wanted to cry but knew he couldn't — a dull butter knife trying to puncture the back of his throat. He looked up, expecting the worst, and was grateful to see they were separated now. Gillian was talking to Jackie, and Erica was floating on her noodle, off somewhere else.

*I just want you back,* he tried to beam from his brain into hers.

...

Someone had started up the campfire, and its leaping flames and heavy smoke smell against the cooling twilight in the woods gave Adam a cozy feeling, despite the sadness like an anvil on his chest.

Gillian was on her Waste Disposal shift, and not knowing what to do with himself, Adam sat on a log and watched the fire. He was that guy, the weirdo staring into the fire, probably coming to terms with all his past mistakes and making silent vows for a stronger, braver future. He felt self-conscious but also kind of didn't care. Everyone here was already so weird, it almost made sense to just stare into the fire, a creepy force field of "private moment" around you.

"Excuse me, would you like some dinner?"

Adam looked up. A short boy — or girl — with a bandanna around his neck was standing a few feet away holding out a bowl. He was respecting Adam's "space."

"Um, sure," said Adam. He stood up and took the bowl and spoon. "Thanks." The boy smiled and nodded, then turned around, leaving Adam to his moment.

Adam sat back down and looked into the bowl. It was so dark out by now, he had no idea what was in there. He tilted the bowl toward the fire and caught flickers of something gray and grainy. He stuck the spoon in and brought a little toward his tongue.

"It's millet," said Casey, plunking down beside him, almost knocking Adam over, like she was drunk, but he knew it was just that she was clumsy and often not aware of where her body was actually going. She didn't care about giving him "space." His space was her space, and he felt a pulse of love for her. They had both rattled around in their mom's uterus. Disgusting really, but they both had been there. And no one else in the world had.

"What the fuck is millet?" he said.

"It's good for you," said Casey, heaping a large spoonful into her mouth. "Just imagine you're lost out here, have been wandering for days, and came upon some natives brewing a special 'of the land' porridge in their cauldron, and they're offering it to you, and it's the first food you've eaten in a week and the most glorious thing you've ever tasted. That's what I'm doing."

Adam ran the fantasy quickly through his head and took a bite. Not bad.

Hazel's voice rang out from a cluster of campers. "The word got out and what I'm hearing from my people inside is that the Camp Trans dance party tonight is *the* event at the Michigan Womyn's Music Festival."

A skinny trans guy with large round glasses ran in front of Adam and Casey toward the group.

"Oh, no. Are you telling me that upward of *one thousand people* are going to be coming here tonight?!" said Round Glasses.

Adam had gathered that along with Hazel, Round Glasses was "in charge."

"What we need to focus on right now is how to make this a safe space for trans women," said Hazel. "I think the campfire and zones one and two should be 'No Wristband.'"

"That's not very welcoming to festies," said another girl. "It's supposed to be about inclusion. We're not setting an example if —"

"All I care about right now is protecting my girls," said Hazel, and she stormed off. Her face glowed in the campfire light for a flash, and it looked like she was crying. The girl named Blaise ran after her.

"You want to go?" Adam said to Casey, nodding after Hazel.

"No . . . We had a 'talk' in her tent," said Casey. "We're, like, officially unofficial."

"Oh. Sorry . . ."

"It's OK," said Casey. "After what I did to June, I probably deserve it."

They were quiet for a moment. Adam thought about June. What was she doing right now? Home alone in her room? Taking one of her baths? Staring in the mirror in the same position as Adam always did? He kind of wished she were here. He thought about Ethan and then put the thought away. He stared out across the campsite, trying to see if he could find Gillian. He couldn't. Only the scarce, crookedly constructed tents and dark dapples of people moving. The sky had gone completely dark. If you looked up, you could see stars. He'd forgotten all about them — like, as a thing that existed. In New York the stars were the lights on cars and buildings, the mysterious sparkles on some of the sidewalks. He thought about him and Gillian, running down the sidewalk, escaping Bound, and how they'd kissed on the street corner and how for that moment, their bodies pressed together, it had felt like they were standing on the exact center of the world. He kept looking out at the camp but still couldn't find any shape that might be her. Hopelessness descended.

"I'm going to tell Mom and Dad," said Casey.

"What?"

"That I'm gay."

"I thought you were 'queer'?"

"Shut up."

"You're the one that said it!"

"Whatever . . . I'm going to tell them I like girls. Women."

"Why?"

"Because lying is stupid. And lonely."

They were silent for a while more. Adam saw a future in which he never told Gillian. He just returned to Piedmont and they never spoke again. No one would ever know what he had done. He would die with it. Alone.

"I never should have let Mom talk about Sam the way she did," said Casey. "I should have told her we were girlfriends. That Sam was butch, not 'confused.' That that's what I like."

"Why do you like boyish girls?" Adam asked.

"I just do," Casey said. "I can't explain it, and I know a lot of people don't get it, but I just think masculine women are the sexiest people on earth."

Adam thought Casey might ask him something about Gillian then. What their plans were. If they were going to keep dating after the summer. If he was going to have to tell her his real age. But she didn't.

"I can't believe I ate this entire bowl of millet," Casey said. She stared into her empty bowl. Adam hadn't touched his after that one bite.

"I'm going to go throw up in the woods now," she said. She smiled at Adam, and stood up and walked away.

...

The rally had begun, soon to be followed by the dance party. Upward of one thousand people from the Womyn's Festival across the road had not shown up. Maybe about fifteen festies were there, and they trailed in a line with Hazel leading, shouting, "One word! One word! That word is INCLUSION!" Someone was beating a drum.

The festies and the Camp Transers formed a circle, and Adam, Gillian, Jackie, and Lionel, who had been standing and watching, joined. Hazel walked into the center.

"We're gonna win this thing!" Hazel shouted. She wasn't using the bullhorn, probably because there were only about thirty people. "Maybe not next year, and maybe not the year after that, but we are GOING TO WIN!"

Everyone cheered.

Jackie stood next to Adam, then some person named Pirate, then Gillian. Gillian hadn't even tried to stand next to him. They'd barely spoken three words since the swimming hole.

"They're never gonna win," Jackie said to Adam in a low voice.

"What?"

"Lisa Vogel is never going to change the policy. She's said, 'Over my dead body will the policy be changed.' Or something like that. But I guess it's important to make a statement."

"Yeah," said Adam.

"Think you'll come back next year?"

"I'm not sure."

He was finding it difficult to talk. The pain in his body was so loud, it drowned out any noise coming from his mouth. He felt acutely aware of how his mouth had to move in specific positions in order to make different words. The glowing green bulb of the subway had meant that anything was possible.

A group of people in the middle of the circle was performing a skit. Adam couldn't really follow it, something about various kinds of people being turned away from Man Land and Woman-Born-Woman Land. And a trans woman being turned away from both. Everyone started clapping before the punch line came, and it was awkward when the group had to tack on the last couple lines after the applause quieted down.

"Portrait of the man as a young girl."

It was the boy with the bandanna who had given Adam the bowl of millet. Now he was standing in the center, holding a piece of paper and reading from it. His body had a jaunty swagger, but Adam could see that his hands holding the paper were trembling.

"When I told my parents I was a boy, they said it felt like someone had died . . . which is kind of funny because I felt like I had finally been born."

Adam wondered how old the boy was. How long he'd had to wait to finally be born. For the first time, it occurred to Adam how alienating it must be to grow up in a body you don't recognize as your own. Like people with brain injuries who can't recognize their mother's face. In all Adam's research and cramming of trans facts, he'd never thought about how that singular experience actually felt. And here was this boy, with his shaking hands, trying to explain to you, and probably himself, what it was like.

The boy finished his poem and left the circle to more applause. He had a huge sheepish smile on his face.

Next, a short girl with a blond ponytail entered the circle.

"Julia Serano!" Hazel called out.

"This one's for Nelly Chua," the girl named Julia said. And everyone roared and stamped their feet.

"We are often told that we are living in a man's world," she shouted in a bold voice, "and in this culture no image represents power more than the phallic symbol, and if the penis equals power, then I am illegally armed."

Julia was also reading from a piece of paper, but no part of her was trembling. She stood with her feet planted square and looked around the circle, her gaze seeming to cast light on each person she turned her head toward.

"They say it's not the size of the wand but the magic that it does. Well, after months on estrogen, my penis is pretty darn small, but she has supernatural powers, she's like some pissed-off ancient Greek goddess, and she can make the most entitled cat-callers and womanizers scurry away with their tails between their legs all because of six small words: 'I used to be a man.' And that may make me an object of ridicule, but I am not the butt of any-one's jokes because I know people make fun of trannies because we are the one thing they fear the most. I am more bad-ass than any gangster, more dangerous than an entire Marine Corps; my penis is more powerful than the cocks of a million alpha males all put together."

The circle grew tighter and stronger. Through the flickering dark, Adam could see people beating their chests. Their eyes fixed on Julia, riveted, like she was finally explaining to them everything they'd ever wanted to know.

"See, my penis can be deadly, especially to me, and I've heard almost every true crime story about what frightened macho boys do to trannies, every bludgeoning and mutilation, bodies beaten beyond recognition —"

"We love you, Nelly!" someone shouted.

"— and I've imagined it all happening to me first person. I can feel myself morph into a slow-moving target, and when I walk to my car alone in the dark, I'll be holding my breath, half expect-ing that inevitable blow to the back of my head, and sometimes I wonder why it hasn't happened yet, and sometimes I wonder why they don't just get it over with —"

Adam felt something huge rushing through him, taking over his body.

"— See, I never wanted to be dangerous, and I spent most of my life wishing that I didn't have a penis, and some mornings I can barely get out of bed because my body is so weighed down with ugly meanings that my culture has dumped all over me — see, I've been made to feel shame and self-loathing so that everyone else can take comfort in what their bodies mean. And if I seem a bit cocky, well, it's because I refuse to make apologies for my body anymore."

And the people were cheering and throwing their fists in the air, and before he knew it, Adam found himself screaming, *"Whooo!"* and stomping his feet and clapping as hard as he could because he felt it, he really did, and he knew he was sad, and he knew he had thought his life was over, but in that moment, with Julia in front of him, shouting out at the crowd and everyone in the circle cheering as one, saying, *"Fuck you"* to the haters, *"we are all different and that is fucking awesome,"* he felt happy and lucky — lucky to be part of this.

"Some women have a penis, some men don't, and the rest of the world is just going to have to get the fuck over it!" yelled Julia, and she marched out of the circle as everyone went wild.

Adam looked over and saw Gillian. She was looking at him too, and he knew, he just knew, she was thinking what he was. With his heart thudding, he walked toward her.

"Hey," he said.

"Hey," she said.

She was still hiding something, there was still a thing *wrong,* but her face was softer, something had changed, and he knew there was a chance. They just needed to talk.

"Do you want to go back out to the lake?" Adam asked.

"OK," said Gillian.

They began walking away from the campsite just as the music started blasting.

"Now let's have a fucking DANCE PARTY!!" someone shouted into the bullhorn.

They walked along the same path on the shoulder of the road as they had this afternoon. Now there were no cars driving by, and everything was dark and still. Just the forest sounds and music and yells from back at the camp.

"Did you eat the millet?" said Adam.

"Tried," said Gillian. "Someone gave Jackie a peanut butter and Nutella sandwich they'd brought, and she gave me half."

They kept walking, moments of silence interspersed with random comments — "I wonder if more people from the festival are actually coming" — and even though it was stilted and definitely weird, Adam could feel hope all around them, pushing them along, urging them toward the lake, where for some reason he felt they needed to go.

When they got to the rocky cove, Adam could only make out hints of how it had looked earlier. Most of the land was mottled gray and indecipherable, but the lake spread out before them under the moon, an endless glistening black.

"Let's go in," said Gillian. She took off her shorts but kept her shirt on, and walked toward the water. Adam did the same. He folded his jeans and put them on a rock. He'd been wearing the ACE bandage for over twenty-four hours, and it hung loose but still functional around his hips, under his boxers.

"Eek!" Gillian said, her customary exclamation, as she stepped her foot into the water. And for that moment, her voice sounded normal again. Just her. Adam's heart squeezed at the sound.

"Ack! It *is* cold," he said, stepping in. More than cold, the craggy, barnacled surface of the lake bed punctured at the soft pads of his feet. It was kind of excruciatingly painful.

"I'm going in!" Gillian said, and she dove into the water, immediately swimming as hard as she could out toward the middle of the lake.

Adam dove in too and, after the brief shock of cold, the water felt delicious all over his limbs. He dunked his head with a splash, and everything went dark for a moment; then he burst back out, and it was fresh and cool as the water evaporated off his face and the lake looked brighter than ever, a startling iridescence. All he could see was the infinite water and the looming sky above and the small black dot of Gillian bobbing ahead of him. He dove back in and swam toward her.

"Let's play Open Water," said Gillian as he approached.

"Open Water?"

"Like the movie," she said. "We pretend we're in *Open Water*."

*Open Water* was a movie that had come out a couple years ago about a couple who go on a tourist snorkeling trip and end up stranded in the open water. Adam hadn't seen it, but the trailer had given him chills. The sharks could come at any moment.

"It's after the storm where we lose the group and we get separated from each other," Gillian instructed. "I'll go over there." She splashed back in and began swimming at her rapid pace as fast as she could from Adam.

Adam swam a little ways away and closed his eyes. He imagined he was alone. He imagined he was in the ocean. The sharks were swimming somewhere below him. If he cut himself on anything, they would smell the blood and come find him. He looked away from Gillian, where it was only the open expanse. It was just him in the open water. The purest version of alone.

"Adam! Adam!" Gillian was shouting. He turned his head and saw her, miles and miles off it seemed. It was the part of the game where they finally see each other. She had seen him first.

"Gillian!" he shouted. And they started swimming furiously toward each other. And they were still in the movie, they were swimming through the shark-infested ocean in their black and orange wetsuits, but when they came together and clasped hands, their dripping faces almost touching, excited and relieved, he wasn't sure if they were still acting, or if this was the real them now, if they were smiling at each other.

Gillian's whole body was shaking.

"You're cold?" he said.

She nodded.

"We should go back," he said. Adam held Gillian's hand, and they swam back to the shore. The rocks were so rough they could barely walk on them, and they veered to the left, up onto a grassy patch, surrounded by woods. They lay on their backs and stared up at the towering trees leading into the moonlit sky. It was silent and Adam listened to his heart. Always there. He wondered if they would lie here all night like this and fall asleep.

"There's something I have to tell you," said Gillian.

The sound of his heart grew louder.

"Yes?" he whispered.

*I think I'm actually gay. I like girls.*

She was silent for a moment.

"I have this problem with depression."

"You do?" Adam said. This wasn't what he had been expecting at all.

"I've had it since I was a kid. Like nine. I used to lie down at school and then just not get up. We'd be in the middle of gym, and all of a sudden I would just feel like I couldn't move. Like even the thought of moving was so depressing to me, I just couldn't keep doing it, and everyone would be playing some volleyball game, and I would just lie down in the middle of everything."

She was silent for another moment.

"What happened?" said Adam, unsure of what his question was referring to.

"When I was twelve, it started happening really often, and one time they had to, like, carry me to the car, so I started seeing a therapist. I got a little better after that, but it's never completely gone away. Sometimes I'll feel fine for months or even a year, and then I'll feel it creeping back, the same fear and anxiety. This thing I can't stop thinking about no matter how hard I try. Like it's trapped in my brain. I've gotten better at hiding it, but I know it will never completely go away. I could feel it starting to happen again a couple weeks ago, and I wanted to tell you, to talk to you about it, but then you were just off with Brad, and I felt like I couldn't. It felt like everything was always about you. And then you're just going to leave, go back to Piedmont, and I thought maybe I shouldn't even tell you. It's my thing. I have to figure out how to deal with it."

Adam looked at Gillian's face and felt something break open inside him.

"Gillian?" he said.

"Yeah?"

"I love you."

And she broke too.

"I hate you," she said. But she was smiling.

"You don't have to say it back," he said.

"I do," she said. "I love you, too."

And they leaned in and squeezed each other in their heavy wet shirts on the prickly, dirty grass.

Adam thought about how he'd always thought he loved her, had said the words to her inside his head a million times, but how he'd never actually really known her until right now. Why was it that the saddest part of oneself was the most true? She was exposed now, and there was something about this that made his whole body glow with no other feeling but pure love. But as he realized this, a shadow of a thought cursed the edges. If what he loved about her was this private vulnerability, this precious internal shame, what if that was also what she felt for him? The built-in

vulnerability of being trans. The private shame that hovers somewhere, sometimes spoken of, sometimes not. Was this what she
thought of when she said she loved him? And would she still love
him without it?

They were kissing now, their hands grabbing at their wet shirts,
dragging dirt and grass through each other's hair. Her tongue in
his mouth and the way she tasted and smelled and how there was
nothing he could ever want more than this. They rolled in the
grass and groped desperately at each other.

"I wish I could feel you in me," she said.

"I know," he said.

"Just you, not the thing."

"I know."

"I want it so bad," she said.

They were silent for a moment. Kissing, grabbing. Adam could
hear the faint music and shouts from the Camp Trans dance party
still going strong.

"Are you wearing it?" she said.

"Yes," he said.

"I want you."

"Just a minute," he said. And he staggered off her and stumbled
slightly down the hill, where his jeans were folded. His whole
body was buzzing with an unreal sensation, like he was sleepwalk-
ing or lucid dreaming. He took his wallet out of his back pocket
and the condom that was inside it. He had put it in there sopho-
more year. For two years it had stayed there, stuck between an old
ID and his Claremont gym membership. He unraveled his ACE
bandage, dropped it on the ground, put the condom over his hard
penis, and stepped back into his jeans.

Back on the shadowed grassy patch, Gillian had taken her
clothes off. She was shivering in the cold air, but as Adam lay himself over her, her body relaxed and leaned into his. They started
kissing again and she spread her legs around him, raised her hips

the way she always did, and Adam reached down and into his zipper, his hand grabbing his stiff penis with the condom around it, and he closed his eyes and leaned forward and pushed the head inside of Gillian, and she let out sounds of pleasure and opened her legs wider, and he pushed in deeper, and now he was all the way in and he was moving in and out and she was moving along with him, and a new song came on over at Camp Trans and someone let out a holler, and he moved faster and faster and she pushed harder, and then her knees squeezed together and her hands clenched on his back and she said, "I think I'm gonna come, Adam, I'm coming," and hearing her say this, suddenly he was too — it was shooting out of him and into her, unimaginable waves of pleasure as his whole body shook, and he realized he was sobbing, tears were streaming down his face, and these sounds were coming from his throat, these startling crow calls he could barely recognize as his own, and the tears were falling on Gillian, and she stared up at him as he cried and sobbed. His head fell into her neck, her arms around him.

"Gillian?" he said.

"Yeah?"

"I'm not trans."

"I know," she said.

And they held each other in the middle of the sprawling dark woods.

# Chapter 16

BACK IN PIEDMONT at home, Adam would sometimes wake up in the middle of the night and think he was still in the closet-room in New York. But unlike that room, where no matter how long you waited, it always remained an impenetrable black, the objects in this room would slowly come into focus, and he would remember where he was. All his old objects had new meanings now, though. Everything did.

That night with Gillian in the forest, they'd staggered back to the campsite, clutching hands but not talking. They'd been awake for almost forty-two hours and were so exhausted that as soon as their bodies reached their sleeping bags, they'd instantly fallen asleep.

A couple hours later, when the morning sun came blinding in through the thin green tent, Adam woke up to Gillian's open eyes, her face resting close to his.

"Last night actually happened, didn't it?" she said.

Adam nodded, nervous.

Everything came out then, the torrent that had been building the past month and a half. How he was not twenty-two but in high school, the plan for the summer with Casey, Calypso in the bathroom at The Hole, the panicked lie at the Gay Marriage party, the attempt and failure to tell Gillian over pizza, the godforsaken ACE bandage, and how once he was inside the lie, he couldn't get out. How she said she would never date a bio guy and sometimes he would stare at her and think, *I'm sorry. I'm sorry. I don't know what to do.*

Gillian stared at him now and took it in, her expression only receptive.

"Did you really actually know?" Adam asked.

Gillian paused and looked down for a moment. "Well, I definitely didn't know you were — how old are you?"

"Um, seventeen, eighteen in six and a half weeks."

"Which could get me thrown in jail."

"No! No one has to know!" said Adam, instantly embarrassed by how girlish and frantic he sounded.

Gillian shifted and looked at Adam out of the corner of her eyes. "It still feels a little creepy..."

"You're not creepy. If anything, I'm the one who's creepy."

He still wasn't sure what she was thinking. What it meant that it was all out there. She wasn't screaming at him, but he still didn't know, and his whole body stayed tensed with hope. He reached down and fiddled with the zipper on his sleeping bag.

"What about ... the other thing," he said.

Gillian was silent for a while longer.

"Yeah," she said. "That."

She told him how ever since they'd had sex that night after Bound, she had started thinking of him as a bio guy, fantasized about him as a bio guy, with a real penis. That in a way, he had ceased being trans to her. She said when they started having sex on the grass in the woods and she realized what was happening, it was terrifying and exhilarating all at once. But that it was also as if some buried part of her had known all along.

"It's still kind of crazy..." she said. She sat up and curled her arms around her knees, looking away from Adam, at the tent's door. "Like I can't stop replaying everything now that I know... I mean, it's a little humiliating —"

"No!" said Adam, sitting up too. Her expression had gone cold, and for a moment he thought it was over.

"I mean, it's kind of like, who *are* you?" She shot him a look.

"I'm *me*," he said desperately.

They looked at each other.

"I swear that's it," he said.

"You swear?"

"I swear."

"You *swear*."

"I *swear* . . . I'm a seventeen-year-old boy who lives in Piedmont and pretended to be trans. That's it. Everything else is true."

And he watched as Gillian's face shifted into that same amused, curious look, like the one she gave him the night he threw the drink on her.

"Do you still like me?" Adam whispered.

"Yes," Gillian whispered back.

They lay down and inched closer, their hands slowly moving onto each other.

"I love you," said Adam.

"I love you, too," she said.

They had sex that morning in the tent, both of them completely naked for the first time.

. . .

As soon as Adam returned to Piedmont, he informed his parents that he was going to be taking four extra classes that semester in order to graduate early and move back to New York in January, where he would get a job (if nothing else, June's old comic book shop was sure to take him) and then start college in the fall. His parents didn't believe him and he didn't care. He studied his ass off. The only thing that mattered was getting back to Gillian. He imagined moving into her colorful little room in Fort Greene, giddy at the thought of waking up next to her every morning.

The apartment at Scholes Street had dismantled. Casey and June had moved back into the Columbia dorms, *not* as roommates. Ethan was elsewhere. He hadn't been home when Adam returned from Michigan, and a few days later Adam flew back to California. He had thought about texting Ethan before he left, wanted to, but didn't.

Casey and June didn't really talk anymore, but Casey told Adam she saw June around campus with her girlfriend, a freshman from Iowa who was newly gay and appeared to worship June. Casey herself was dating a twenty-eight-year-old lawyer named Lucile. She was a public defender who had guest lectured at one of Casey's classes. Adam's mom had come to him in distress over the photo Casey e-mailed her of this über-butch woman, her arm draped proprietarily over Casey's shoulder.

"But I just don't understand," his mom had said. "Casey's *beautiful*."

Adam had responded, "Uh, Casey being beautiful has nothing to do with it? Get over it, Mom. Casey likes her. Deal."

And the more Adam said it, and soon got his never-really-cared-anyway dad to start saying it too, his mom, outnumbered and getting nowhere, eventually switched from freaking out about Casey being gay to the fact that Lucile was "a little too old for Casey. Don't you think? Casey should be with a woman her own age . . ."

Upon dating Lucile, Casey had promptly switched her major from biology to prelaw. "I want to make effective social change in this world," she said. "Not spend my life poring over agar slides." But Adam, in his nights of frenzied studying, had become especially obsessed with his human anatomy class. Even though he wasn't "trans" anymore, his interest in gender remained, and he was amazed to learn it wasn't just chromosomes — XX or XY — that determine a person's sex, but a whole array of factors. He wrote a paper on sexual differentiation, detailing how originally we are all "female," but in "males" a gene on the Y chromosome releases hormones during phases of development. The timing and levels of these hormones, however, fluctuate from person to person, creating different results in each individual's body and brain. He argued that because these sex-determining hormones have unique variation in the development of both XX and XY people and continue to fluctuate throughout life, that means a person's sex is in some sense *physically* on a spectrum rather than the strict male/female dichotomy everyone is taught. That this broad diversity is really what's "natural."

Adam was so excited when he first realized this connection between gender identity and biology that he immediately went on one of the old trans message boards he used to frequent and left a long anonymous post explaining all the scientific details he'd learned. He expected to get a flurry of responses, but, instead, by the next morning there was only one comment: "cool!" and then, four days later, a peeved three-paragraph rant on whether or not people should be allowed to post anonymously. But whatever, Adam thought it was fascinating. He applied to Hunter, LaGuardia, Brooklyn, and Pace, with his projected major as biology.

Adam still hung around Brad and Colin and the rest, but rarely outside of school. He didn't care anymore — they meant nothing to him — and he mainly had homework to do anyway. They could tell he didn't care, and it made them love him.

"Hey, Adam, you coming to the Laserium this Friday?"

"Adam, we're thinking of hitting Yosemite in a few weeks. You're in — right, dude?"

All day he looked forward to the evening when he could talk on the phone or Skype with Gillian. That was the real part of his life, the part that mattered. But then things started to get weird.

It was mid-October when one night Gillian mentioned casually, "If either of us starts dating anyone."

"What do you mean?" Adam said. "*We're* dating."

And she laughed and played it off, and they talked about something else. But a few days later on Skype it came up again and she said, "We're not monogamous, Adam. You live across the country."

"But I'm moving in three months," he said. "I'm coming to you."

And she just looked uncomfortable.

He remained in denial for as long as possible, telling himself she was just busy when she didn't call him back, that her Internet was down when he didn't see her on Skype. When they did talk, he was overly optimistic, a deluge of positivity and plans for the future flowing from his mouth at her pixelated — sometimes distorted, computer-frozen — image, the face that when he first returned to Piedmont had always looked so flushed and eager to talk to him but was now weary, compliant, as if their Skyping were one more thing on a "To Do" list.

Finally, she told him about Rory. "It's getting serious," she said, within the same sentence that she mentioned there was a Rory at all. When she explained who he was, how he worked at the museum with her, wanted to be a curator, her face grew appallingly excited, like she couldn't help it, absolutely could not stop herself from smiling at the thought of him, he was *just that great.*

"A bio guy?" Adam said.

"Yeah, cis guy." And she blushed and looked a little embarrassed but also proud, like she'd finally managed to come into her own, and wasn't Adam happy for her?

And when he got upset — and, OK, maybe a little hysterical — her face turned impassive, and she said in that same cold, measured voice, the one she'd used during those horrible days at the end of New York, "I like him, Adam. And he's my own age."

"Are you having sex?" Adam asked.

"It doesn't matter," she said.

*"Are you?"*

"Yes," she said. And her pixel face computer-froze into a grue-some mask.

A couple nights later, Adam got drunk—more like oblit-erated—chugging from every bottle, including the crème de menthe, down in his parents' liquor cabinet, and sent off a stream of instantly-regrettable-yet-in-the-moment-positively-unstoppa-ble e-mails, dozens of ham-fisted, typo-filled variations on Your a slut, and I hopehe dumpa you andyou die alone. The next morning came her curt response. She didn't think they should talk for a while.

And they didn't. Adam went to school and did his homework and ate lunch with Brad and the gang, as a ghost. At night he lay in bed and imagined Gillian and Rory, their naked bodies pressed together, their mingling fluids. He wondered if she had told Rory about the depression. And Adam would thrash in his sheets and get up and dry heave into the toilet. He would lie back down, pass out for a moment, and then wake with an agonized start. Unable to do anything but get up again and pace around his shadowy room, his heart racing spastically. Every morning felt like waking up into a horror movie. He had no plan, no sense of a future, only buzzing, anxious chaos.

But then, after a few weeks, the anxiety subsided, the pain was somehow slightly less, and Adam was surprised when he was watching TV one night and actually laughed. Soon enough, he started to feel normal more often than not, and a part of this was that the person he really started talking to, some nights for hours at a time, was Ethan.

Adam had seen him on IM one night and sent a tentative hi, even though he was pretty sure it would go ignored. Instead, Ethan had written back right away, and they'd chatted, just super-casual stuff for a bit. The next night they were IM'ing again and decided to switch to the phone. It began kind of awkward, but soon they were talking nonstop, speaking over each other, laughing, just like they were still back on Scholes Street and nothing had changed. Adam divulged the whole trans-lie saga with Gillian — and while at first he was worried that Ethan might be offended, Ethan just laughed and egged him for more details, then said that he was as of now officially optioning Adam's life rights for his next film.

Ethan also told Adam about Rachel.

"Are you guys living together in New York?" Adam asked. "Is it amazing?"

"Um, yeah, not exactly . . ." said Ethan.

"Was she . . . still not OK with you being trans?" Adam asked.

Ever since learning Ethan was trans, Adam had always assumed that he and Rachel had broken up because of Ethan's transition, that this was the big secret — "what had happened" with Rachel. But Ethan said, "No, that was never it," and they stayed up till 3:00 A.M. on the phone, Ethan telling Adam the story he'd never told anyone else.

He'd realized he was trans the beginning of his senior year of high school. Rachel was his friend, and the night he told her, they made out for the first time. His parents had refused to listen at first, but he was so insistent, so desperate, they eventually agreed to let him start on hormones and pay for top surgery when he turned eighteen. Transitioning in high school was so intense that he and Rachel clung to each other, like they were the only two people in the world. After his top surgery, the doctors gave him a prescription for Vicodin, and he and Rachel took the pills together, and when the prescription ran out, they went and found more. Ethan had thought it was just for fun, like getting drunk occasionally, but then he realized Rachel was always taking the pills, that she was on them more often than not, and she'd moved on to stronger ones without telling him. He finally told her parents, even though they already hated him, thought he was a freak. They sent her to a fancy rehab, and when she got back, Ethan thought everything would be better, until he realized nothing had changed, that she was still using all the time. He'd made this big grand speech about him or the pills, and she broke up with him. That's when he moved to New York.

"But what about when she came in August?" said Adam.

"It was horrible," said Ethan. "She was still on pills and kept trying to get me to do them too. I felt like I didn't even know who she was. If I ever really loved her. Or just used to love the pills. It's really scary to see something you held so true — the most true — as false."

They were silent for a moment.

"I told Gillian I loved her," said Adam.

Had that been false too? If she could just leave him like that, move on to someone else, was it ever even really true?

"You did," said Ethan. "That was real."

He and Ethan were quiet awhile more, and Adam felt something welling inside him.

"Hey, Ethan?" Adam said. "I'm sorry. About, you know. In New York. Being a dick."

"It's cool," said Ethan. "I'm sorry too."

Ethan was living in a one-bedroom in Williamsburg, but he'd blown through his trust fund and the rent was bleeding his parents — "They keep saying it's time I paid for my own shit, and they're right" — and one night when Adam told Ethan how he had planned to move back to New York in January but now because of Gillian he wasn't sure anymore, Ethan suggested that the two of them get a place. "Something cheap but cool, a bachelor pad. I mean, only if you want to . . ."

Adam almost exploded with joy.

At the beginning of December, Adam was accepted into Hunter for the fall, and at the end of the month, he walked into the noisy, bustling San Francisco Airport. And as he looked out at all the different people rushing around, names and flight gates blasting from the intercom, he felt a familiar surge of terror and excitement remembering how he had stood in this exact same spot last June on the brink of the summer unknown, same heavy bags, same red duffel strapped over his back, same boarding pass to NYC-LAGUARDIA, crumpled sweaty in his hand. Except this time his flight was leaving at 11:00 A.M., not ridiculous 6:15. He'd booked the ticket his damn self. Why had he ever thought it was so difficult?

# Acknowledgments

Greatest thanks to my editor, Lauren Wein, and my agent, Merrilee Heifetz; to Molly Axtmann, Tania Schrag, Frederic Schrag, Julia Fuller, Toby Wincorn, Melissa Plaut, Kris Peterson, Anna Sochynsky, Gabrielle Bell, Liz Brown, Melissa Anderson, Kevin Seccia, and Charlotte Wells.

# About the Author

Ariel Schrag grew up in Berkeley, California. She is the author of the graphic memoirs *Awkward, Definition, Potential,* and *Likewise.* She lives in Brooklyn.

S
R